ON THE ROAD TO PERDITION

BOOK 2: SANCTUARY

writer
MAX ALLAN COLLINS

artist
STEVE LIEBER

PARADOX PRESS  NEW YORK, NEW YORK

PARADOX PRESS / DC COMICS
Dan Didio, VP-Editorial · Joan Hilty, Editor
Harvey Richards, Assistant Editor · John J. Hill, Art Director
Paul Levitz, President & Publisher · Georg Brewer VP-Design & Retail Product Development
Richard Bruning, Senior VP-Creative Director · Patrick Caldon, Senior VP-Finance & Operations
Chris Caramalis, VP-Finance · Terri Cunningham, VP-Managing Editor · Alison Gill, VP-Manufacturing
Lillian Laserson, Senior VP & General Counsel · Jim Lee, Editorial Director-WildStorm
David McKillips, VP-Advertising & Custom Publishing · John Nee, VP-Business Development
Cheryl Rubin, VP-Brand Management · Bob Wayne, VP-Sales & Marketing

Cover artist: JOSÉ LUIS GARCÍA-LÓPEZ
Cover colors and separations: DAVE McCAIG

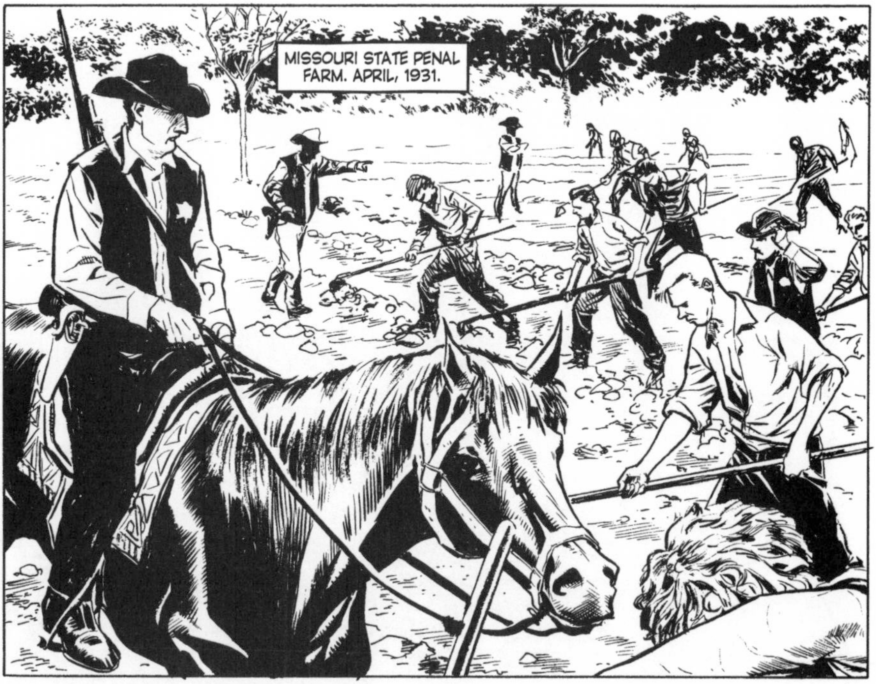
MISSOURI STATE PENAL FARM. APRIL, 1931.

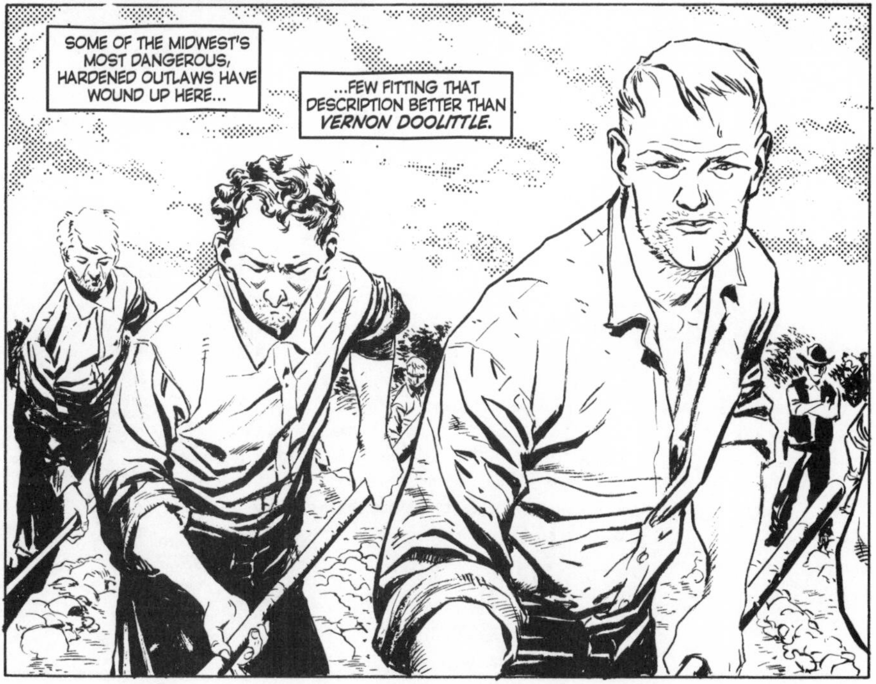
SOME OF THE MIDWEST'S MOST DANGEROUS, HARDENED OUTLAWS HAVE WOUND UP HERE...
...FEW FITTING THAT DESCRIPTION BETTER THAN *VERNON DOOLITTLE*.

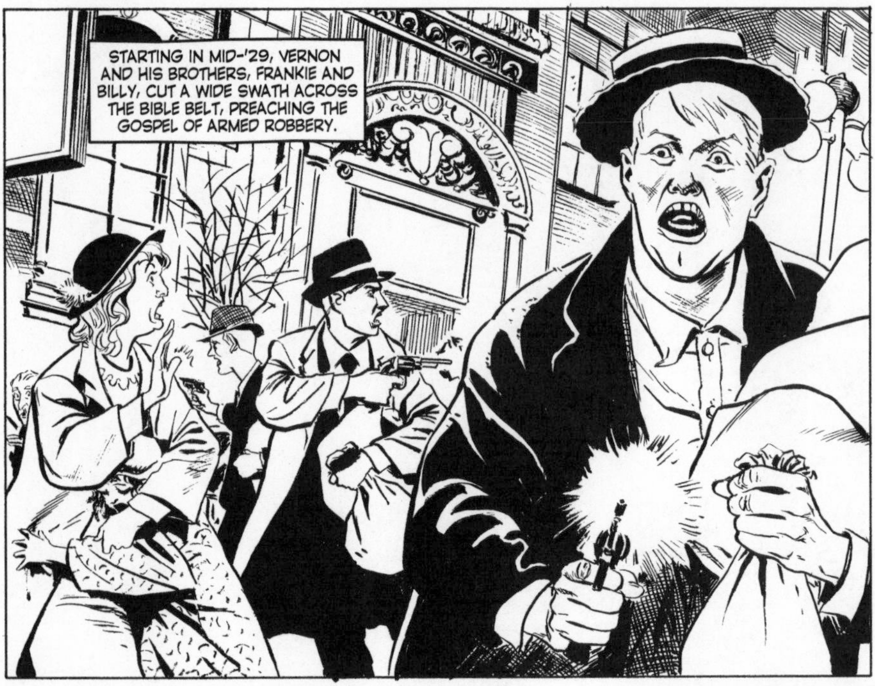
STARTING IN MID-'29, VERNON AND HIS BROTHERS, FRANKIE AND BILLY, CUT A WIDE SWATH ACROSS THE BIBLE BELT, PREACHING THE GOSPEL OF ARMED ROBBERY.

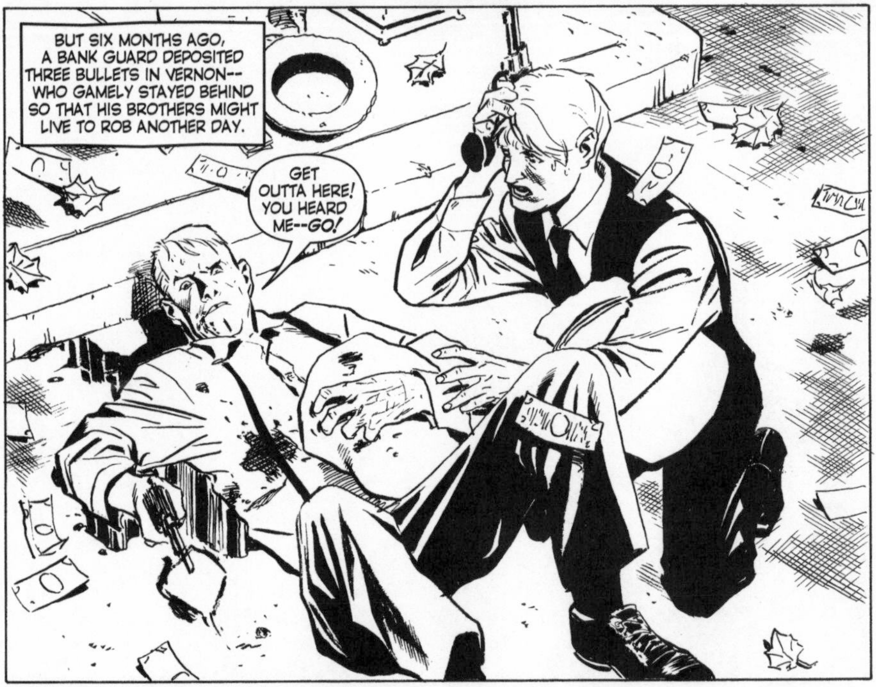
BUT SIX MONTHS AGO, A BANK GUARD DEPOSITED THREE BULLETS IN VERNON--WHO GAMELY STAYED BEHIND SO THAT HIS BROTHERS MIGHT LIVE TO ROB ANOTHER DAY.
GET OUTTA HERE! YOU HEARD ME--GO!

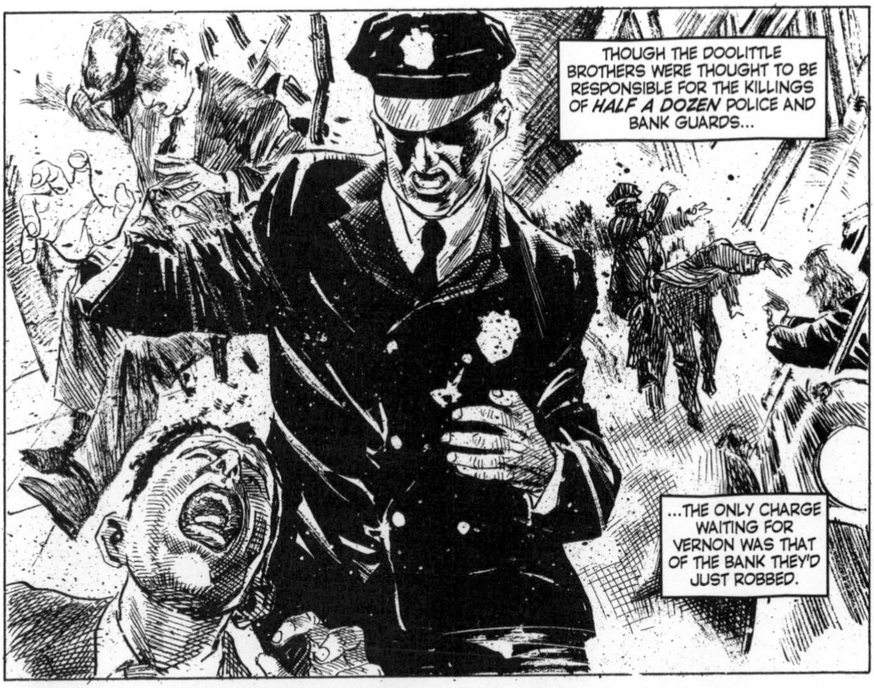
THOUGH THE DOOLITTLE BROTHERS WERE THOUGHT TO BE RESPONSIBLE FOR THE KILLINGS OF *HALF A DOZEN* POLICE AND BANK GUARDS...
...THE ONLY CHARGE WAITING FOR VERNON WAS THAT OF THE BANK THEY'D JUST ROBBED.

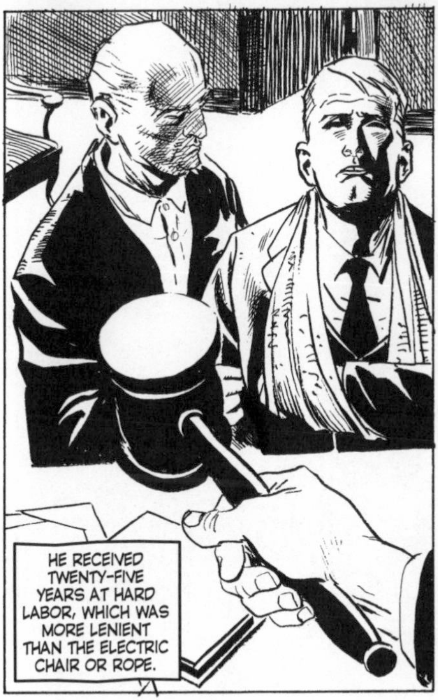
HE RECEIVED TWENTY-FIVE YEARS AT HARD LABOR, WHICH WAS MORE LENIENT THAN THE ELECTRIC CHAIR OR ROPE.

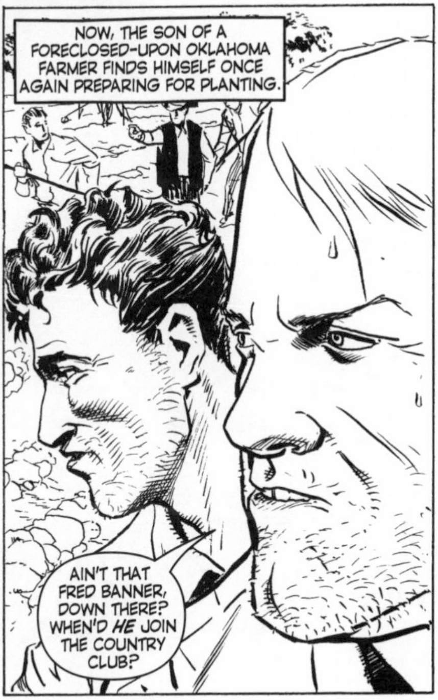
NOW, THE SON OF A FORECLOSED-UPON OKLAHOMA FARMER FINDS HIMSELF ONCE AGAIN PREPARING FOR PLANTING.
AIN'T THAT FRED BANNER, DOWN THERE? WHEN'D *HE* JOIN THE COUNTRY CLUB?

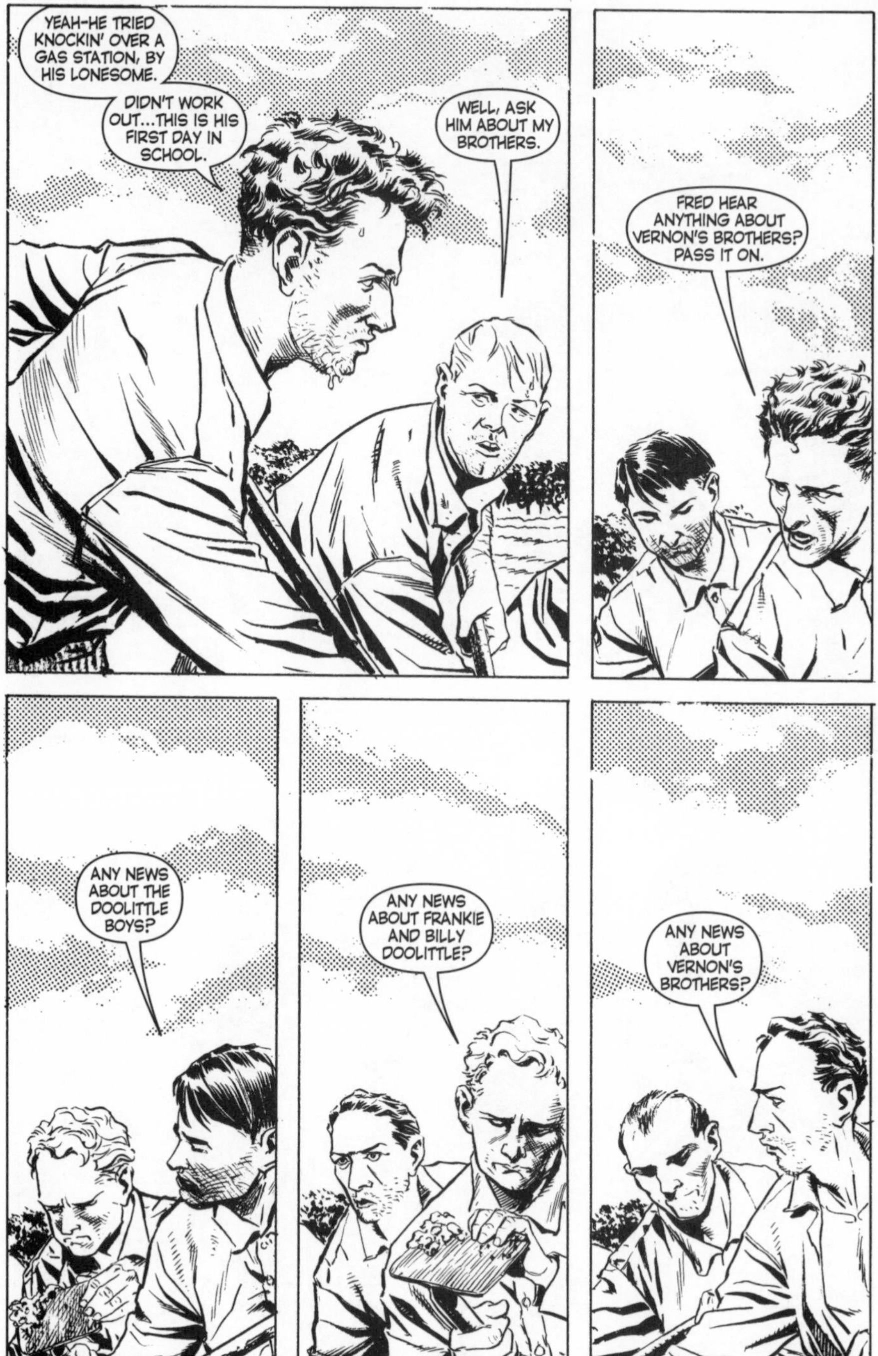
YEAH–HE TRIED KNOCKIN' OVER A GAS STATION, BY HIS LONESOME.
DIDN'T WORK OUT...THIS IS HIS FIRST DAY IN SCHOOL.
WELL, ASK HIM ABOUT MY BROTHERS.
FRED HEAR ANYTHING ABOUT VERNON'S BROTHERS? PASS IT ON.
ANY NEWS ABOUT THE DOOLITTLE BOYS?
ANY NEWS ABOUT FRANKIE AND BILLY DOOLITTLE?
ANY NEWS ABOUT VERNON'S BROTHERS?

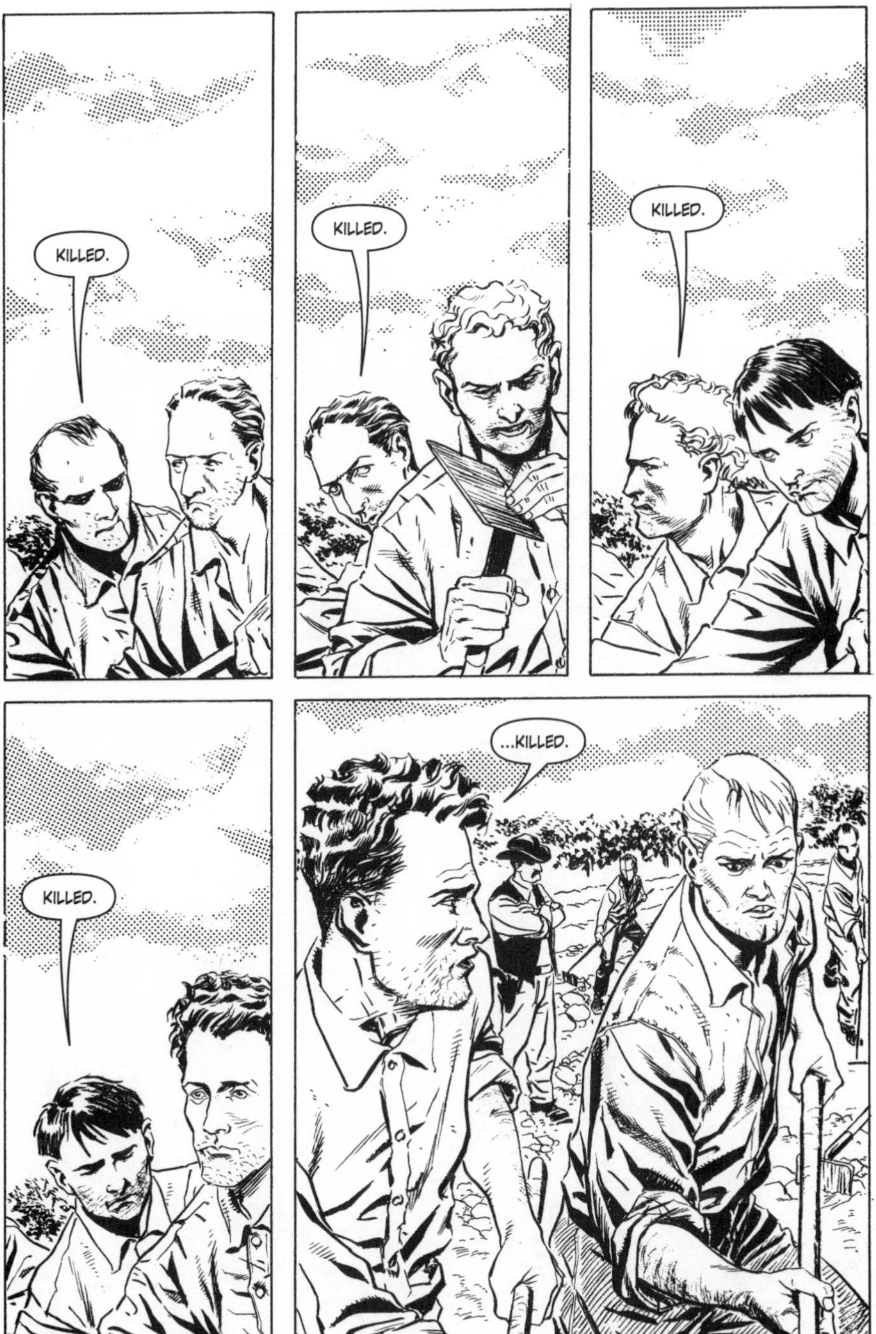
KILLED.
KILLED.
KILLED.
KILLED.
...KILLED.

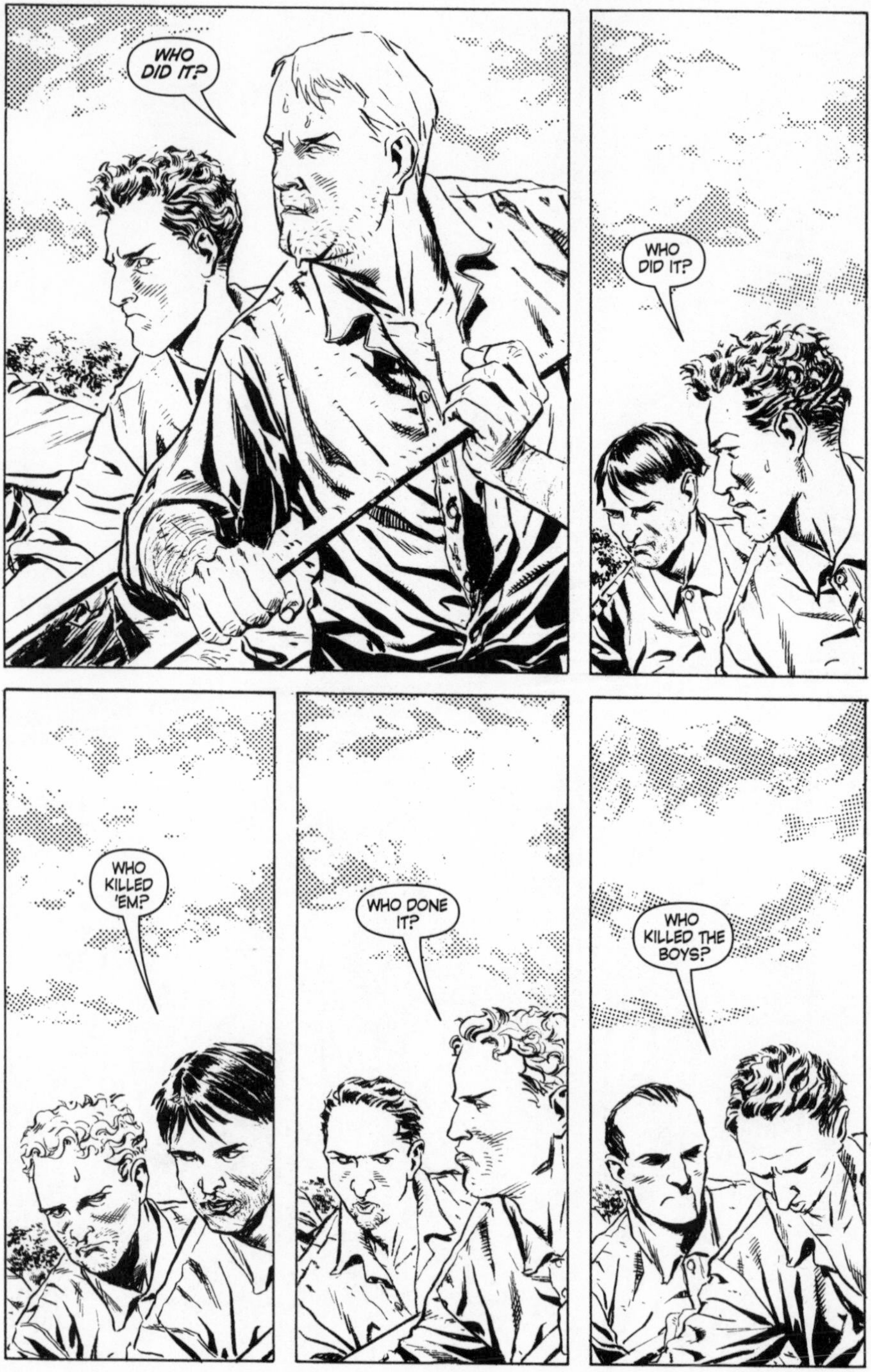
WHO DID IT?
WHO DID IT?
WHO KILLED 'EM?
WHO DONE IT?
WHO KILLED THE BOYS?

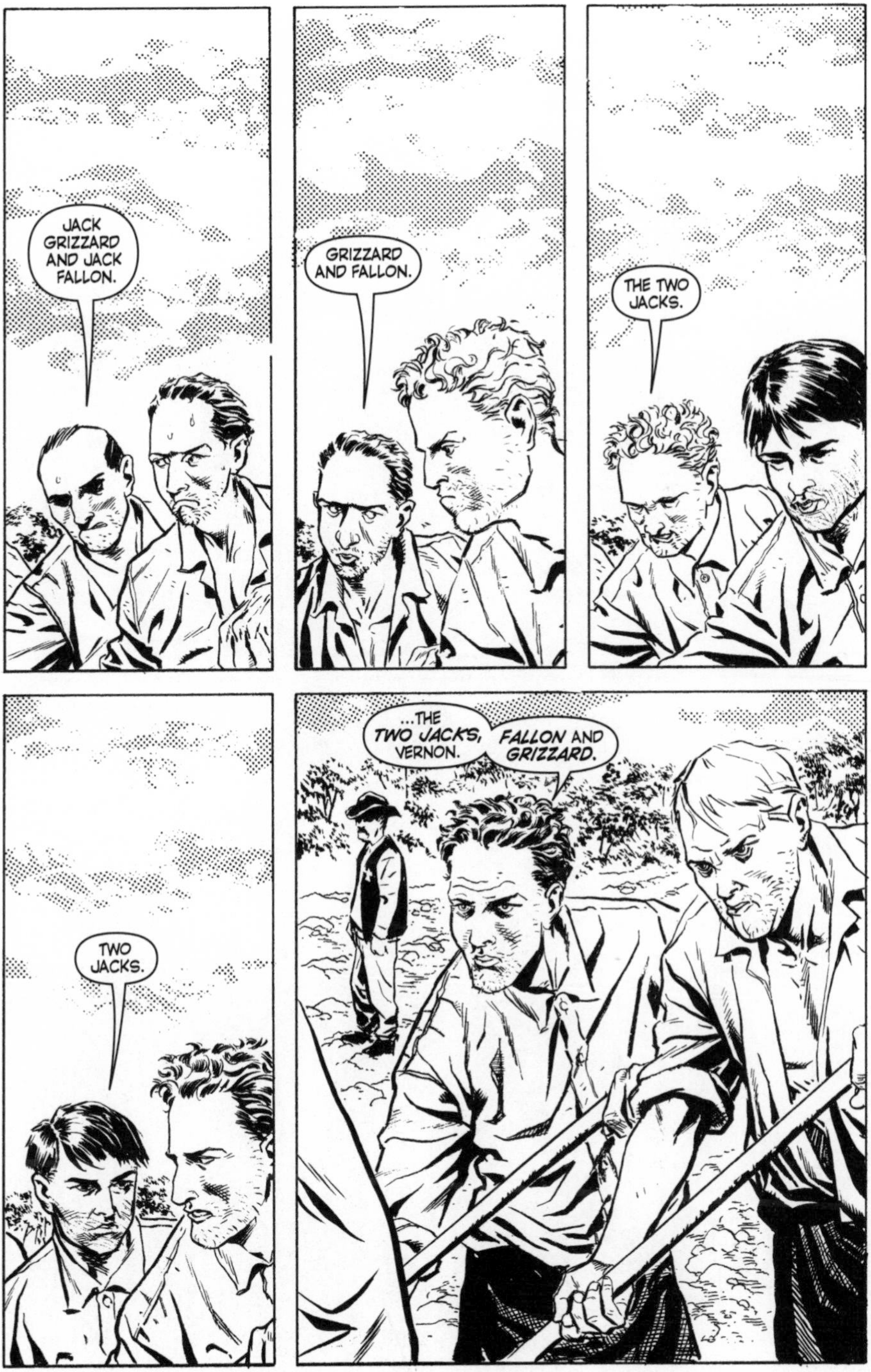
JACK GRIZZARD AND JACK FALLON.
GRIZZARD AND FALLON.
THE TWO JACKS.
TWO JACKS.
...THE *TWO JACKS,* VERNON.
FALLON AND *GRIZZARD.*

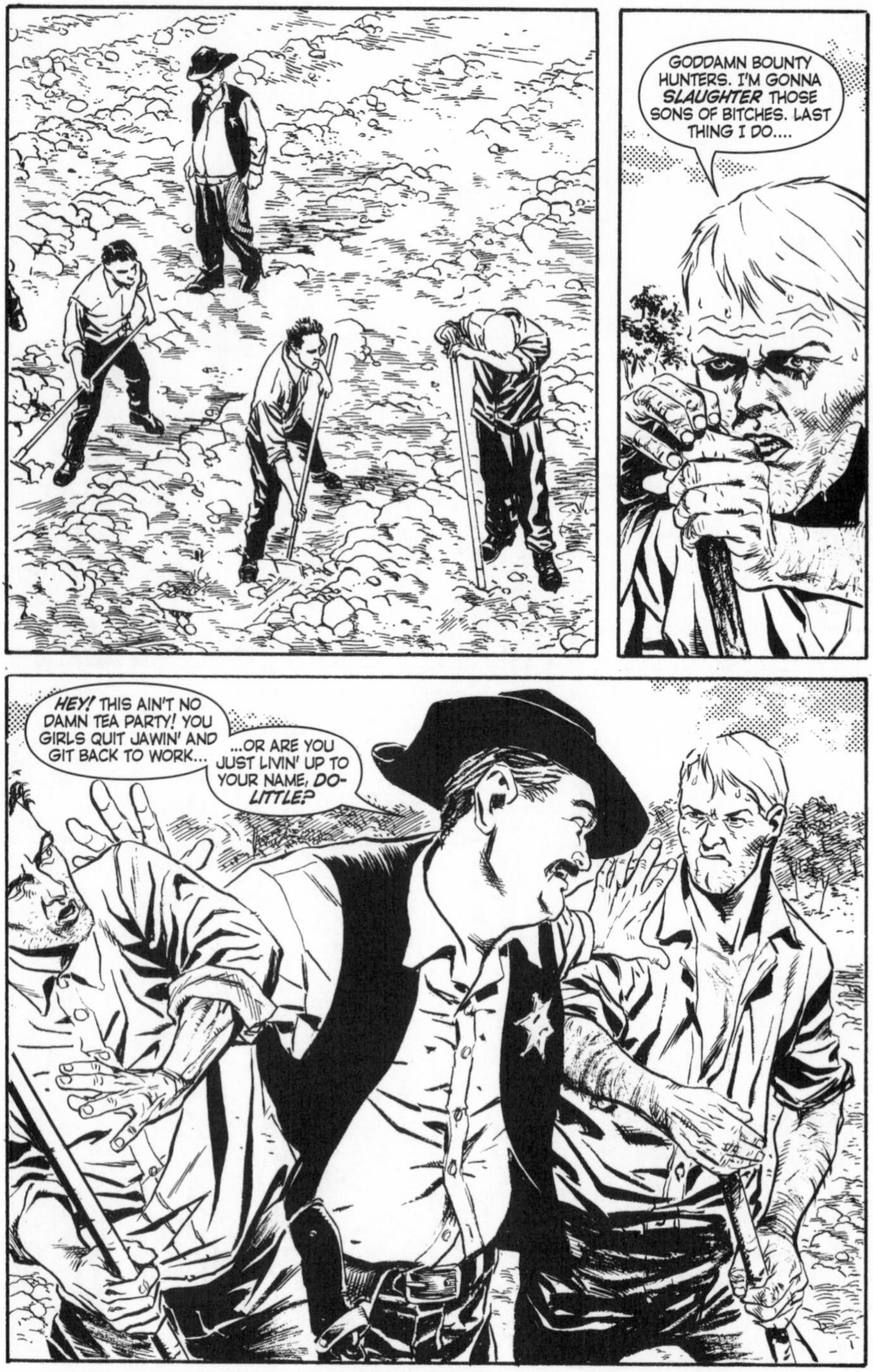
GODDAMN BOUNTY HUNTERS. I'M GONNA *SLAUGHTER* THOSE SONS OF BITCHES. LAST THING I DO....
HEY! THIS AIN'T NO DAMN TEA PARTY! YOU GIRLS QUIT JAWIN' AND GIT BACK TO WORK...
...OR ARE YOU JUST LIVIN' UP TO YOUR NAME, *DO-LITTLE?*

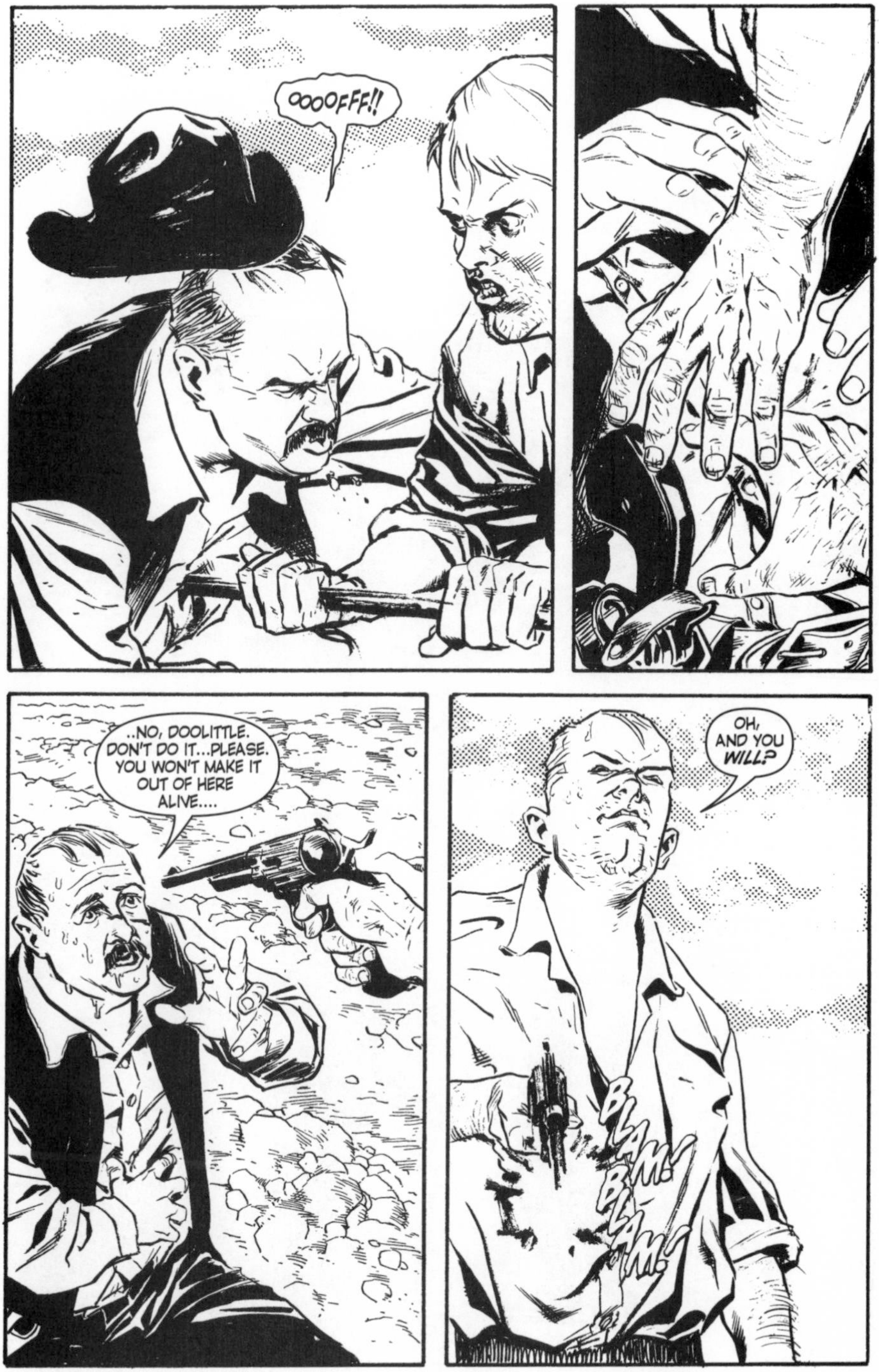
OOOOFFF!!
..NO, DOOLITTLE. DON'T DO IT...PLEASE. YOU WON'T MAKE IT OUT OF HERE ALIVE....
OH, AND YOU WILL?
BLAM!
BLAM!
BLAM!

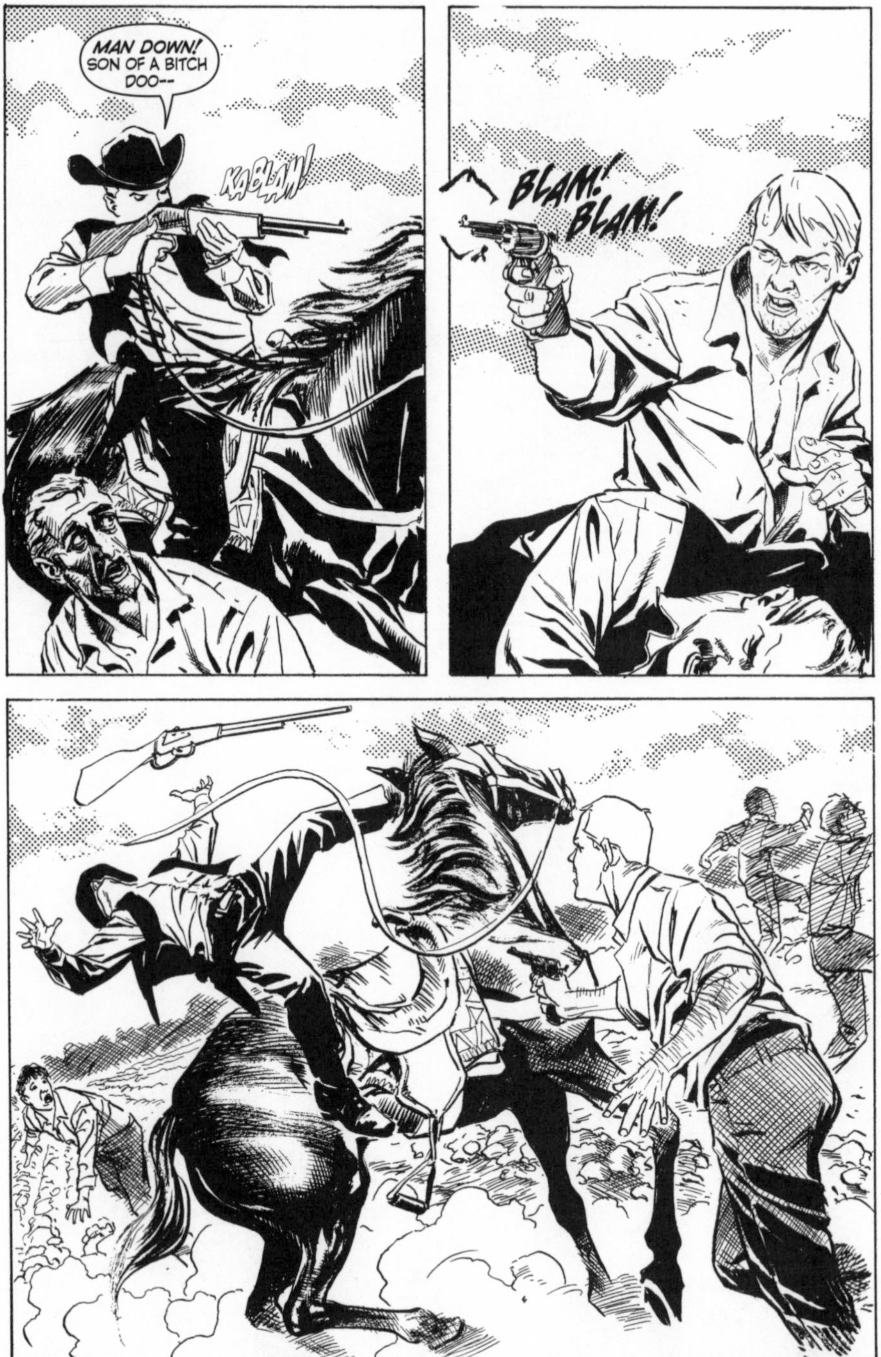
MAN DOWN! SON OF A BITCH DOO--
KABLAM!
BLAM! BLAM!

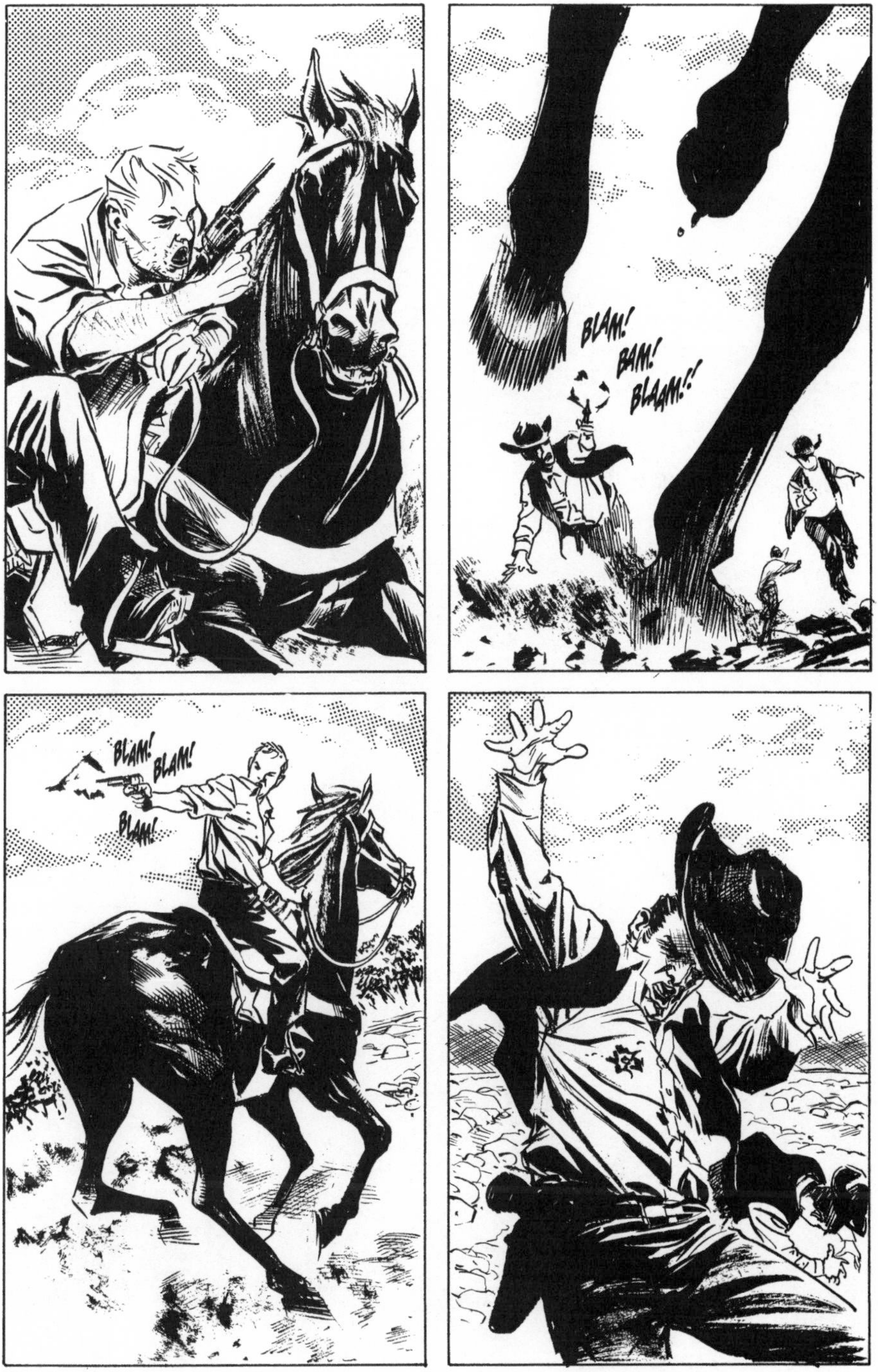
BLAM!
BAM!
BLAAM!?!
BLAM!
BLAM!
BLAM!

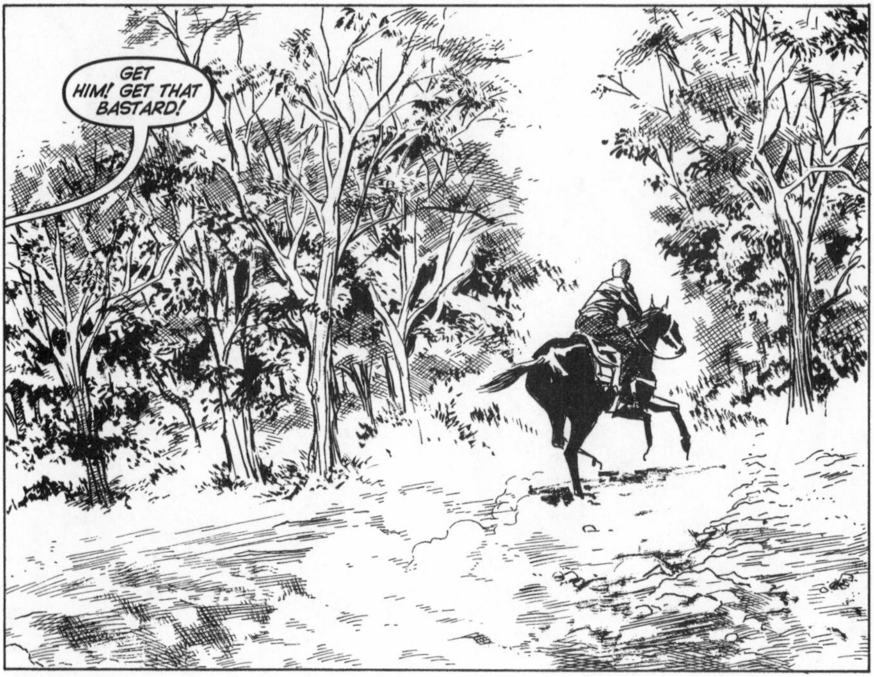
GET HIM! GET THAT BASTARD!

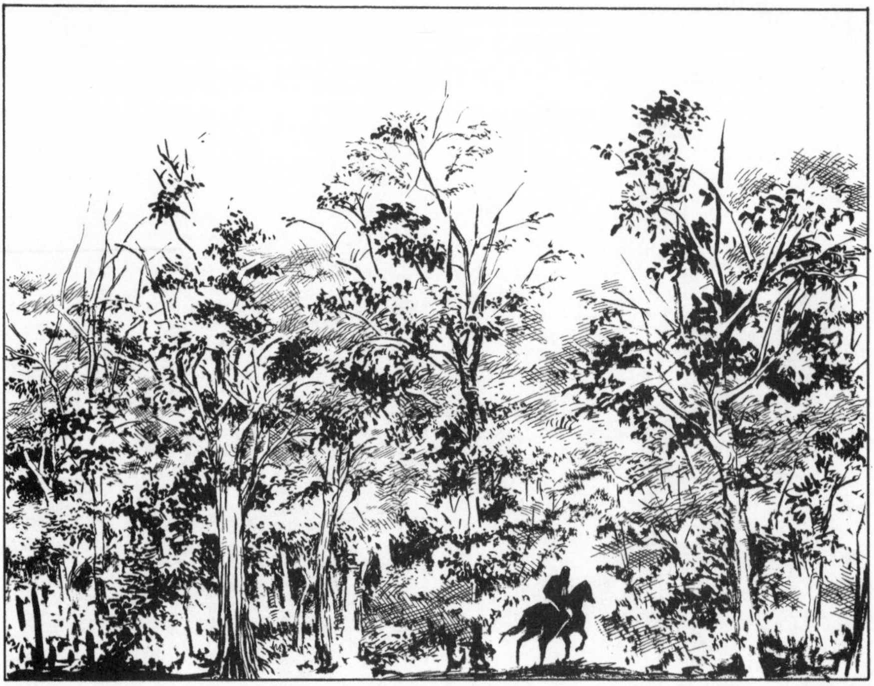

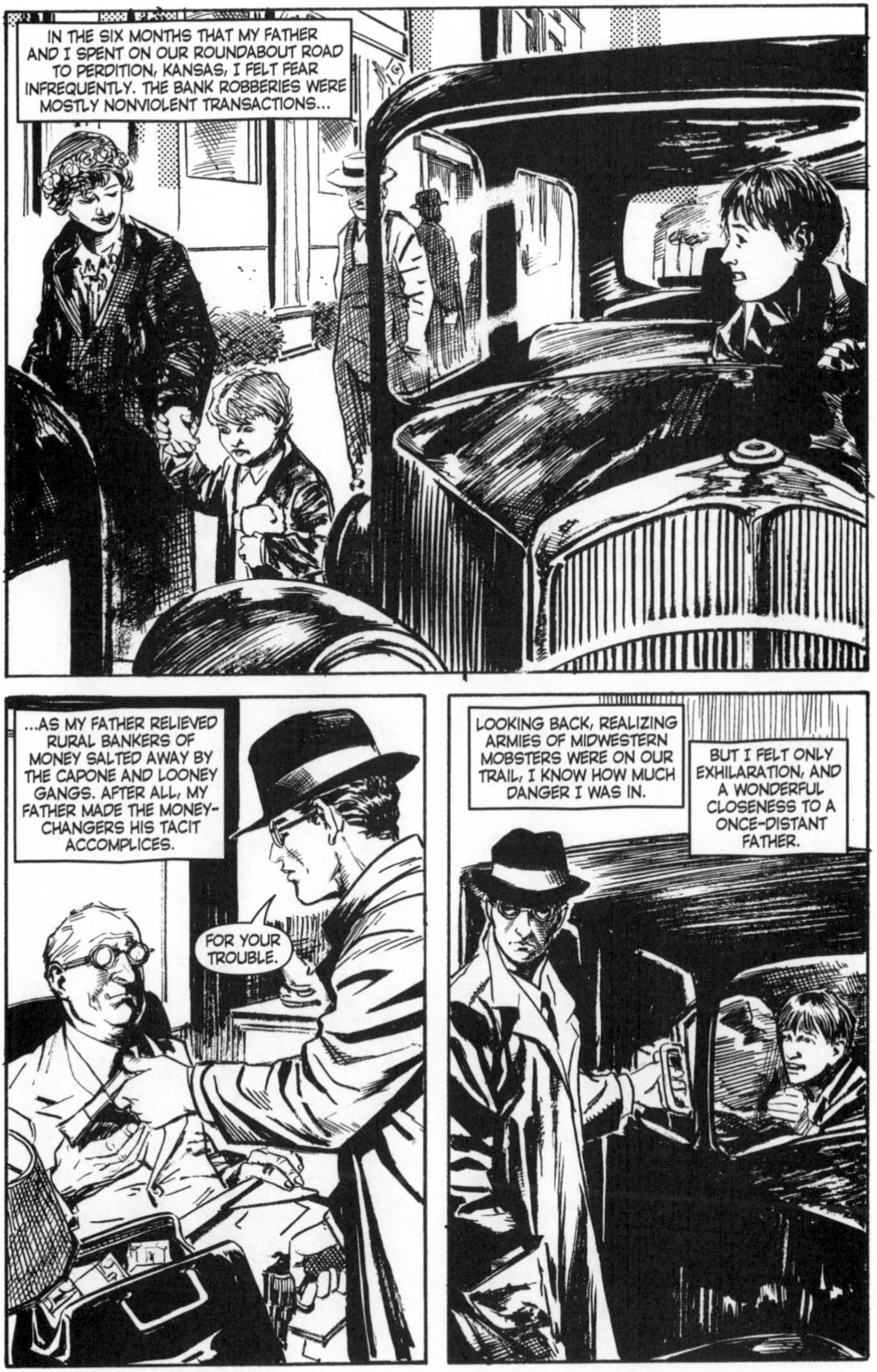
IN THE SIX MONTHS THAT MY FATHER AND I SPENT ON OUR ROUNDABOUT ROAD TO PERDITION, KANSAS, I FELT FEAR INFREQUENTLY. THE BANK ROBBERIES WERE MOSTLY NONVIOLENT TRANSACTIONS...
...AS MY FATHER RELIEVED RURAL BANKERS OF MONEY SALTED AWAY BY THE CAPONE AND LOONEY GANGS. AFTER ALL, MY FATHER MADE THE MONEY-CHANGERS HIS TACIT ACCOMPLICES.
FOR YOUR TROUBLE.
LOOKING BACK, REALIZING ARMIES OF MIDWESTERN MOBSTERS WERE ON OUR TRAIL, I KNOW HOW MUCH DANGER I WAS IN.
BUT I FELT ONLY EXHILARATION, AND A WONDERFUL CLOSENESS TO A ONCE-DISTANT FATHER.

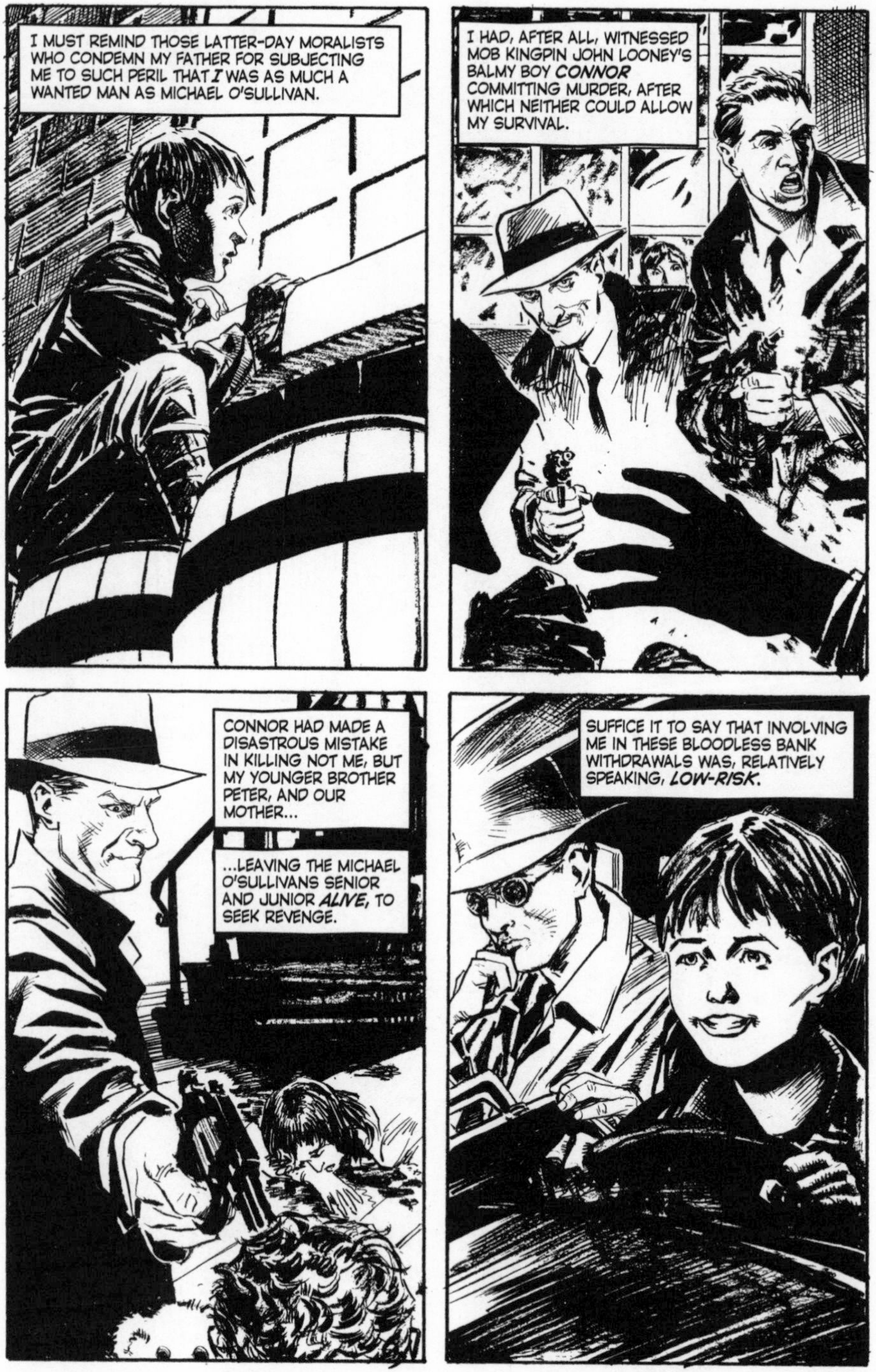
I MUST REMIND THOSE LATTER-DAY MORALISTS WHO CONDEMN MY FATHER FOR SUBJECTING ME TO SUCH PERIL THAT *I* WAS AS MUCH A WANTED MAN AS MICHAEL O'SULLIVAN.
I HAD, AFTER ALL, WITNESSED MOB KINGPIN JOHN LOONEY'S BALMY BOY ***CONNOR*** COMMITTING MURDER, AFTER WHICH NEITHER COULD ALLOW MY SURVIVAL.
CONNOR HAD MADE A DISASTROUS MISTAKE IN KILLING NOT ME, BUT MY YOUNGER BROTHER PETER, AND OUR MOTHER...
...LEAVING THE MICHAEL O'SULLIVANS SENIOR AND JUNIOR ***ALIVE***, TO SEEK REVENGE.
SUFFICE IT TO SAY THAT INVOLVING ME IN THESE BLOODLESS BANK WITHDRAWALS WAS, RELATIVELY SPEAKING, ***LOW-RISK***.

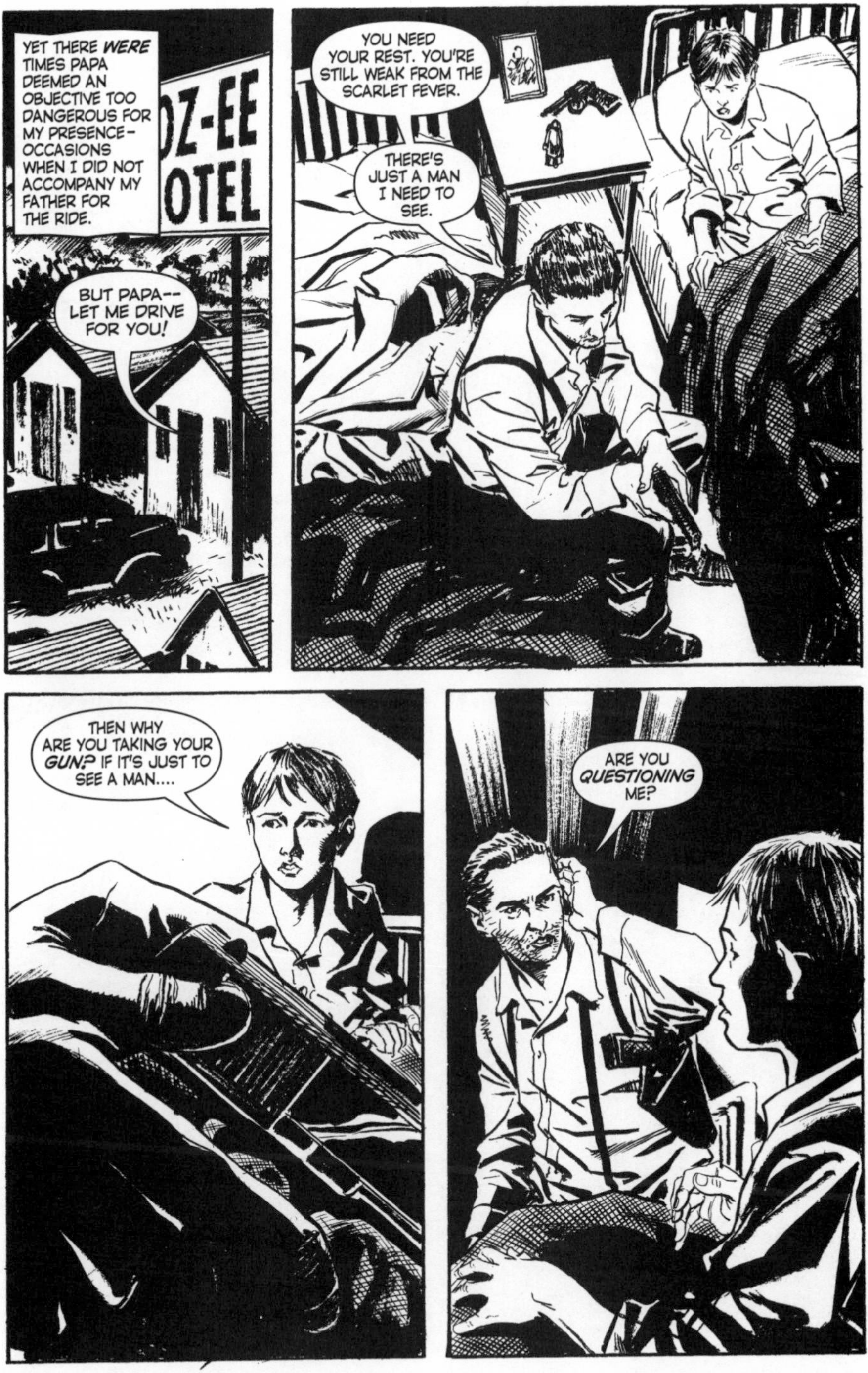
YET THERE *WERE* TIMES PAPA DEEMED AN OBJECTIVE TOO DANGEROUS FOR MY PRESENCE-OCCASIONS WHEN I DID NOT ACCOMPANY MY FATHER FOR THE RIDE.
OZ-EE
OTEL
BUT PAPA-- LET ME DRIVE FOR YOU!
YOU NEED YOUR REST. YOU'RE STILL WEAK FROM THE SCARLET FEVER.
THERE'S JUST A MAN I NEED TO SEE.
THEN WHY ARE YOU TAKING YOUR *GUN?* IF IT'S JUST TO SEE A MAN....
ARE YOU *QUESTIONING* ME?

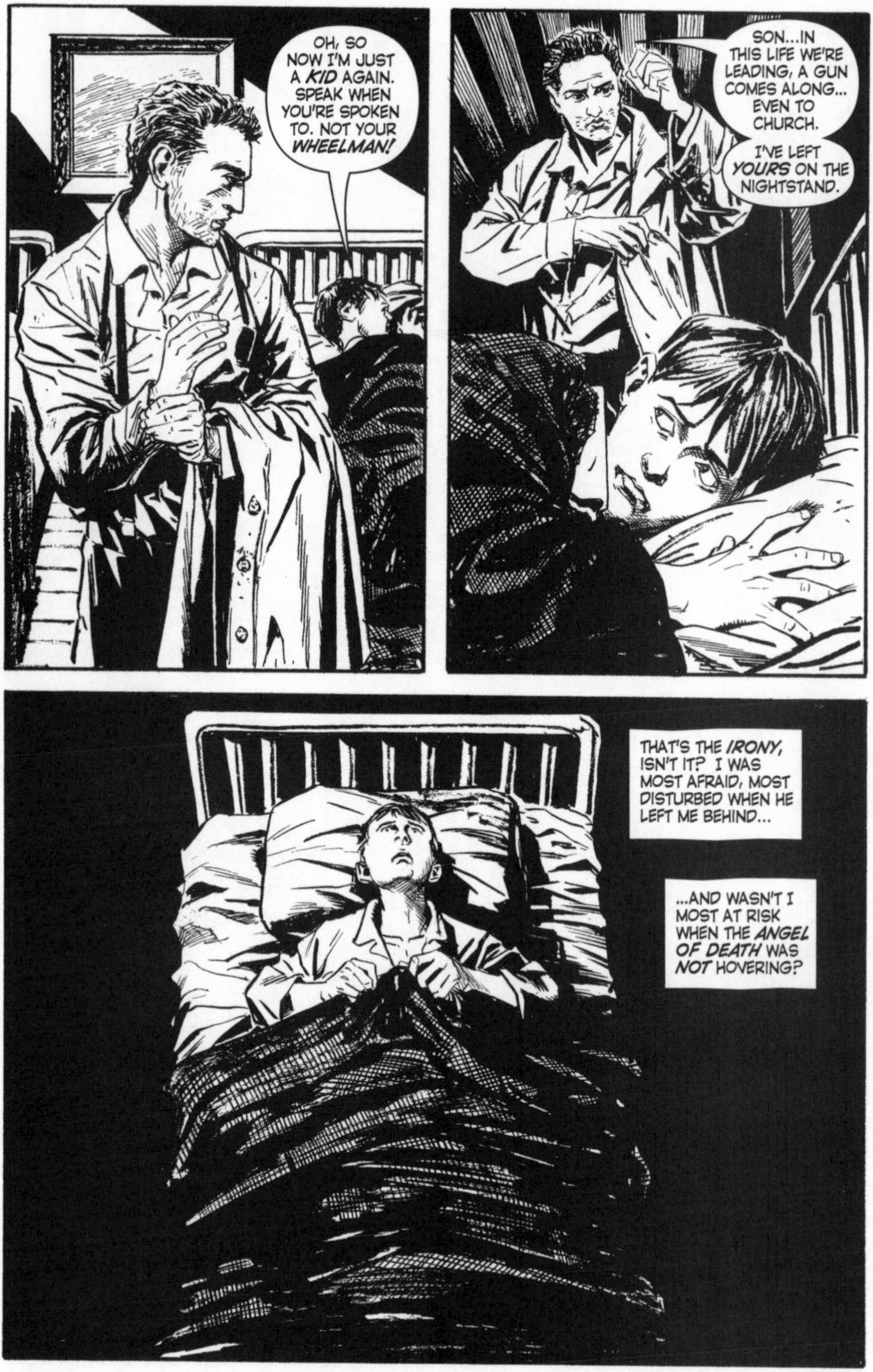
OH, SO NOW I'M JUST A *KID* AGAIN. SPEAK WHEN YOU'RE SPOKEN TO. NOT YOUR *WHEELMAN!*
SON...IN THIS LIFE WE'RE LEADING, A GUN COMES ALONG... EVEN TO CHURCH.
I'VE LEFT *YOURS* ON THE NIGHTSTAND.
THAT'S THE *IRONY*, ISN'T IT? I WAS MOST AFRAID, MOST DISTURBED WHEN HE LEFT ME BEHIND...
...AND WASN'T I MOST AT RISK WHEN THE *ANGEL OF DEATH* WAS *NOT* HOVERING?

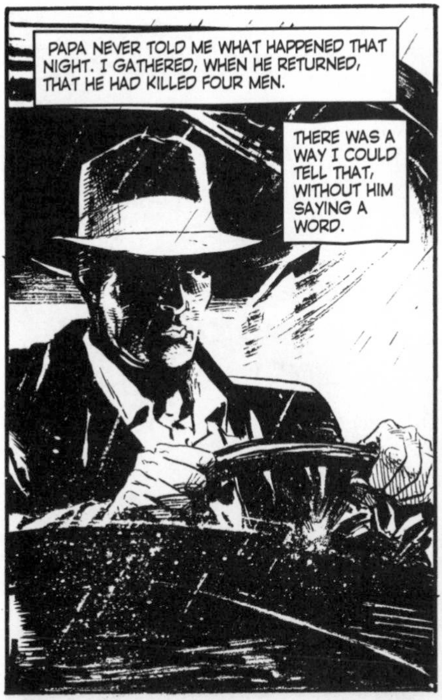
PAPA NEVER TOLD ME WHAT HAPPENED THAT NIGHT. I GATHERED, WHEN HE RETURNED, THAT HE HAD KILLED FOUR MEN.
THERE WAS A WAY I COULD TELL THAT, WITHOUT HIM SAYING A WORD.

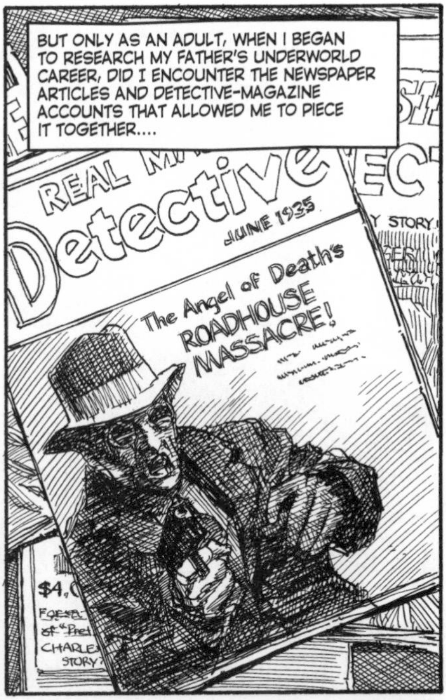
BUT ONLY AS AN ADULT, WHEN I BEGAN TO RESEARCH MY FATHER'S UNDERWORLD CAREER, DID I ENCOUNTER THE NEWSPAPER ARTICLES AND DETECTIVE-MAGAZINE ACCOUNTS THAT ALLOWED ME TO PIECE IT TOGETHER....
Detective
JUNE 1935
The Angel of Death's
ROADHOUSE MASSACRE!

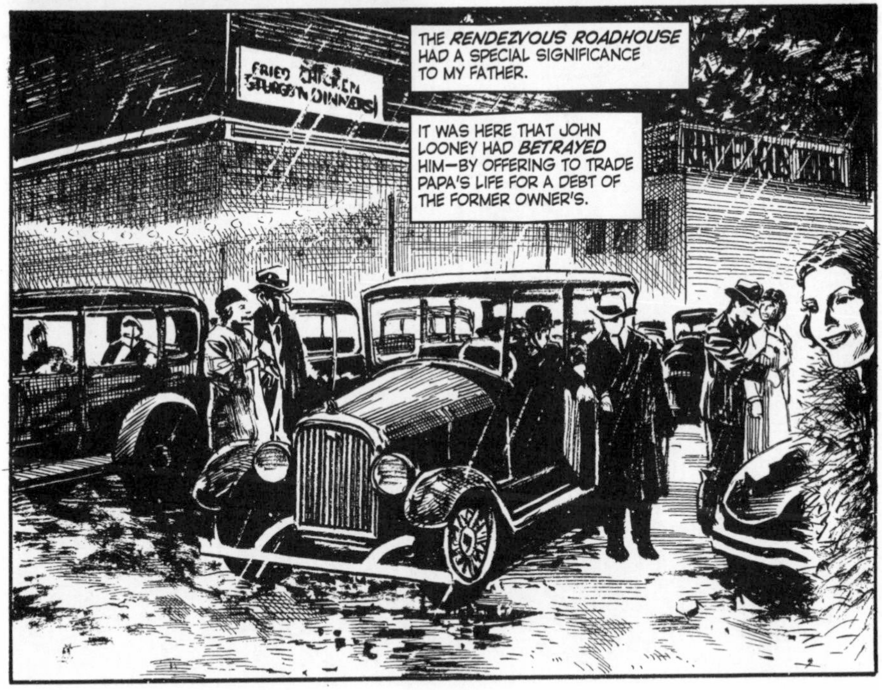
THE *RENDEZVOUS ROADHOUSE* HAD A SPECIAL SIGNIFICANCE TO MY FATHER.
FRIED CHICKEN
STURGEON DINNERS
IT WAS HERE THAT JOHN LOONEY HAD *BETRAYED* HIM—BY OFFERING TO TRADE PAPA'S LIFE FOR A DEBT OF THE FORMER OWNER'S.

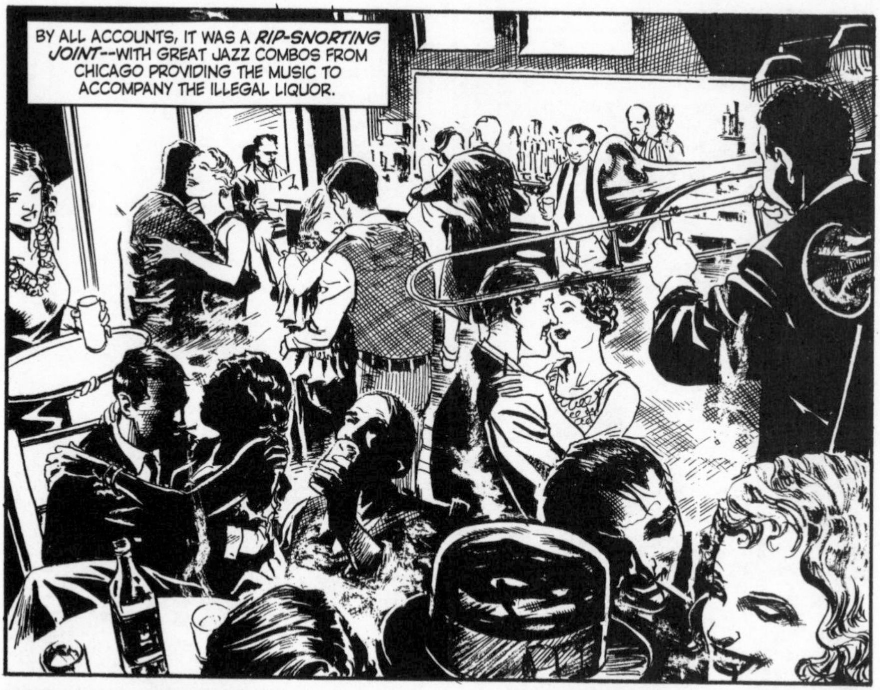
BY ALL ACCOUNTS, IT WAS A *RIP-SNORTING JOINT*--WITH GREAT JAZZ COMBOS FROM CHICAGO PROVIDING THE MUSIC TO ACCOMPANY THE ILLEGAL LIQUOR.

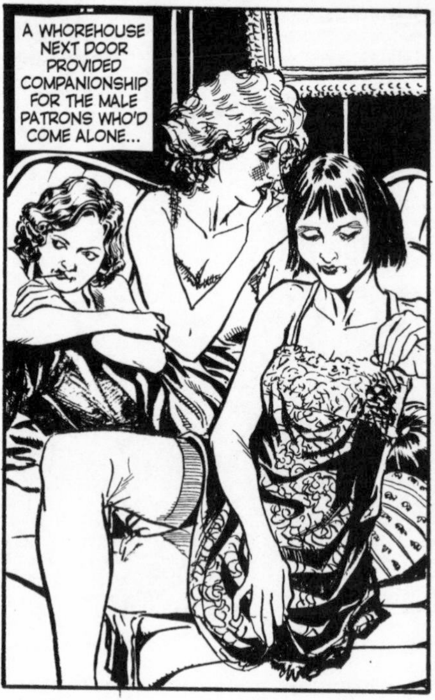
A WHOREHOUSE NEXT DOOR PROVIDED COMPANIONSHIP FOR THE MALE PATRONS WHO'D COME ALONE...

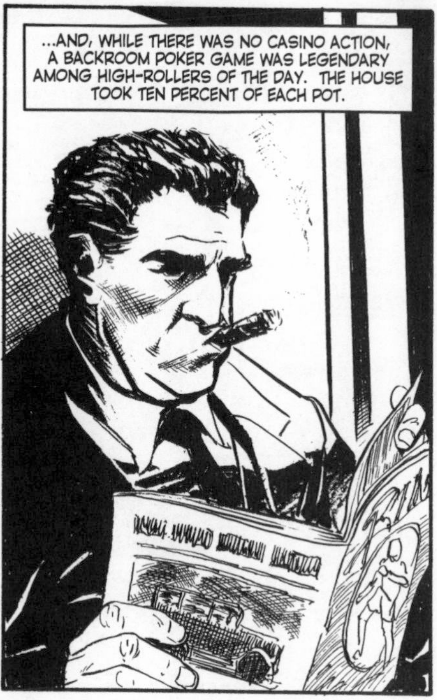
...AND, WHILE THERE WAS NO CASINO ACTION, A BACKROOM POKER GAME WAS LEGENDARY AMONG HIGH-ROLLERS OF THE DAY. THE HOUSE TOOK TEN PERCENT OF EACH POT.

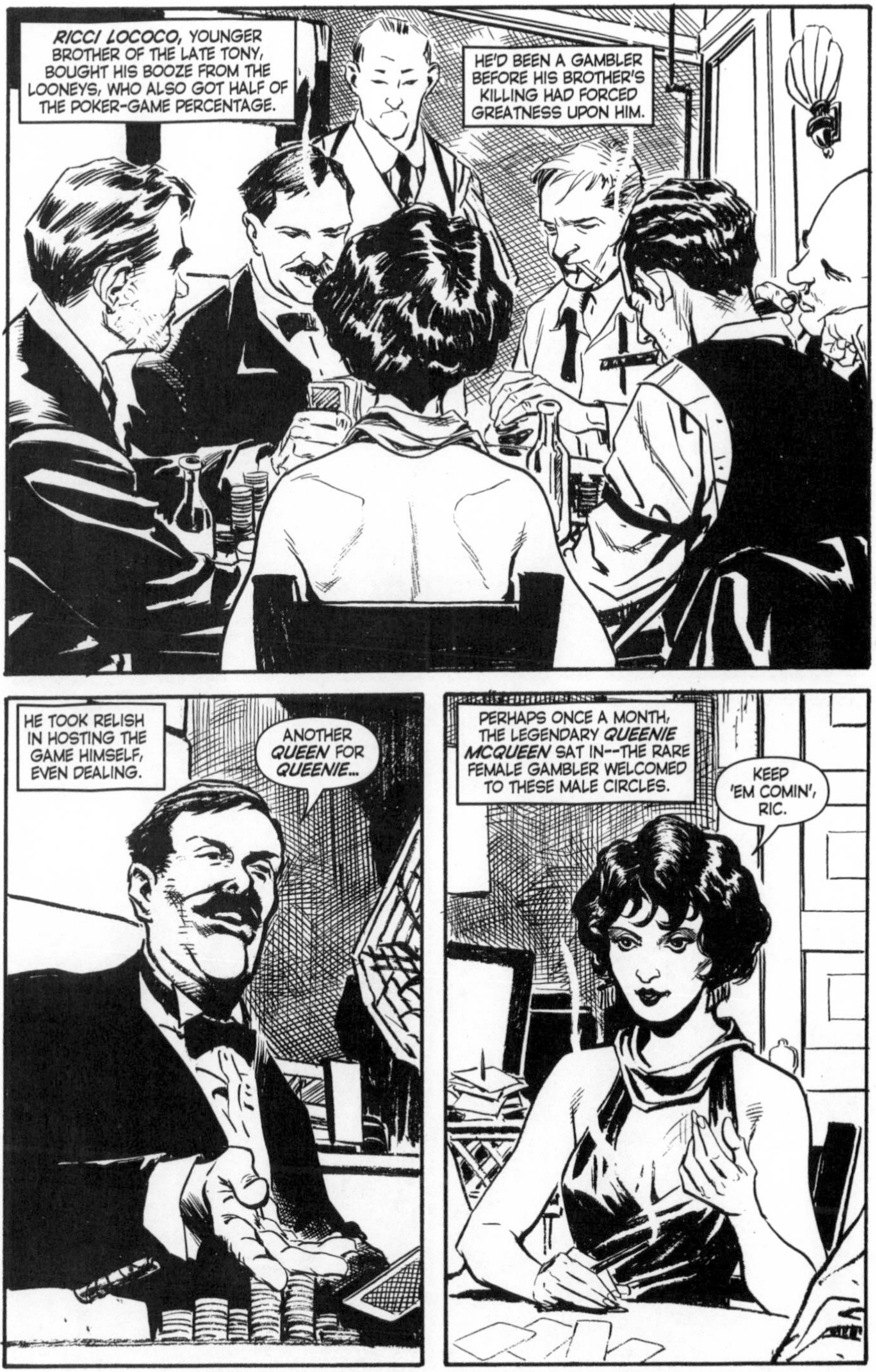
RICCI LOCOCO, YOUNGER BROTHER OF THE LATE TONY, BOUGHT HIS BOOZE FROM THE LOONEYS, WHO ALSO GOT HALF OF THE POKER-GAME PERCENTAGE.
HE'D BEEN A GAMBLER BEFORE HIS BROTHER'S KILLING HAD FORCED GREATNESS UPON HIM.
HE TOOK RELISH IN HOSTING THE GAME HIMSELF, EVEN DEALING.
ANOTHER QUEEN FOR QUEENIE...
PERHAPS ONCE A MONTH, THE LEGENDARY QUEENIE MCQUEEN SAT IN--THE RARE FEMALE GAMBLER WELCOMED TO THESE MALE CIRCLES.
KEEP 'EM COMIN', RIC.

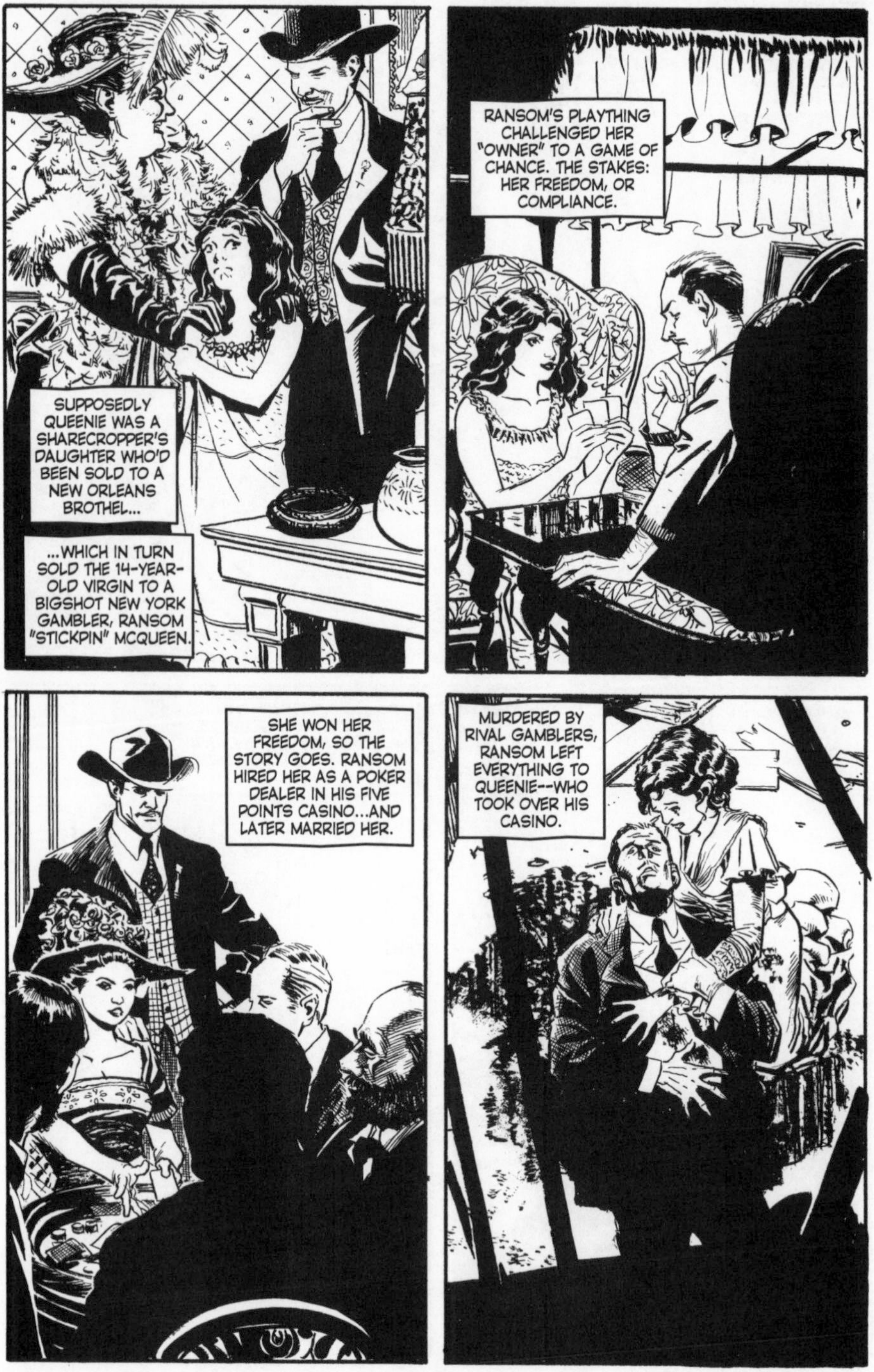
SUPPOSEDLY QUEENIE WAS A SHARECROPPER'S DAUGHTER WHO'D BEEN SOLD TO A NEW ORLEANS BROTHEL...
...WHICH IN TURN SOLD THE 14-YEAR-OLD VIRGIN TO A BIGSHOT NEW YORK GAMBLER, RANSOM "STICKPIN" MCQUEEN.
RANSOM'S PLAYTHING CHALLENGED HER "OWNER" TO A GAME OF CHANCE. THE STAKES: HER FREEDOM, OR COMPLIANCE.
SHE WON HER FREEDOM, SO THE STORY GOES. RANSOM HIRED HER AS A POKER DEALER IN HIS FIVE POINTS CASINO...AND LATER MARRIED HER.
MURDERED BY RIVAL GAMBLERS, RANSOM LEFT EVERYTHING TO QUEENIE--WHO TOOK OVER HIS CASINO.

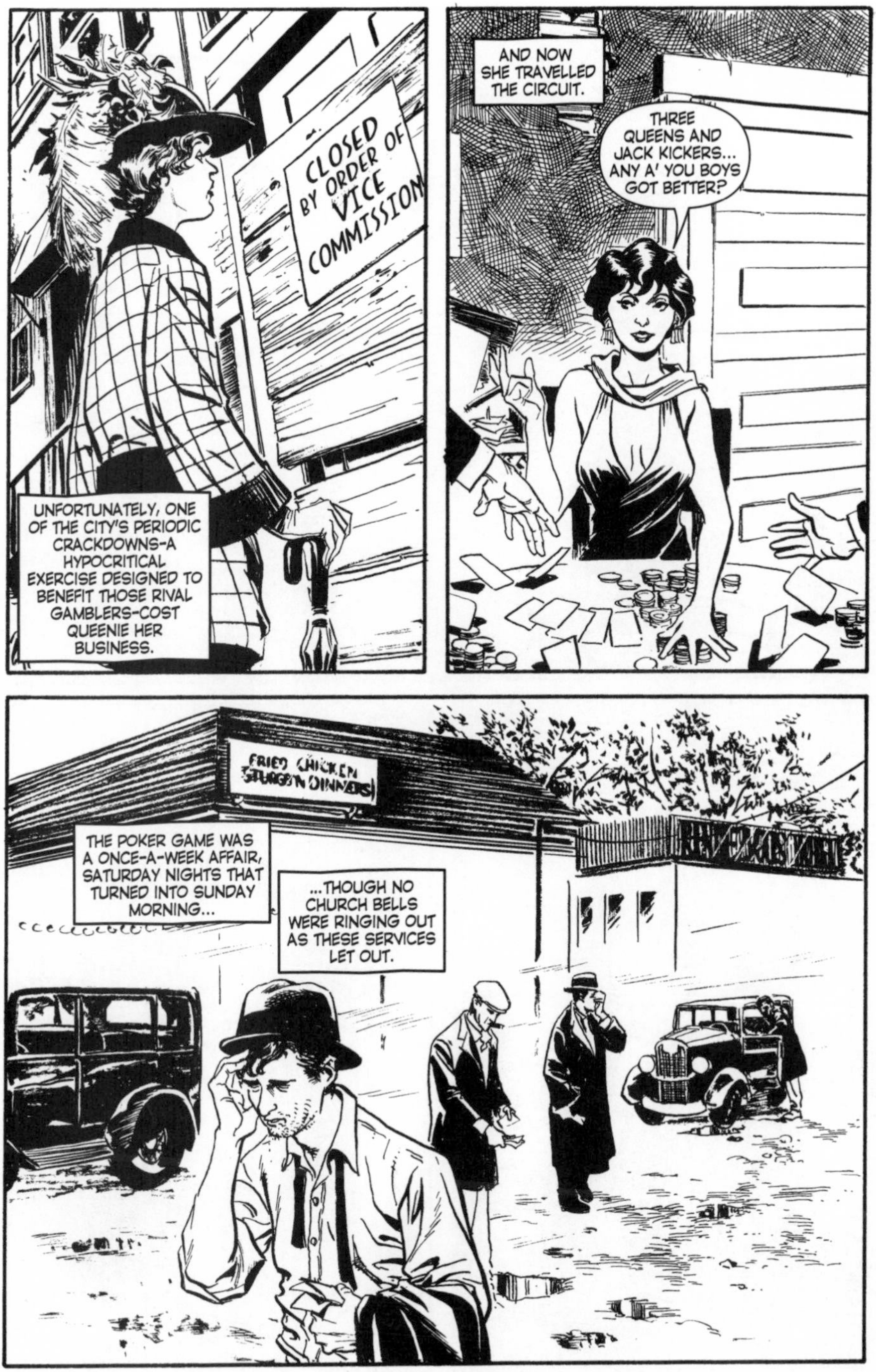
CLOSED BY ORDER OF VICE COMMISSION
UNFORTUNATELY, ONE OF THE CITY'S PERIODIC CRACKDOWNS–A HYPOCRITICAL EXERCISE DESIGNED TO BENEFIT THOSE RIVAL GAMBLERS–COST QUEENIE HER BUSINESS.
AND NOW SHE TRAVELLED THE CIRCUIT.
THREE QUEENS AND JACK KICKERS... ANY A' YOU BOYS GOT BETTER?
FRIED CHICKEN STURGEON DINNERS
THE POKER GAME WAS A ONCE-A-WEEK AFFAIR, SATURDAY NIGHTS THAT TURNED INTO SUNDAY MORNING...
...THOUGH NO CHURCH BELLS WERE RINGING OUT AS THESE SERVICES LET OUT.

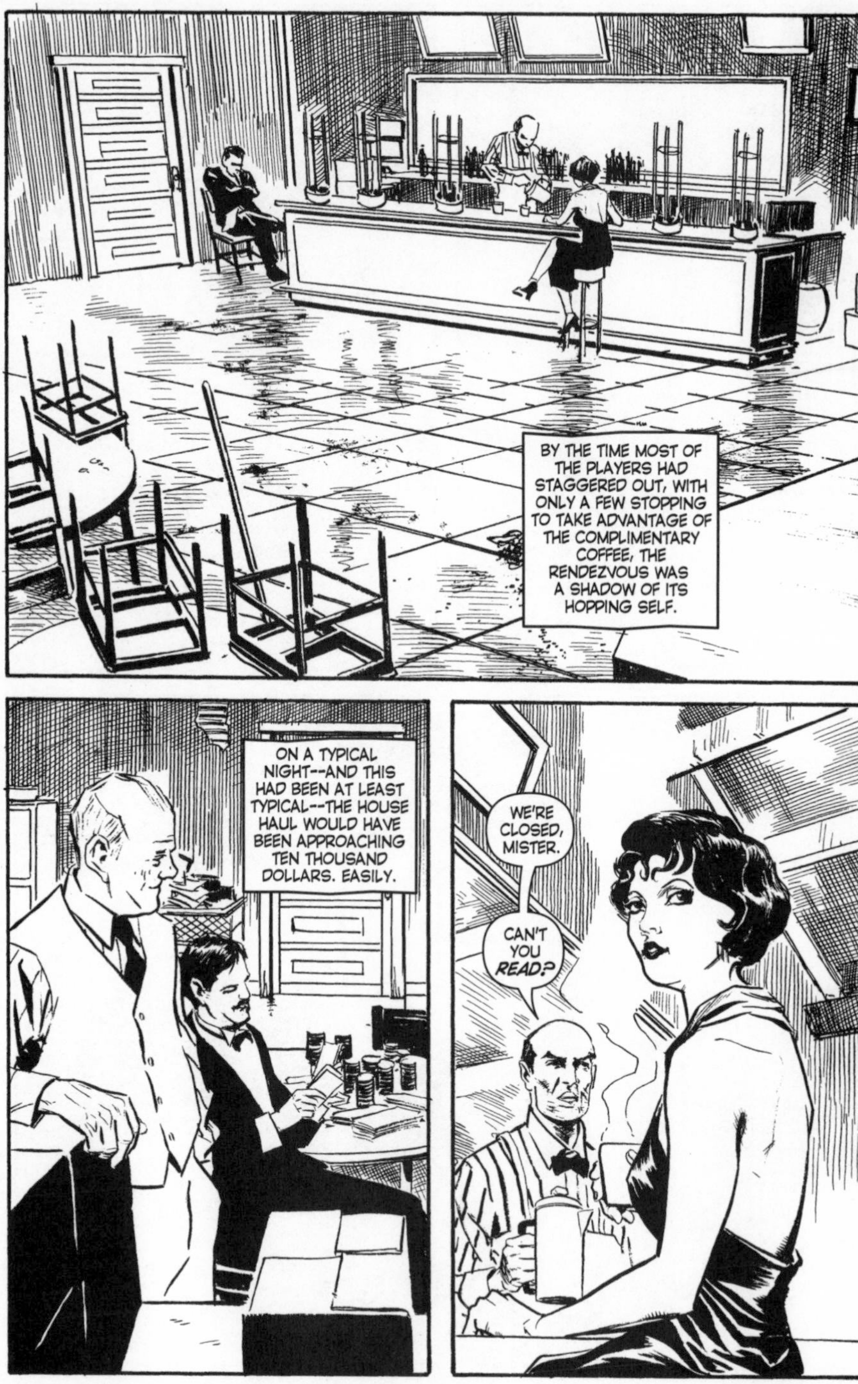
BY THE TIME MOST OF THE PLAYERS HAD STAGGERED OUT, WITH ONLY A FEW STOPPING TO TAKE ADVANTAGE OF THE COMPLIMENTARY COFFEE, THE RENDEZVOUS WAS A SHADOW OF ITS HOPPING SELF.
ON A TYPICAL NIGHT--AND THIS HAD BEEN AT LEAST TYPICAL--THE HOUSE HAUL WOULD HAVE BEEN APPROACHING TEN THOUSAND DOLLARS. EASILY.
WE'RE CLOSED, MISTER.
CAN'T YOU *READ?*

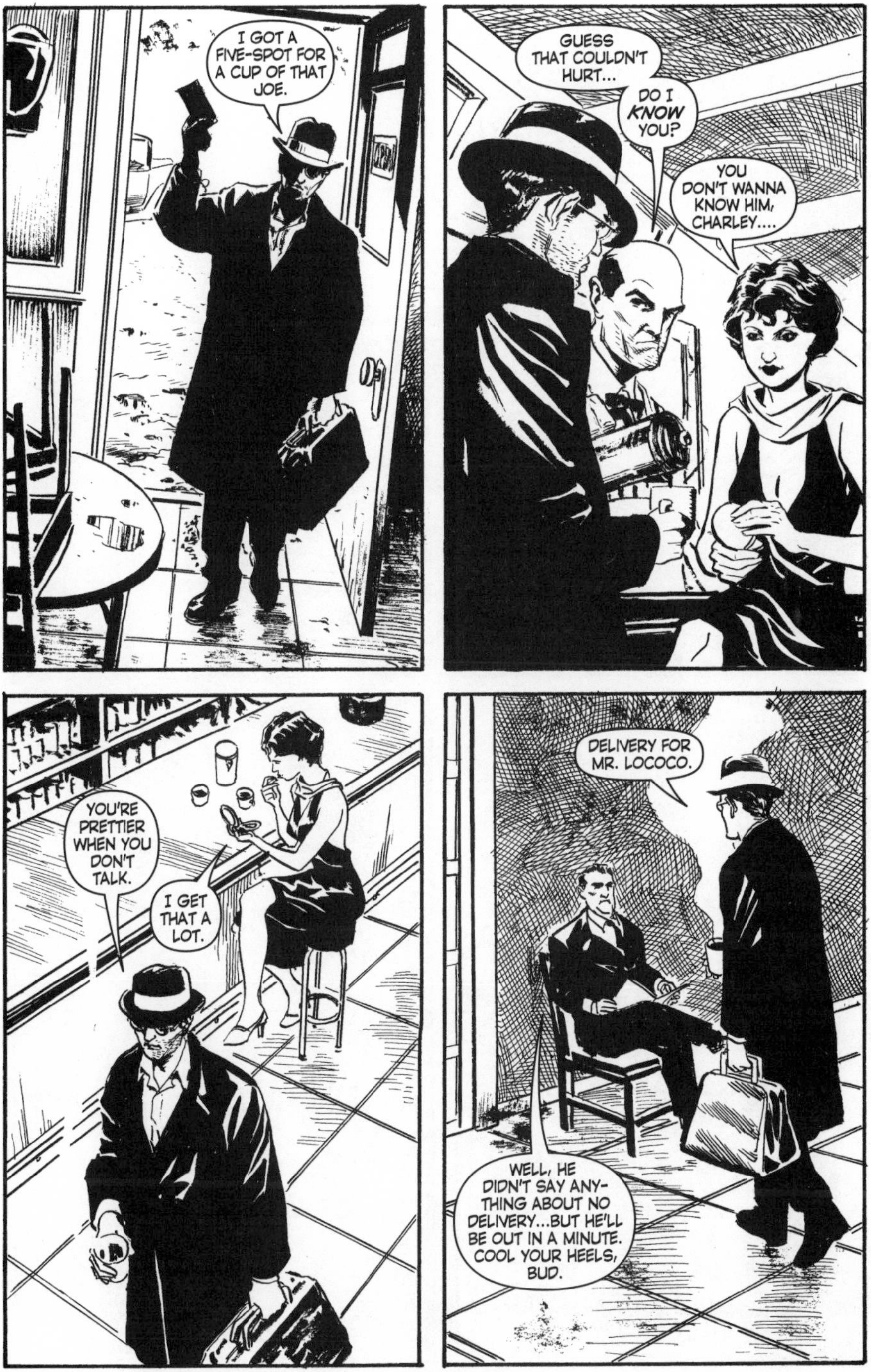
I GOT A FIVE-SPOT FOR A CUP OF THAT JOE.
GUESS THAT COULDN'T HURT...
DO I KNOW YOU?
YOU DON'T WANNA KNOW HIM, CHARLEY....
YOU'RE PRETTIER WHEN YOU DON'T TALK.
I GET THAT A LOT.
DELIVERY FOR MR. LOCOCO.
WELL, HE DIDN'T SAY ANY-THING ABOUT NO DELIVERY...BUT HE'LL BE OUT IN A MINUTE. COOL YOUR HEELS, BUD.

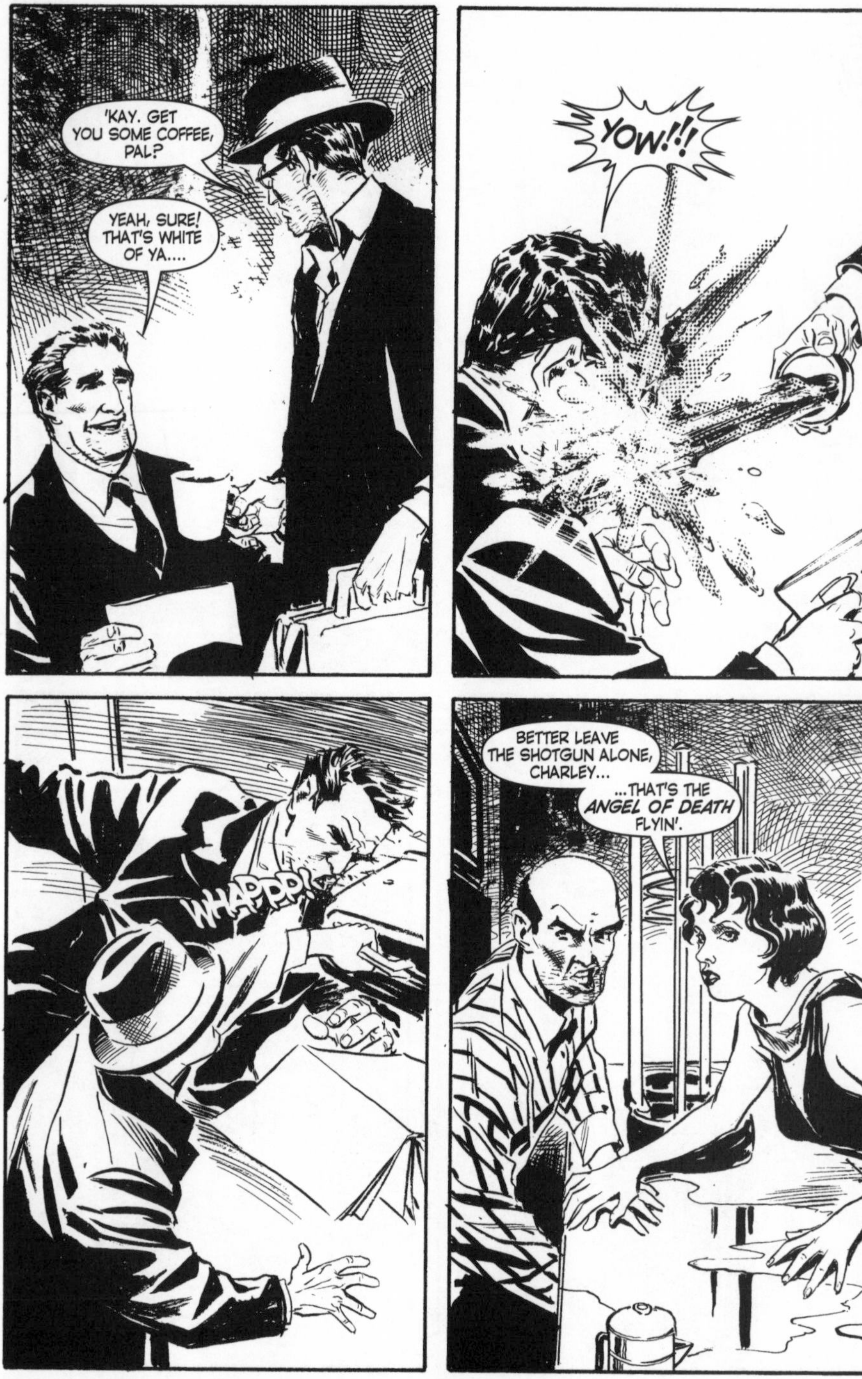
'KAY. GET YOU SOME COFFEE, PAL?
YEAH, SURE! THAT'S WHITE OF YA....
YOW!!!
WHAPPP!
BETTER LEAVE THE SHOTGUN ALONE, CHARLEY...
...THAT'S THE *ANGEL OF DEATH* FLYIN'.

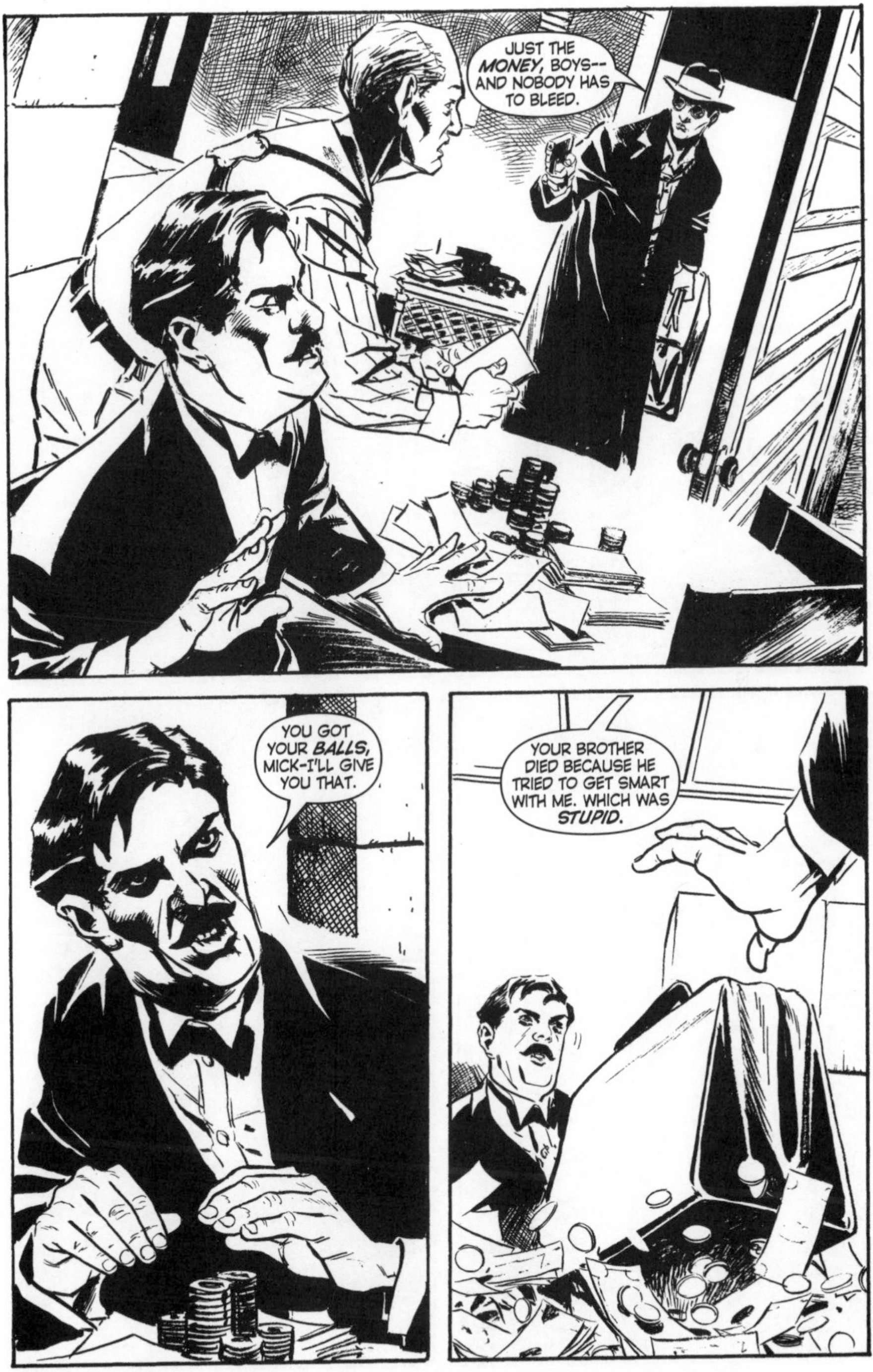
JUST THE MONEY, BOYS-- AND NOBODY HAS TO BLEED.
YOU GOT YOUR BALLS, MICK-I'LL GIVE YOU THAT.
YOUR BROTHER DIED BECAUSE HE TRIED TO GET SMART WITH ME. WHICH WAS STUPID.

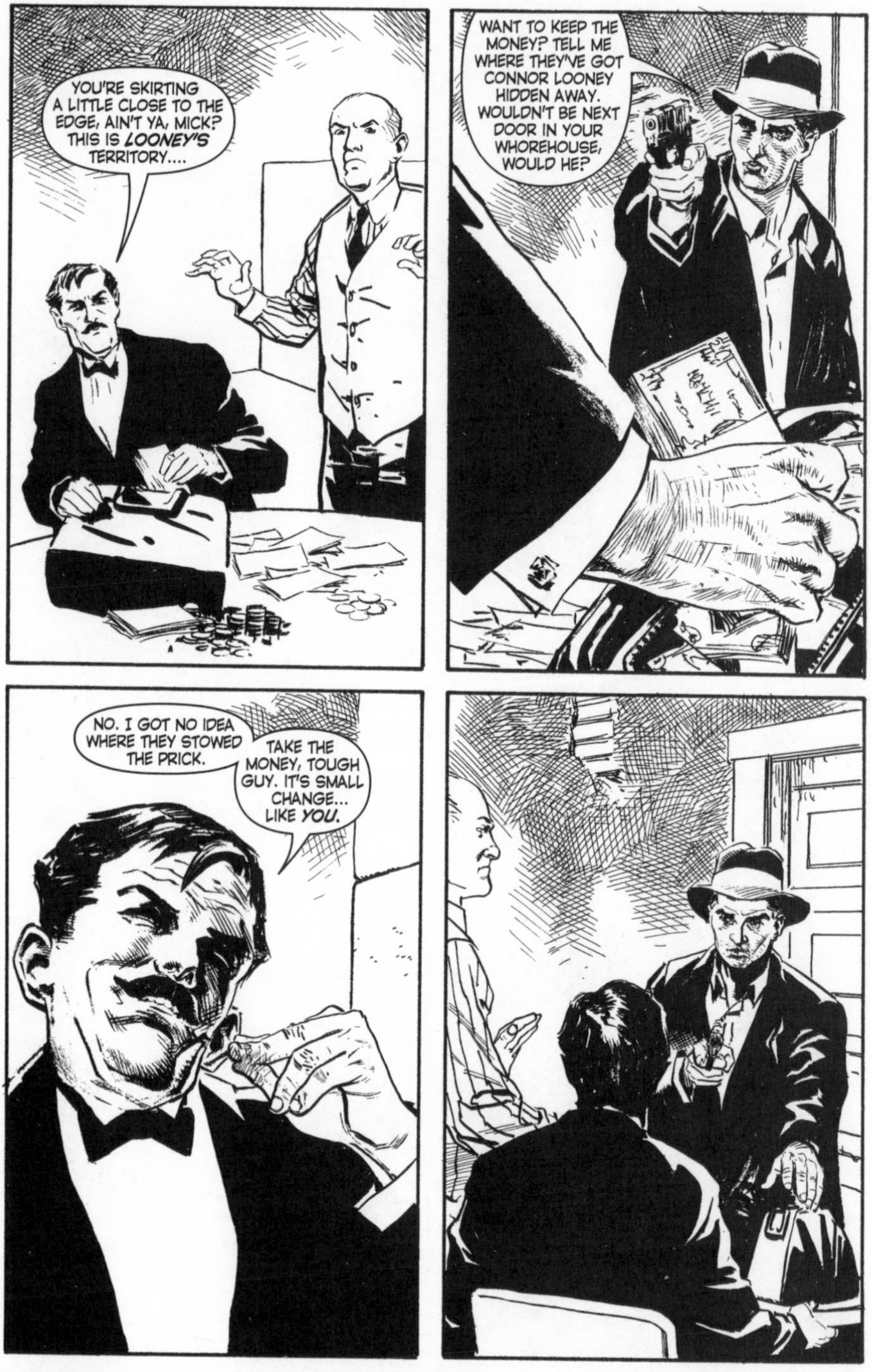
YOU'RE SKIRTING A LITTLE CLOSE TO THE EDGE, AIN'T YA, MICK? THIS IS *LOONEY'S* TERRITORY....
WANT TO KEEP THE MONEY? TELL ME WHERE THEY'VE GOT CONNOR LOONEY HIDDEN AWAY. WOULDN'T BE NEXT DOOR IN YOUR WHOREHOUSE, WOULD HE?
NO. I GOT NO IDEA WHERE THEY STOWED THE PRICK.
TAKE THE MONEY, TOUGH GUY. IT'S SMALL CHANGE... LIKE *YOU*.

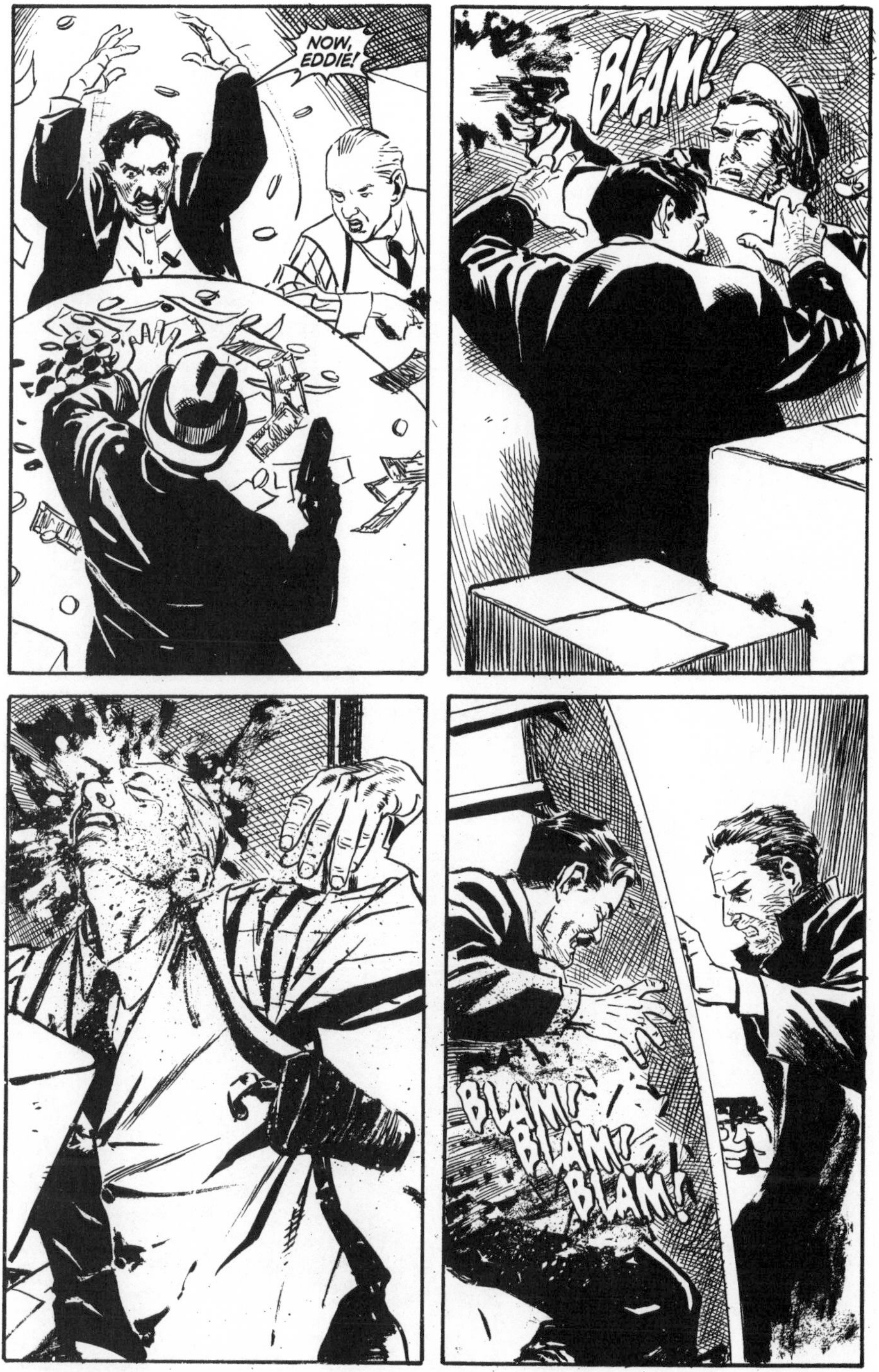
NOW, EDDIE!
BLAM!
BLAM!
BLAM!
BLAM!

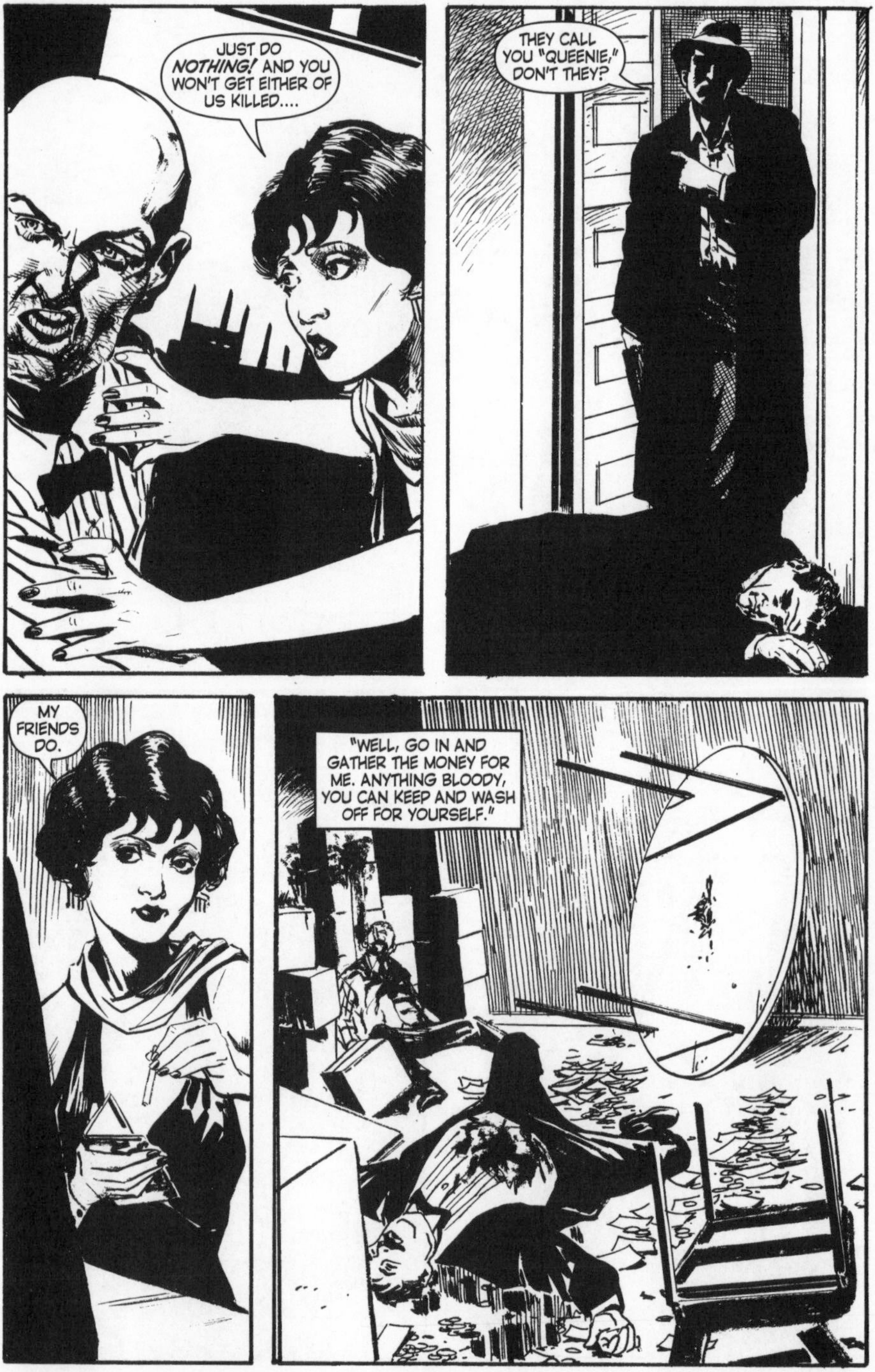

JUST DO NOTHING! AND YOU WON'T GET EITHER OF US KILLED....
THEY CALL YOU "QUEENIE," DON'T THEY?
MY FRIENDS DO.
"WELL, GO IN AND GATHER THE MONEY FOR ME. ANYTHING BLOODY, YOU CAN KEEP AND WASH OFF FOR YOURSELF."

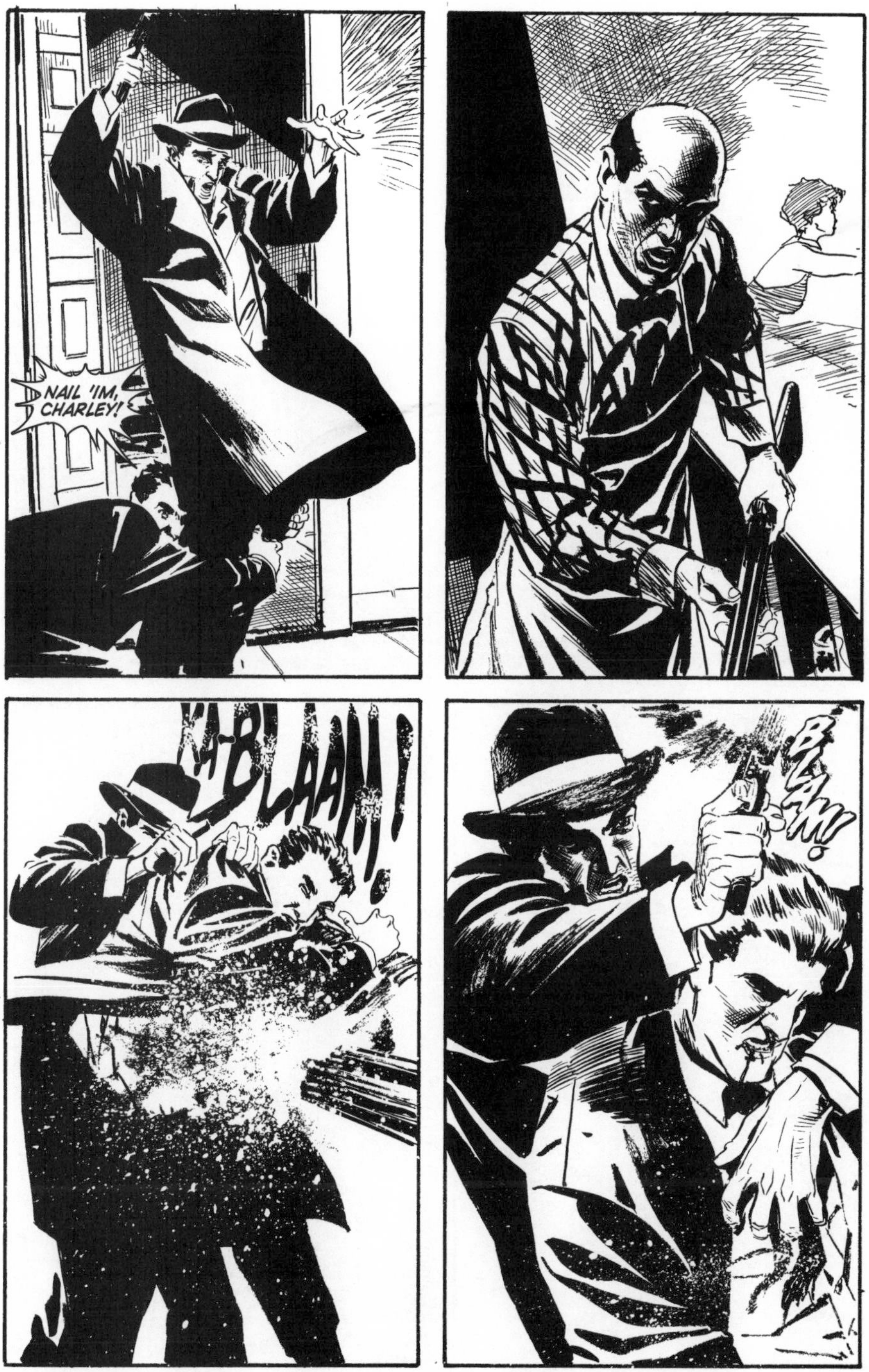
NAIL 'IM, CHARLEY!
KA-BLAAM!
BLAAM!

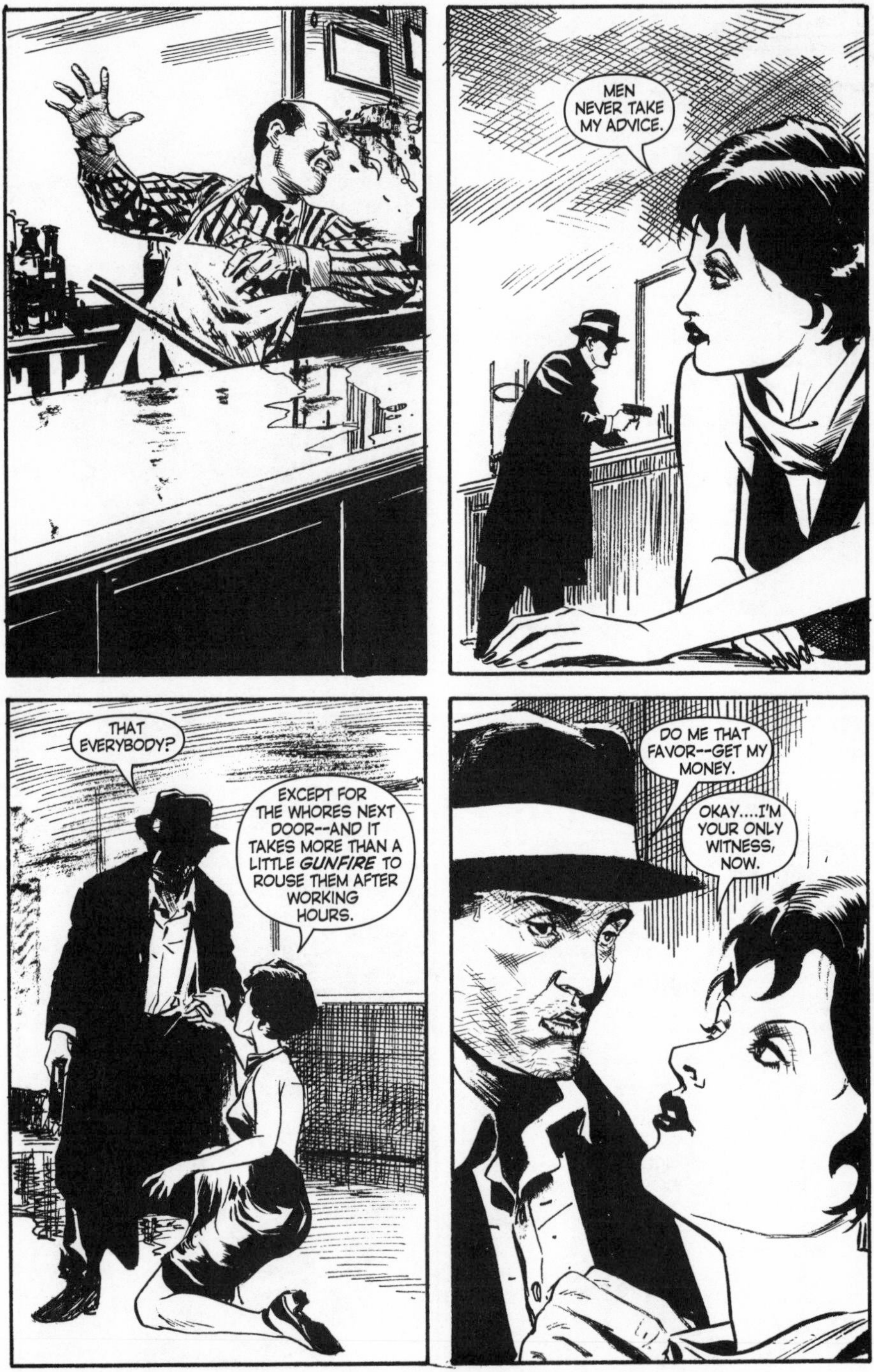
MEN NEVER TAKE MY ADVICE.
THAT EVERYBODY?
EXCEPT FOR THE WHORES NEXT DOOR--AND IT TAKES MORE THAN A LITTLE GUNFIRE TO ROUSE THEM AFTER WORKING HOURS.
DO ME THAT FAVOR--GET MY MONEY.
OKAY....I'M YOUR ONLY WITNESS, NOW.

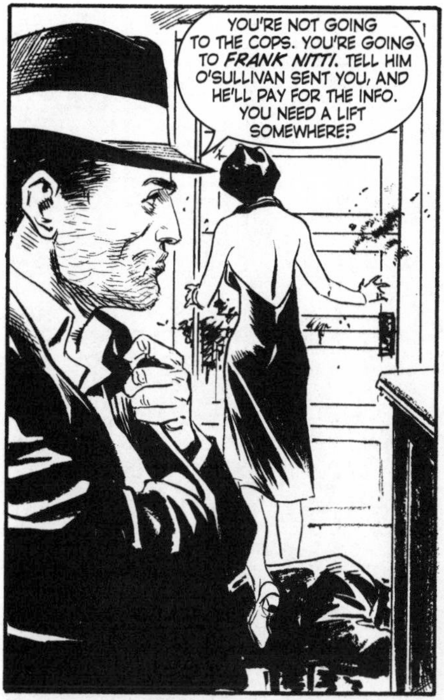
YOU'RE NOT GOING TO THE COPS. YOU'RE GOING TO FRANK NITTI. TELL HIM O'SULLIVAN SENT YOU, AND HE'LL PAY FOR THE INFO. YOU NEED A LIFT SOMEWHERE?

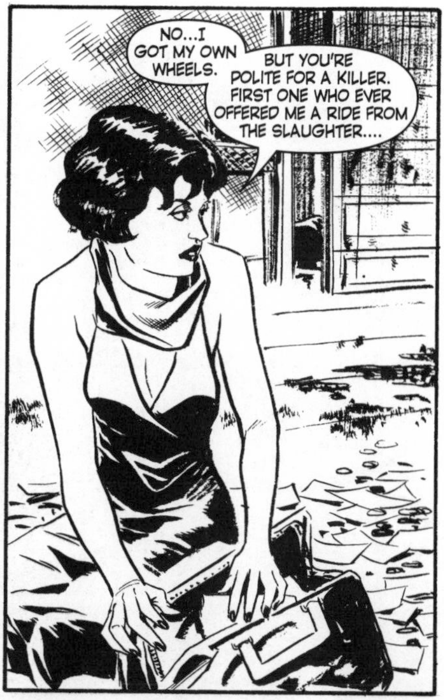
NO...I GOT MY OWN WHEELS.
BUT YOU'RE POLITE FOR A KILLER. FIRST ONE WHO EVER OFFERED ME A RIDE FROM THE SLAUGHTER....

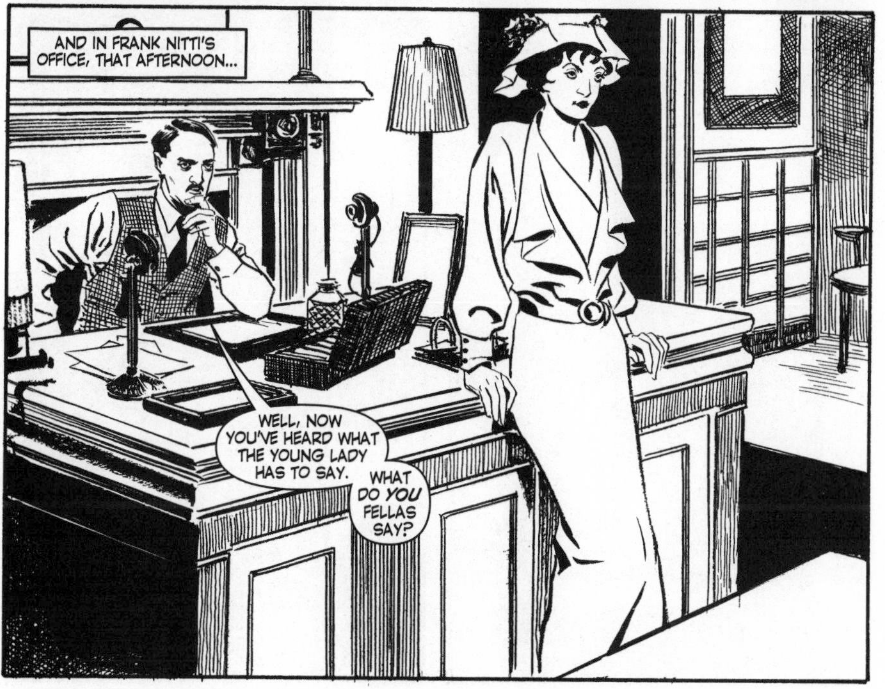
AND IN FRANK NITTI'S OFFICE, THAT AFTERNOON...
WELL, NOW YOU'VE HEARD WHAT THE YOUNG LADY HAS TO SAY.
WHAT DO YOU FELLAS SAY?

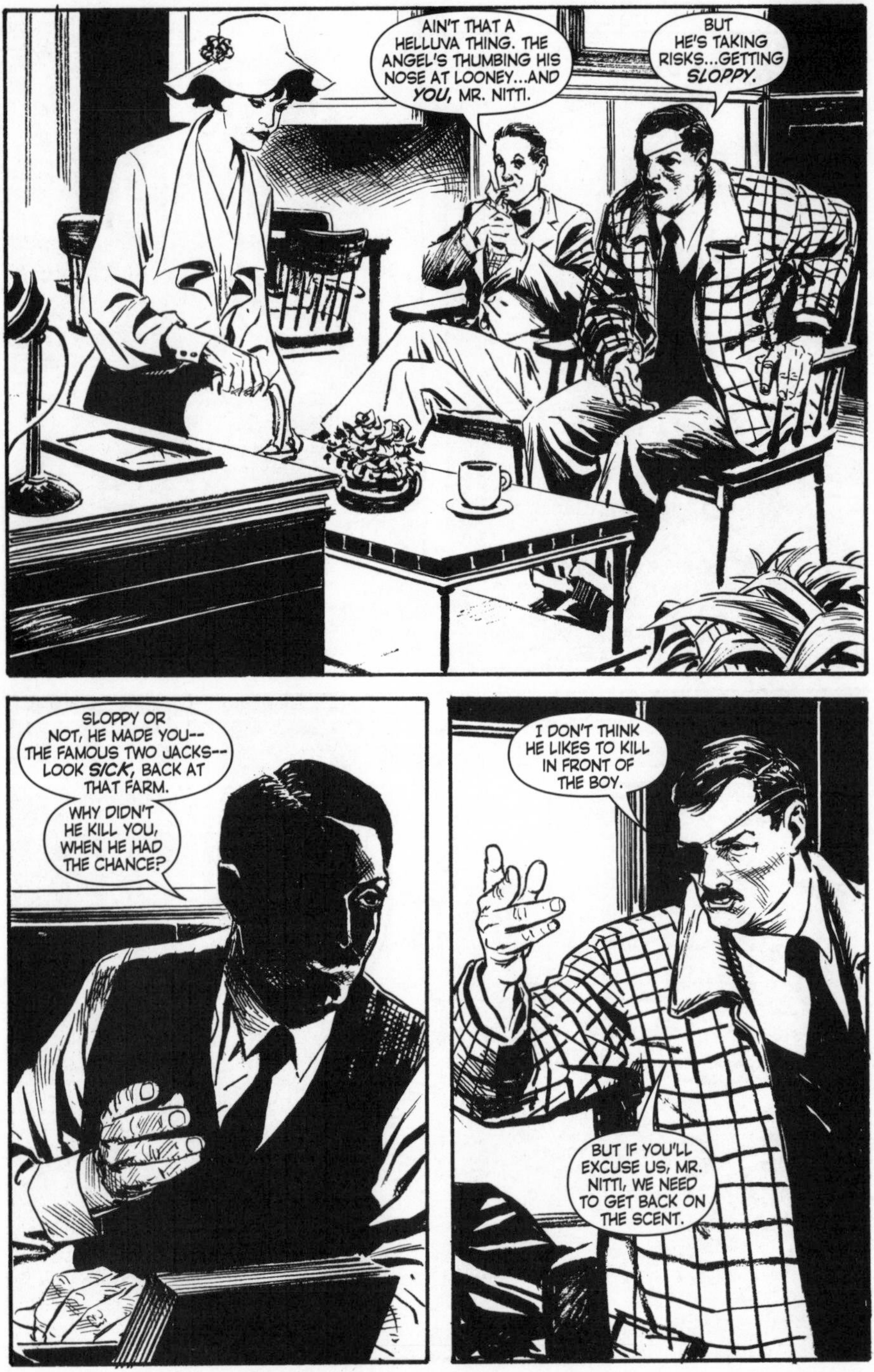
AIN'T THAT A HELLUVA THING. THE ANGEL'S THUMBING HIS NOSE AT LOONEY...AND *YOU*, MR. NITTI.
BUT HE'S TAKING RISKS...GETTING *SLOPPY*.
SLOPPY OR NOT, HE MADE YOU-- THE FAMOUS TWO JACKS-- LOOK *SICK*, BACK AT THAT FARM.
WHY DIDN'T HE KILL YOU, WHEN HE HAD THE CHANCE?
I DON'T THINK HE LIKES TO KILL IN FRONT OF THE BOY.
BUT IF YOU'LL EXCUSE US, MR. NITTI, WE NEED TO GET BACK ON THE SCENT.

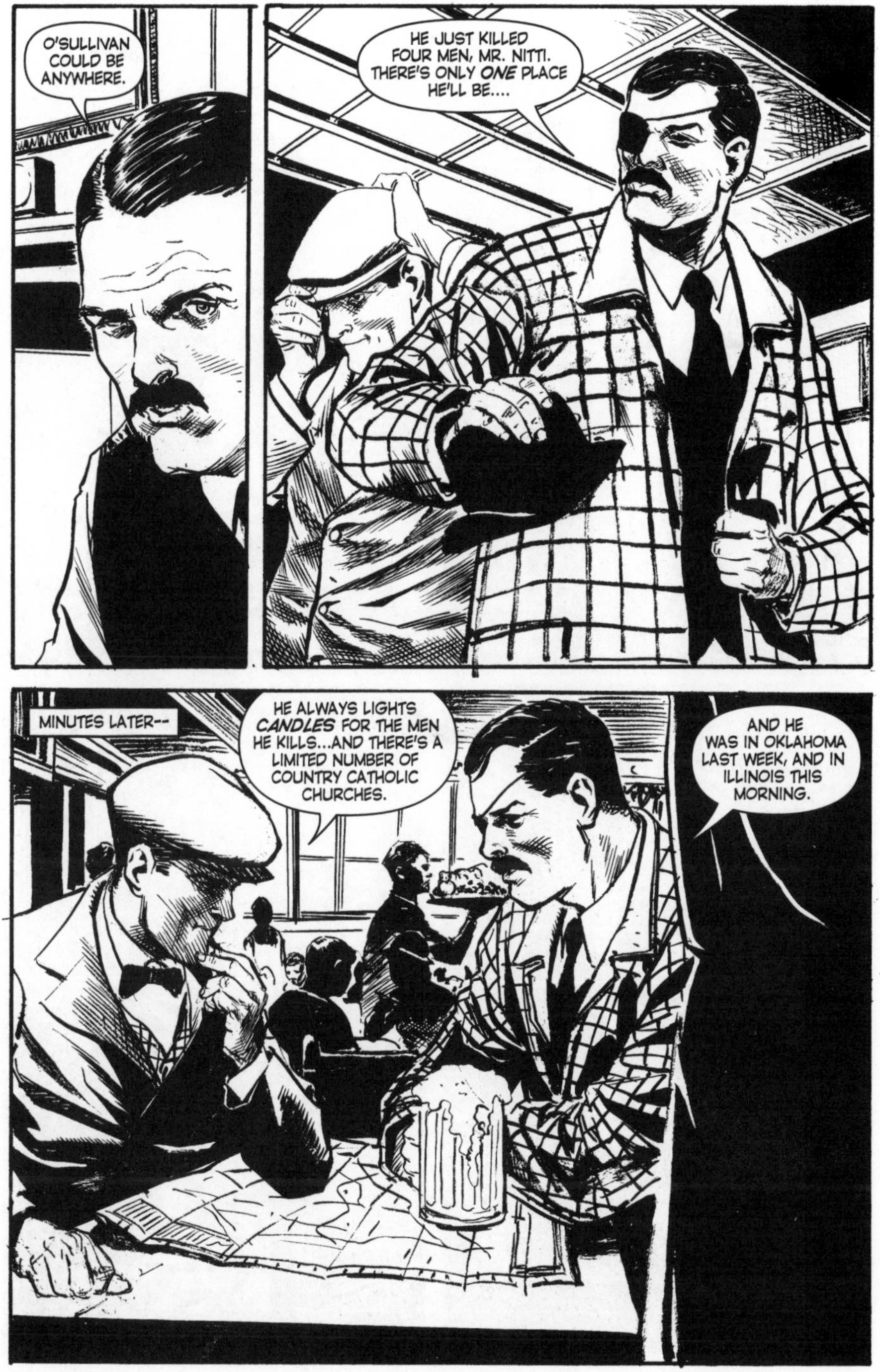
O'SULLIVAN COULD BE ANYWHERE.
HE JUST KILLED FOUR MEN, MR. NITTI. THERE'S ONLY ONE PLACE HE'LL BE....
MINUTES LATER--
HE ALWAYS LIGHTS CANDLES FOR THE MEN HE KILLS...AND THERE'S A LIMITED NUMBER OF COUNTRY CATHOLIC CHURCHES.
AND HE WAS IN OKLAHOMA LAST WEEK, AND IN ILLINOIS THIS MORNING.

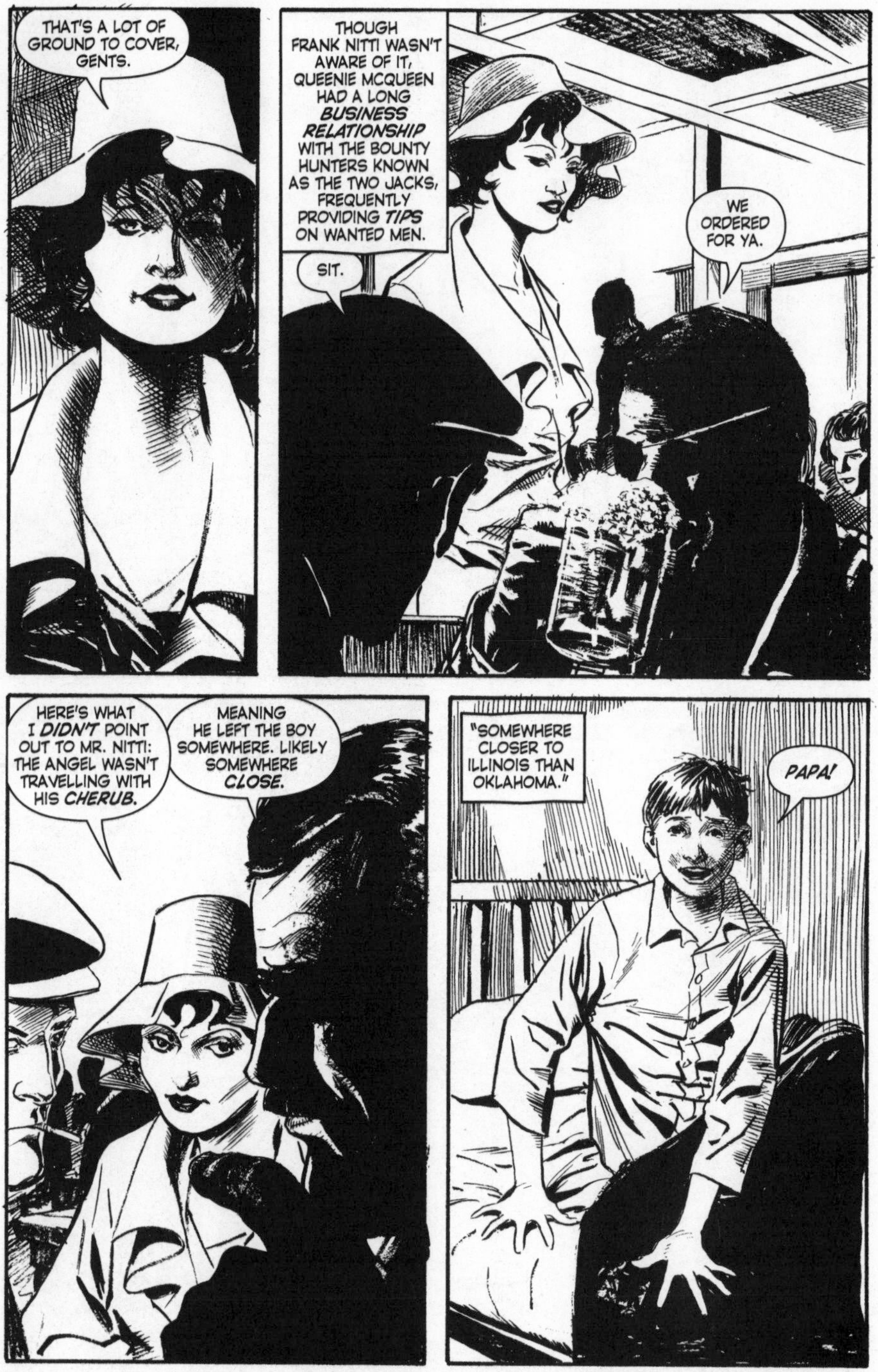

THAT'S A LOT OF GROUND TO COVER, GENTS.
THOUGH FRANK NITTI WASN'T AWARE OF IT, QUEENIE MCQUEEN HAD A LONG BUSINESS RELATIONSHIP WITH THE BOUNTY HUNTERS KNOWN AS THE TWO JACKS, FREQUENTLY PROVIDING TIPS ON WANTED MEN.
SIT.
WE ORDERED FOR YA.
HERE'S WHAT I DIDN'T POINT OUT TO MR. NITTI: THE ANGEL WASN'T TRAVELLING WITH HIS CHERUB.
MEANING HE LEFT THE BOY SOMEWHERE. LIKELY SOMEWHERE CLOSE.
"SOMEWHERE CLOSER TO ILLINOIS THAN OKLAHOMA."
PAPA!

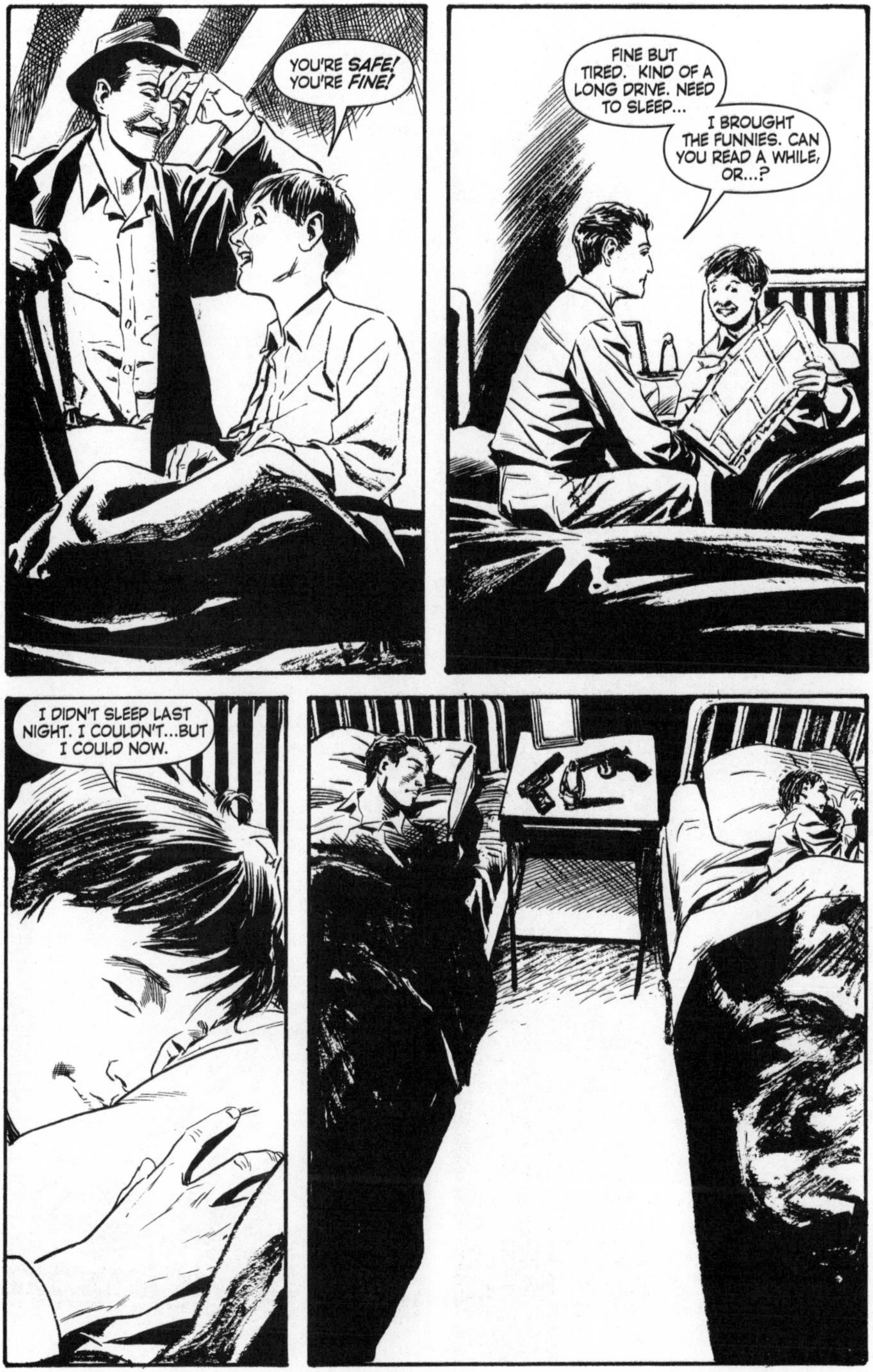
YOU'RE *SAFE!* YOU'RE *FINE!*
FINE BUT TIRED. KIND OF A LONG DRIVE. NEED TO SLEEP...
I BROUGHT THE FUNNIES. CAN YOU READ A WHILE, OR...?
I DIDN'T SLEEP LAST NIGHT. I COULDN'T...BUT I COULD NOW.

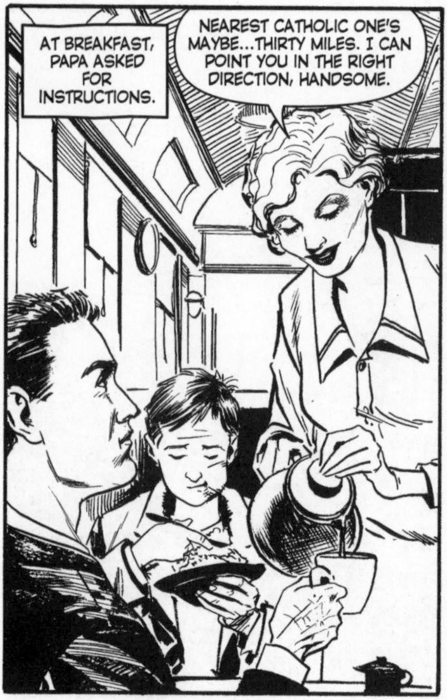
AT BREAKFAST, PAPA ASKED FOR INSTRUCTIONS.
NEAREST CATHOLIC ONE'S MAYBE...THIRTY MILES. I CAN POINT YOU IN THE RIGHT DIRECTION, HANDSOME.

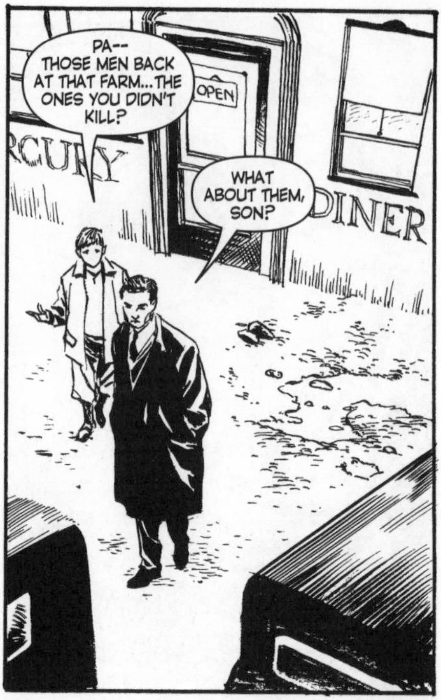
PA-- THOSE MEN BACK AT THAT FARM...THE ONES YOU DIDN'T KILL?
OPEN
RCURY
DINER
WHAT ABOUT THEM, SON?

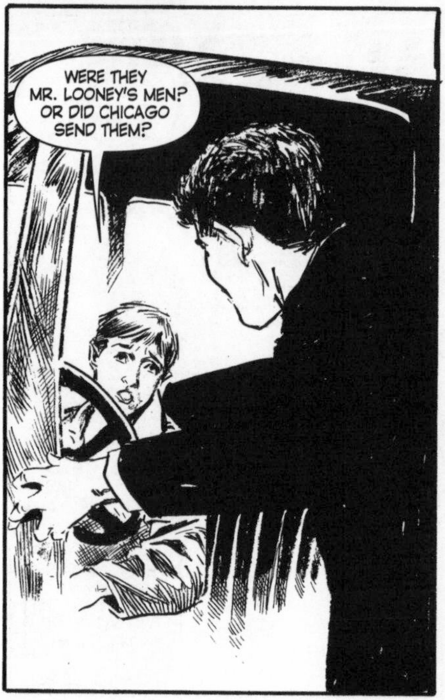
WERE THEY MR. LOONEY'S MEN? OR DID CHICAGO SEND THEM?

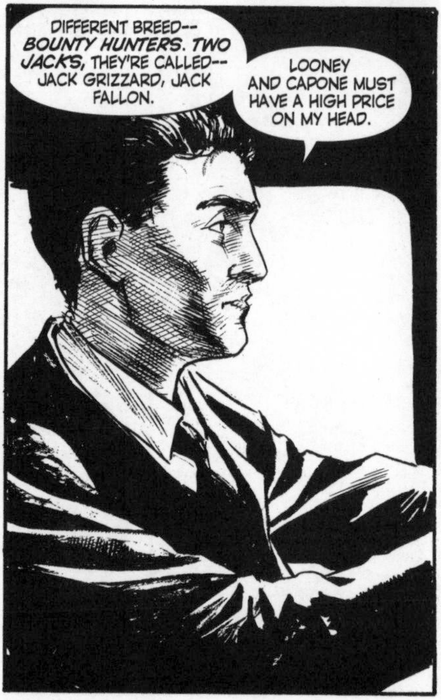
DIFFERENT BREED-- *BOUNTY HUNTERS. TWO JACKS*, THEY'RE CALLED-- JACK GRIZZARD, JACK FALLON.
LOONEY AND CAPONE MUST HAVE A HIGH PRICE ON MY HEAD.

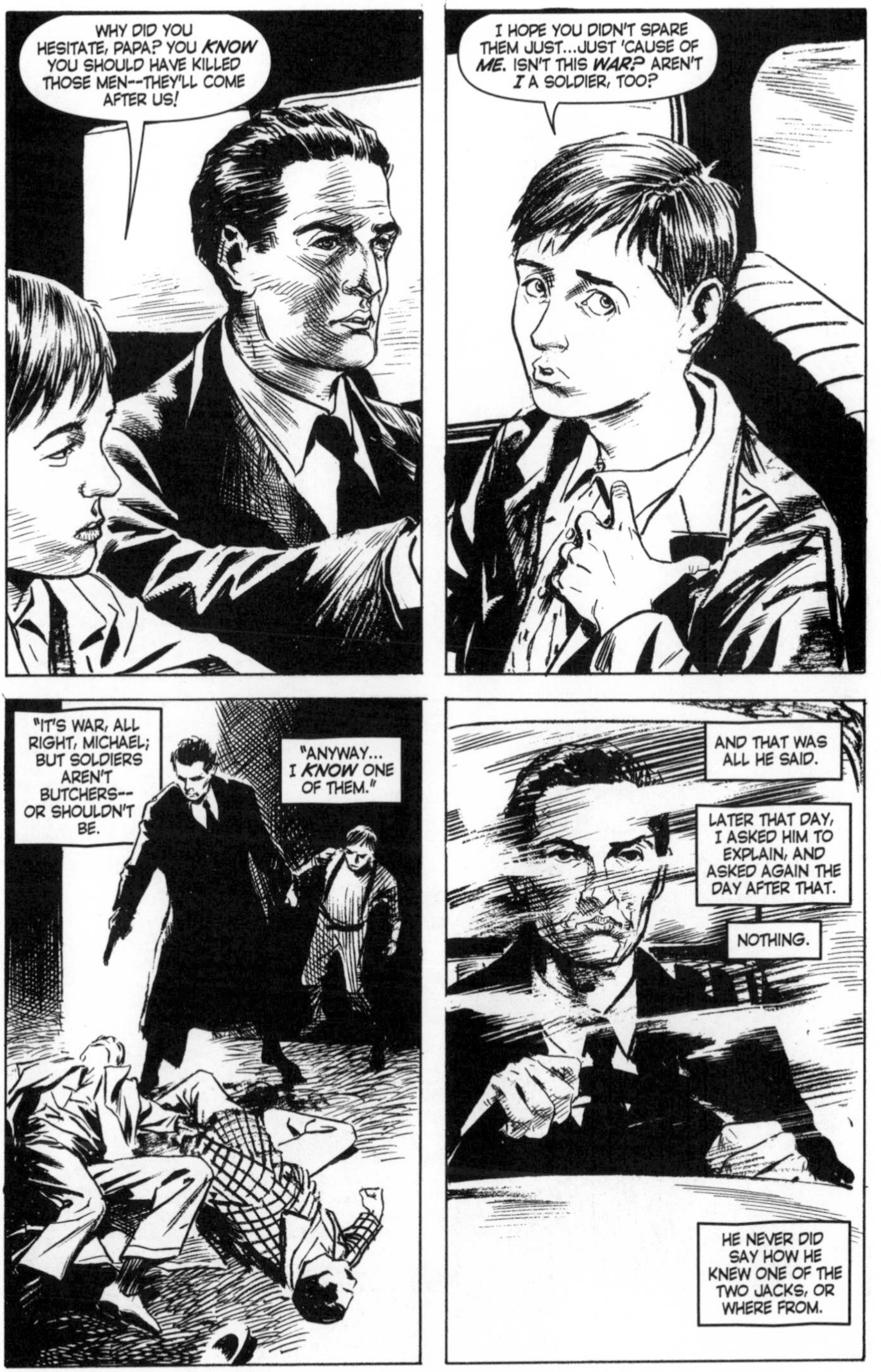
WHY DID YOU HESITATE, PAPA? YOU KNOW YOU SHOULD HAVE KILLED THOSE MEN--THEY'LL COME AFTER US!
I HOPE YOU DIDN'T SPARE THEM JUST...JUST 'CAUSE OF ME. ISN'T THIS WAR? AREN'T I A SOLDIER, TOO?
"IT'S WAR, ALL RIGHT, MICHAEL; BUT SOLDIERS AREN'T BUTCHERS-- OR SHOULDN'T BE.
"ANYWAY... I KNOW ONE OF THEM."
AND THAT WAS ALL HE SAID.
LATER THAT DAY, I ASKED HIM TO EXPLAIN, AND ASKED AGAIN THE DAY AFTER THAT.
NOTHING.
HE NEVER DID SAY HOW HE KNEW ONE OF THE TWO JACKS, OR WHERE FROM.

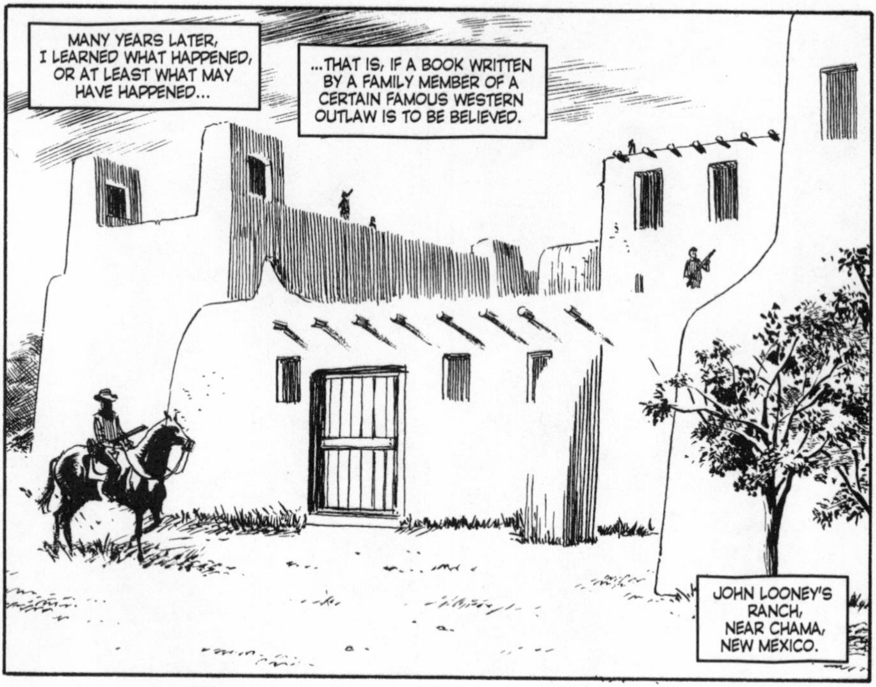
MANY YEARS LATER, I LEARNED WHAT HAPPENED, OR AT LEAST WHAT MAY HAVE HAPPENED...
...THAT IS, IF A BOOK WRITTEN BY A FAMILY MEMBER OF A CERTAIN FAMOUS WESTERN OUTLAW IS TO BE BELIEVED.
JOHN LOONEY'S RANCH, NEAR CHAMA, NEW MEXICO.

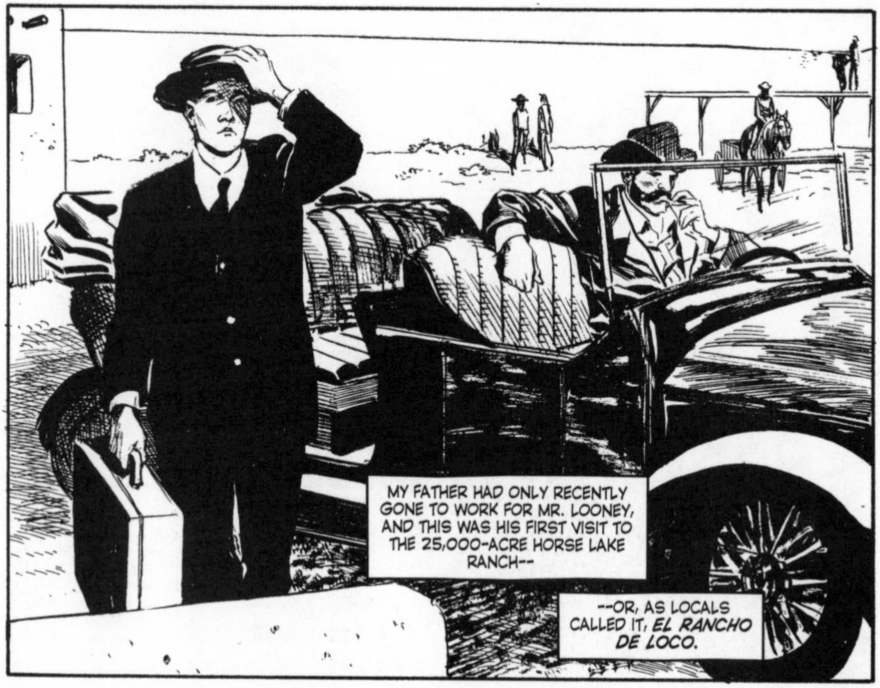
MY FATHER HAD ONLY RECENTLY GONE TO WORK FOR MR. LOONEY, AND THIS WAS HIS FIRST VISIT TO THE 25,000-ACRE HORSE LAKE RANCH--
--OR, AS LOCALS CALLED IT, *EL RANCHO DE LOCO*.

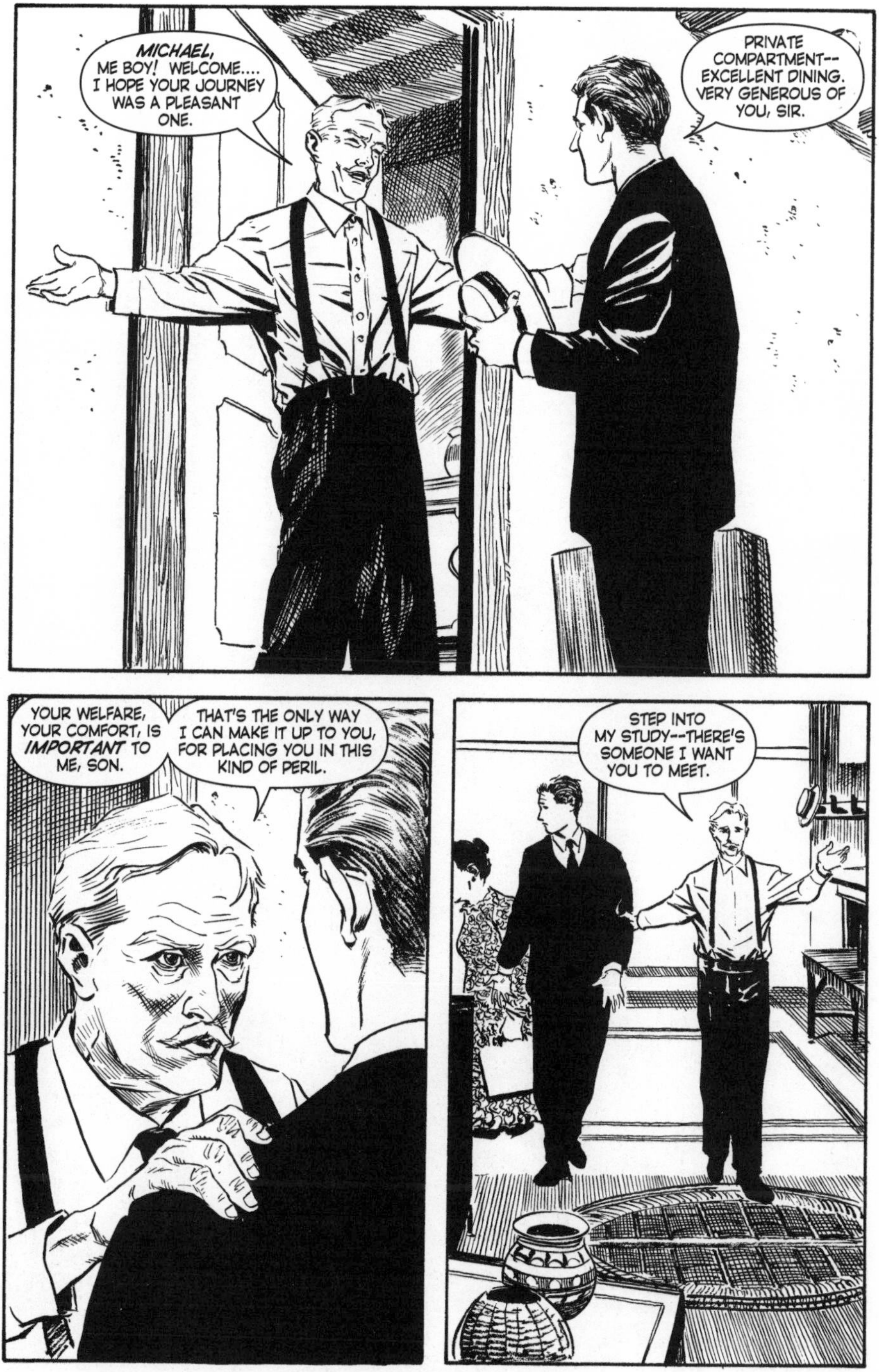
MICHAEL, ME BOY! WELCOME.... I HOPE YOUR JOURNEY WAS A PLEASANT ONE.
PRIVATE COMPARTMENT-- EXCELLENT DINING. VERY GENEROUS OF YOU, SIR.
YOUR WELFARE, YOUR COMFORT, IS *IMPORTANT* TO ME, SON.
THAT'S THE ONLY WAY I CAN MAKE IT UP TO YOU, FOR PLACING YOU IN THIS KIND OF PERIL.
STEP INTO MY STUDY--THERE'S SOMEONE I WANT YOU TO MEET.

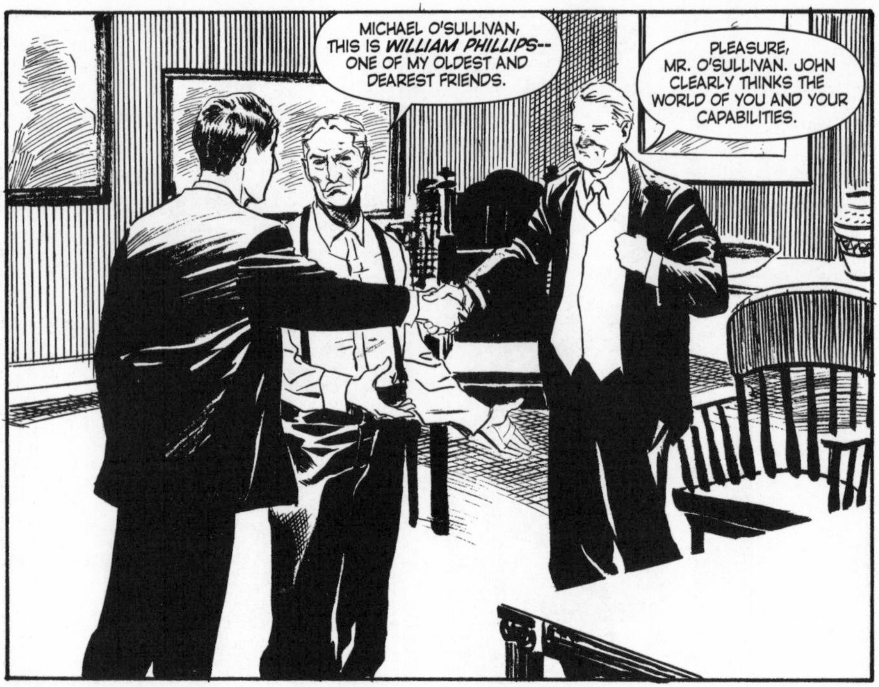
MICHAEL O'SULLIVAN, THIS IS WILLIAM PHILLIPS-- ONE OF MY OLDEST AND DEAREST FRIENDS.
PLEASURE, MR. O'SULLIVAN. JOHN CLEARLY THINKS THE WORLD OF YOU AND YOUR CAPABILITIES.

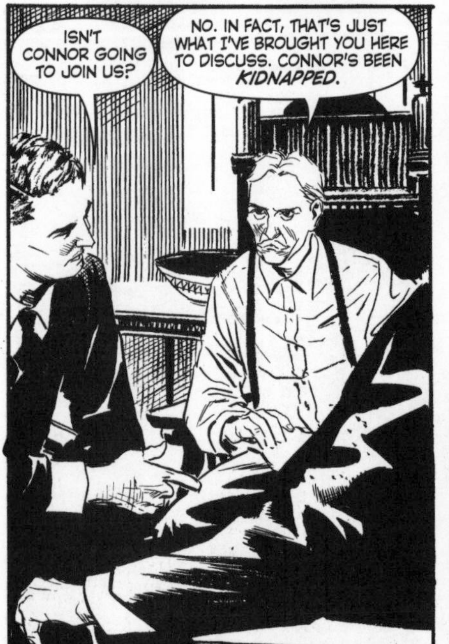
ISN'T CONNOR GOING TO JOIN US?
NO. IN FACT, THAT'S JUST WHAT I'VE BROUGHT YOU HERE TO DISCUSS. CONNOR'S BEEN KIDNAPPED.

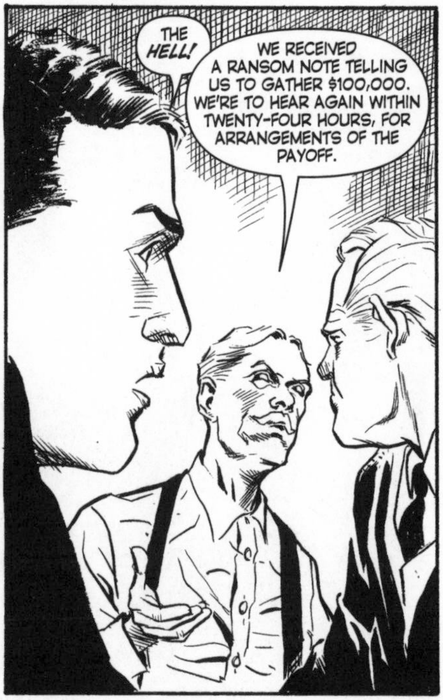
THE HELL!
WE RECEIVED A RANSOM NOTE TELLING US TO GATHER $100,000. WE'RE TO HEAR AGAIN WITHIN TWENTY-FOUR HOURS, FOR ARRANGEMENTS OF THE PAYOFF.

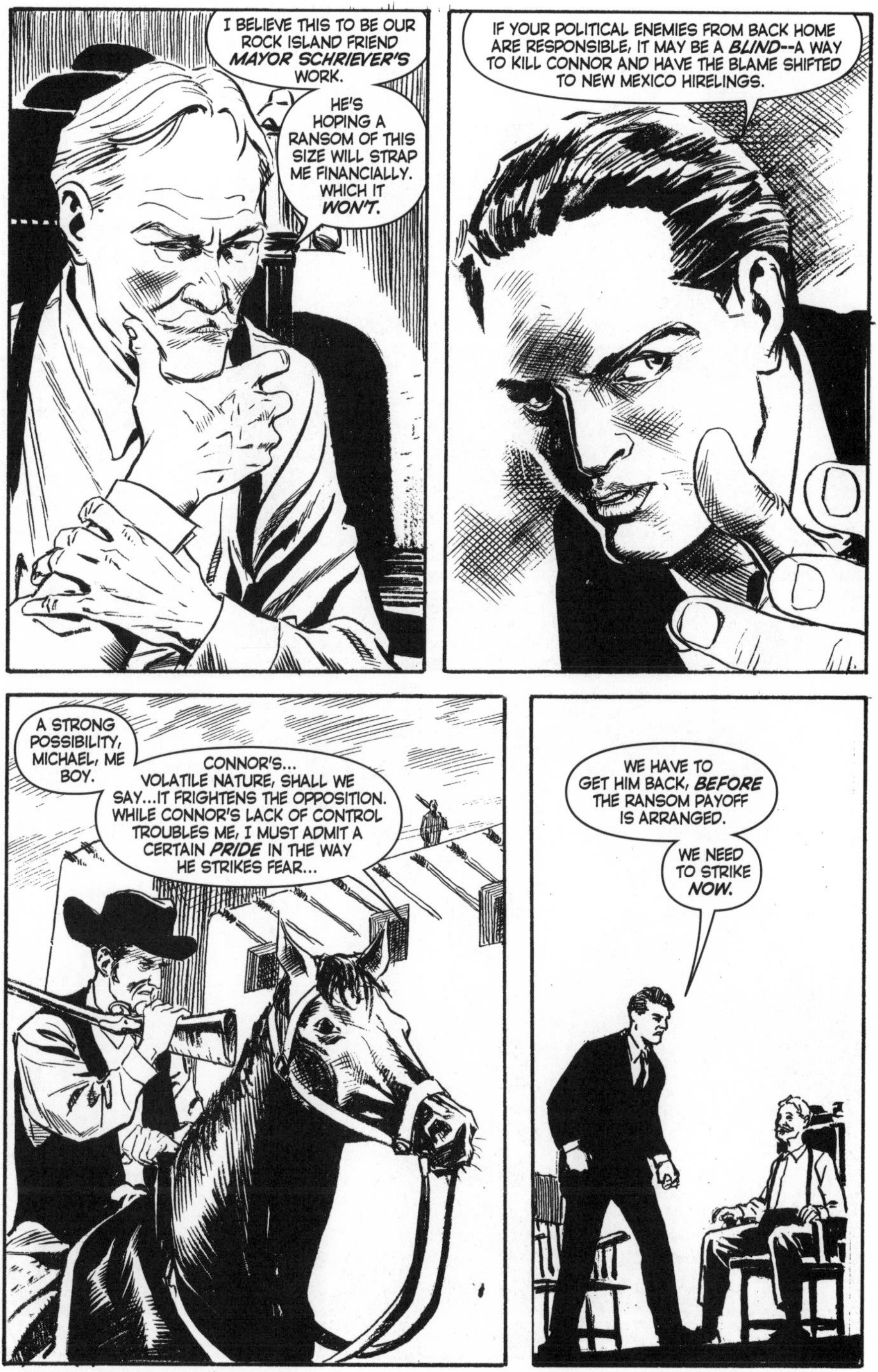
I BELIEVE THIS TO BE OUR ROCK ISLAND FRIEND *MAYOR SCHRIEVER'S* WORK.
HE'S HOPING A RANSOM OF THIS SIZE WILL STRAP ME FINANCIALLY. WHICH IT *WON'T*.
IF YOUR POLITICAL ENEMIES FROM BACK HOME ARE RESPONSIBLE, IT MAY BE A *BLIND*--A WAY TO KILL CONNOR AND HAVE THE BLAME SHIFTED TO NEW MEXICO HIRELINGS.
A STRONG POSSIBILITY, MICHAEL, ME BOY.
CONNOR'S... VOLATILE NATURE, SHALL WE SAY...IT FRIGHTENS THE OPPOSITION. WHILE CONNOR'S LACK OF CONTROL TROUBLES ME, I MUST ADMIT A CERTAIN *PRIDE* IN THE WAY HE STRIKES FEAR...
WE HAVE TO GET HIM BACK, *BEFORE* THE RANSOM PAYOFF IS ARRANGED.
WE NEED TO STRIKE *NOW*.

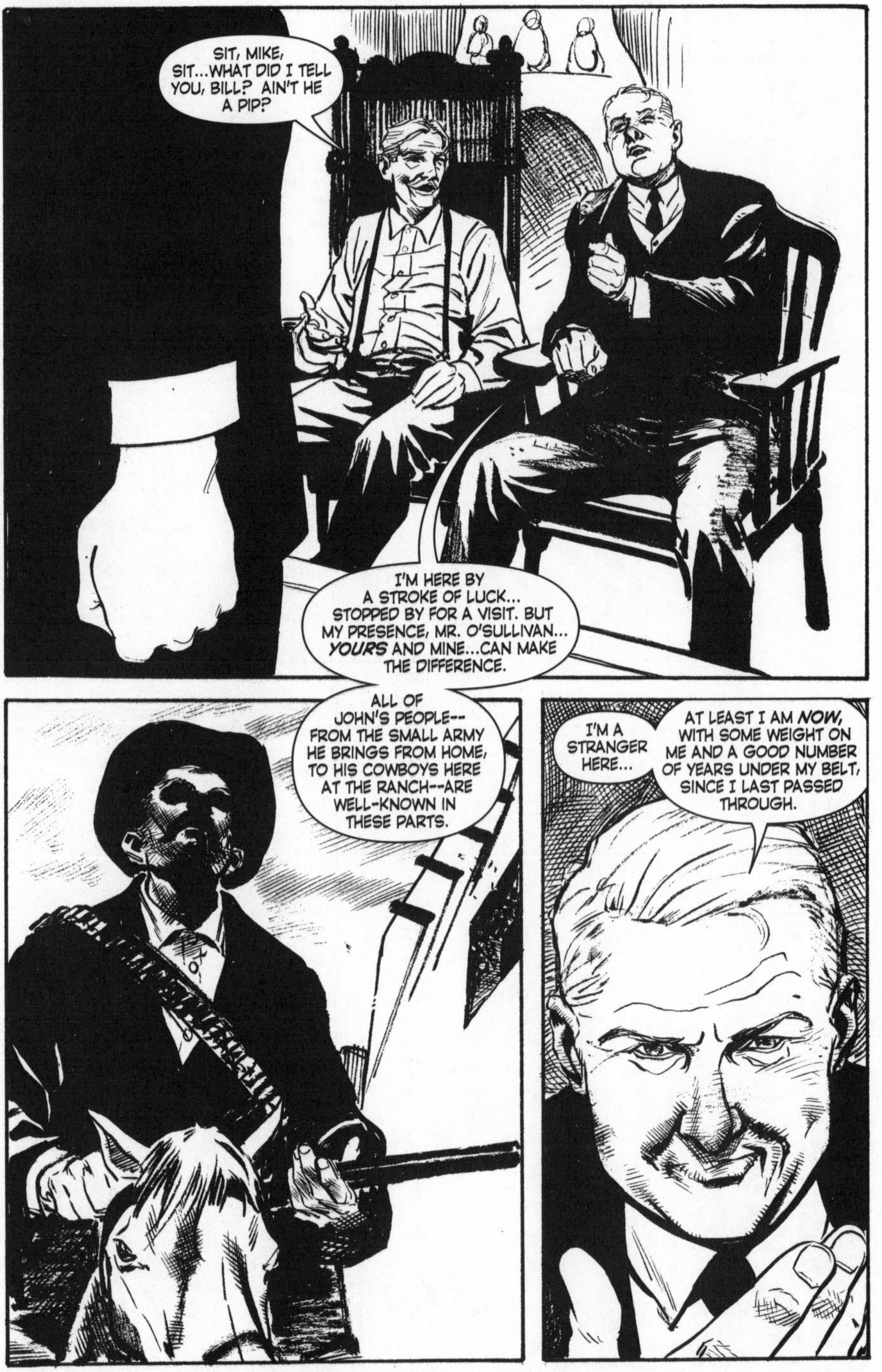
SIT, MIKE, SIT...WHAT DID I TELL YOU, BILL? AIN'T HE A PIP?
I'M HERE BY A STROKE OF LUCK... STOPPED BY FOR A VISIT. BUT MY PRESENCE, MR. O'SULLIVAN... YOURS AND MINE...CAN MAKE THE DIFFERENCE.
ALL OF JOHN'S PEOPLE-- FROM THE SMALL ARMY HE BRINGS FROM HOME, TO HIS COWBOYS HERE AT THE RANCH--ARE WELL-KNOWN IN THESE PARTS.
I'M A STRANGER HERE...
AT LEAST I AM NOW, WITH SOME WEIGHT ON ME AND A GOOD NUMBER OF YEARS UNDER MY BELT, SINCE I LAST PASSED THROUGH.

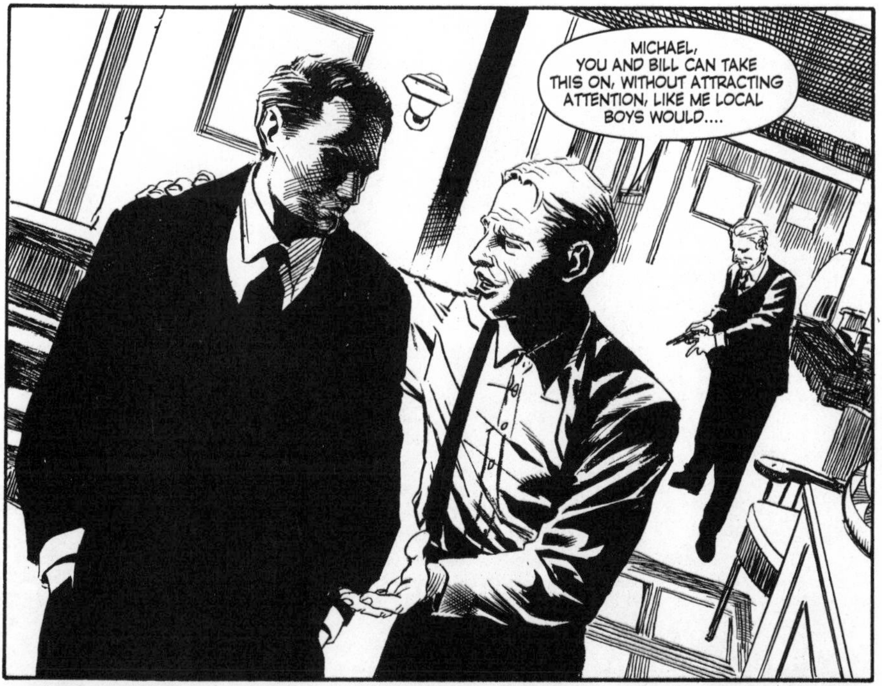
MICHAEL, YOU AND BILL CAN TAKE THIS ON, WITHOUT ATTRACTING ATTENTION, LIKE ME LOCAL BOYS WOULD....

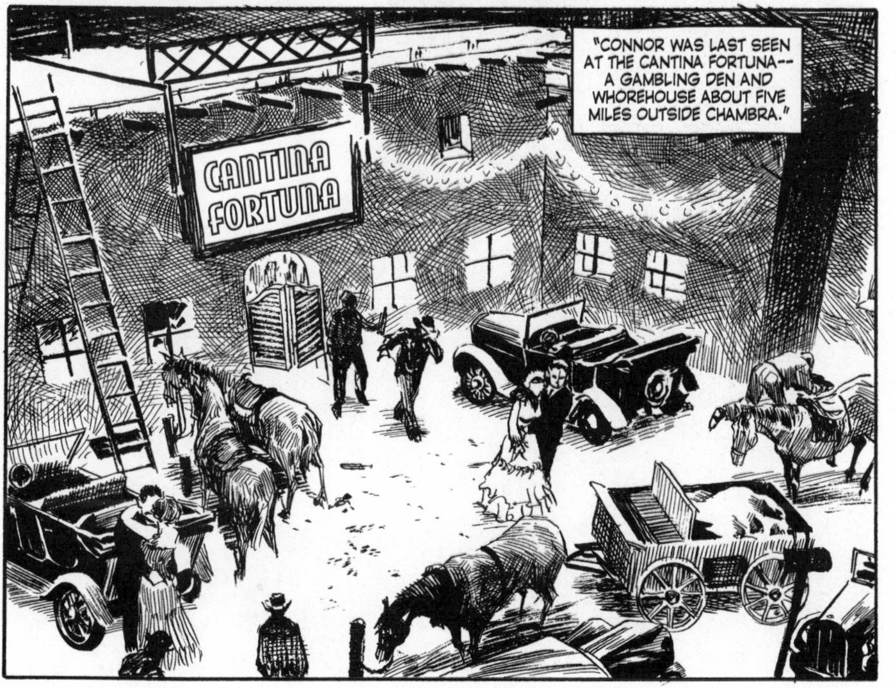
"CONNOR WAS LAST SEEN AT THE CANTINA FORTUNA-- A GAMBLING DEN AND WHOREHOUSE ABOUT FIVE MILES OUTSIDE CHAMBRA."
CANTINA FORTUNA

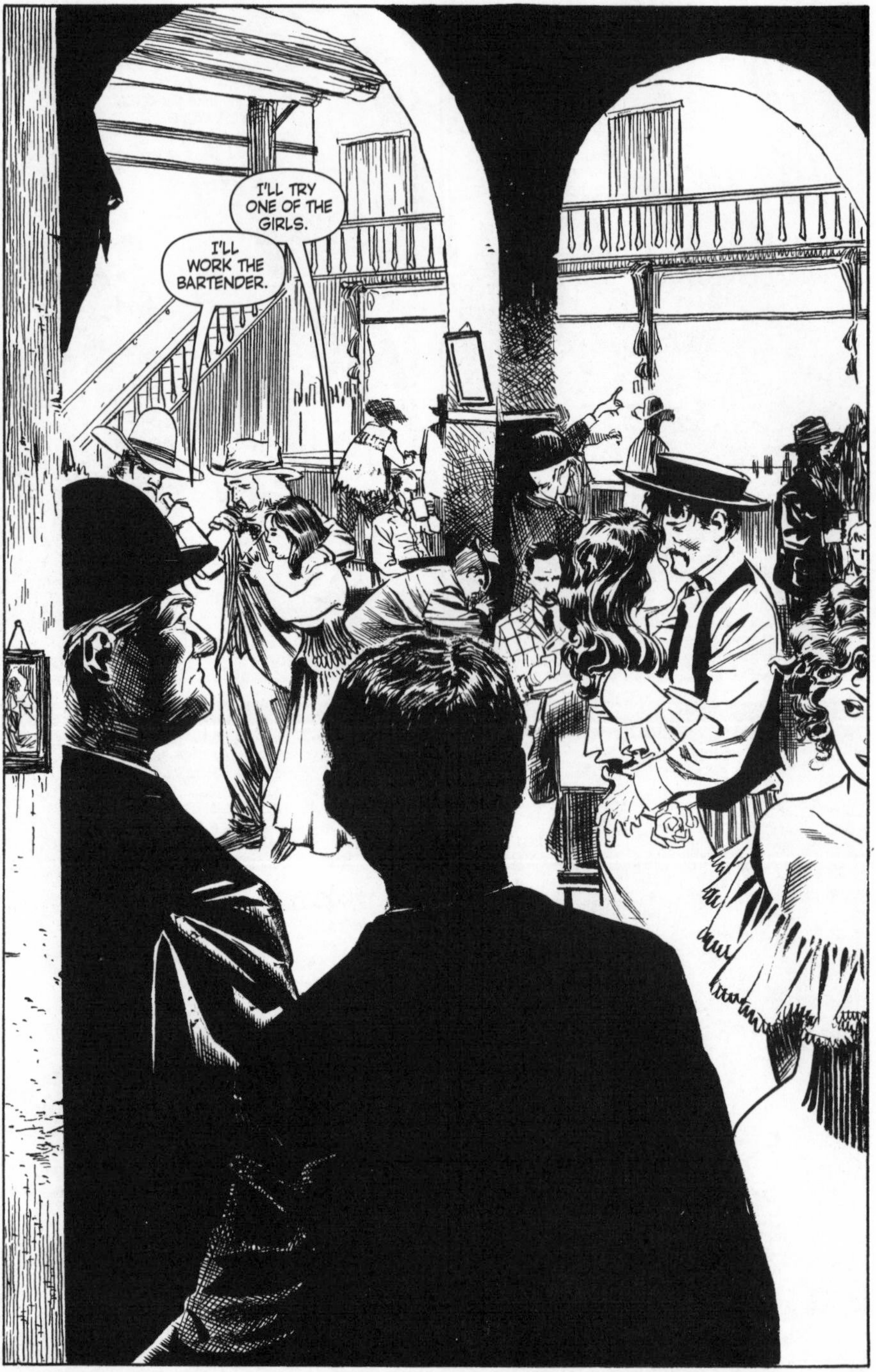
I'LL TRY ONE OF THE GIRLS.
I'LL WORK THE BARTENDER.

SEÑOR-- YOU DO NOT JUST WALK UP THE STAIRS, LIKE YOU THE OWNER.

SEÑORITA, ALL I WANT TO DO IS RENT ONE LITTLE ROOM...AND ONE LITTLE GIRL.

AND YOUR PLEASURE IS?

THE YOUNGER THE BETTER...NO CHEST. A BOY'S BOTTOM. THE KIND A MAN CAN *SPANK*, IF A GIRL IS NAUGHTY....

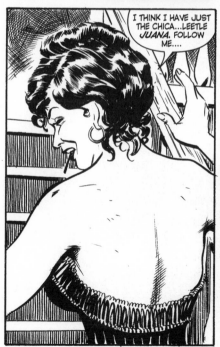

I THINK I HAVE JUST THE CHICA...LEETLE *JUANA.* FOLLOW ME....

YOU CAN GET IN TROUBLE ASKING SUCH QUESTIONS, SEÑOR.

YOU CAN GET WEALTHY *ANSWERING* THEM, AMIGO.

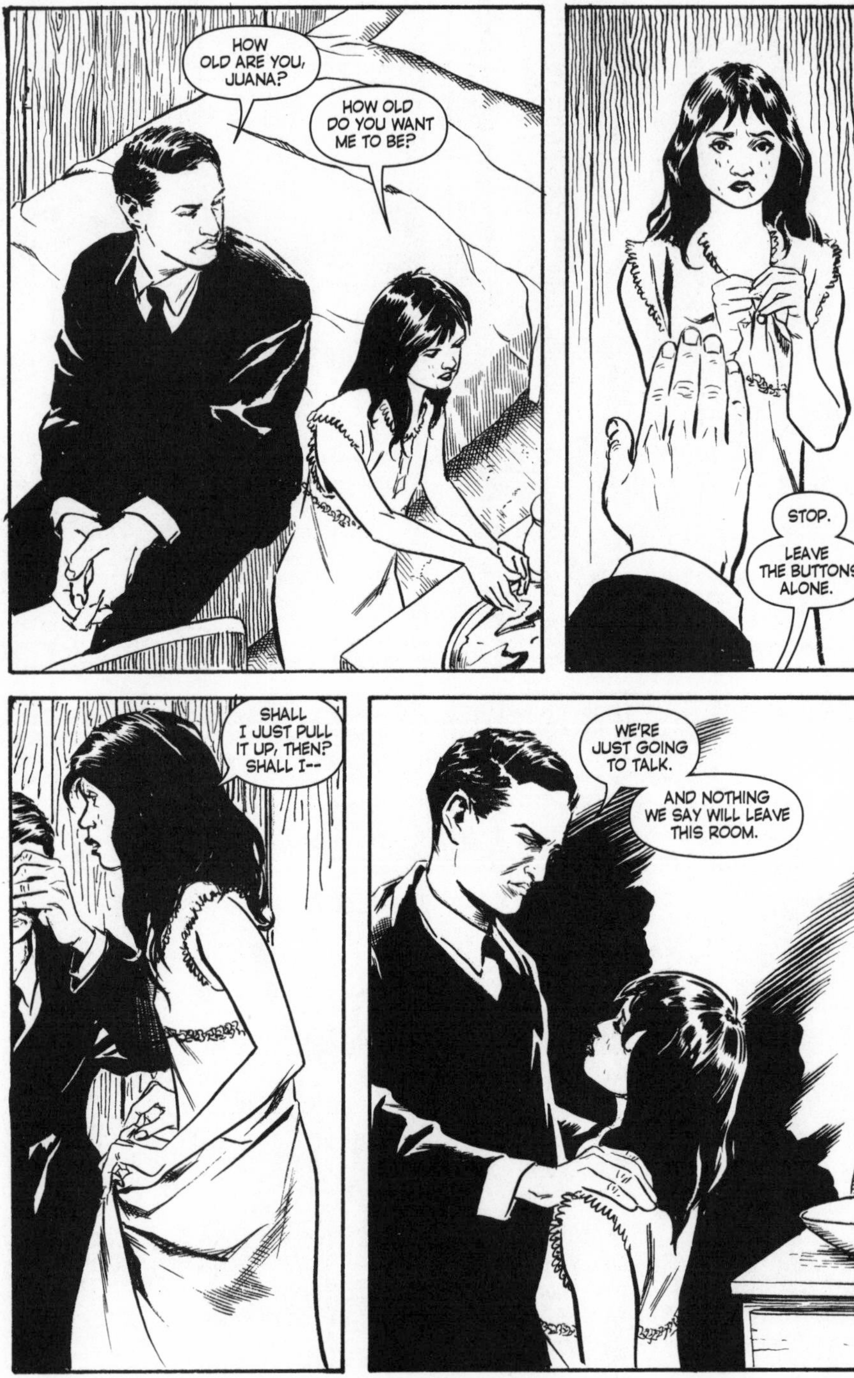
HOW OLD ARE YOU, JUANA?
HOW OLD DO YOU WANT ME TO BE?
STOP.
LEAVE THE BUTTONS ALONE.
SHALL I JUST PULL IT UP, THEN? SHALL I--
WE'RE JUST GOING TO TALK.
AND NOTHING WE SAY WILL LEAVE THIS ROOM.

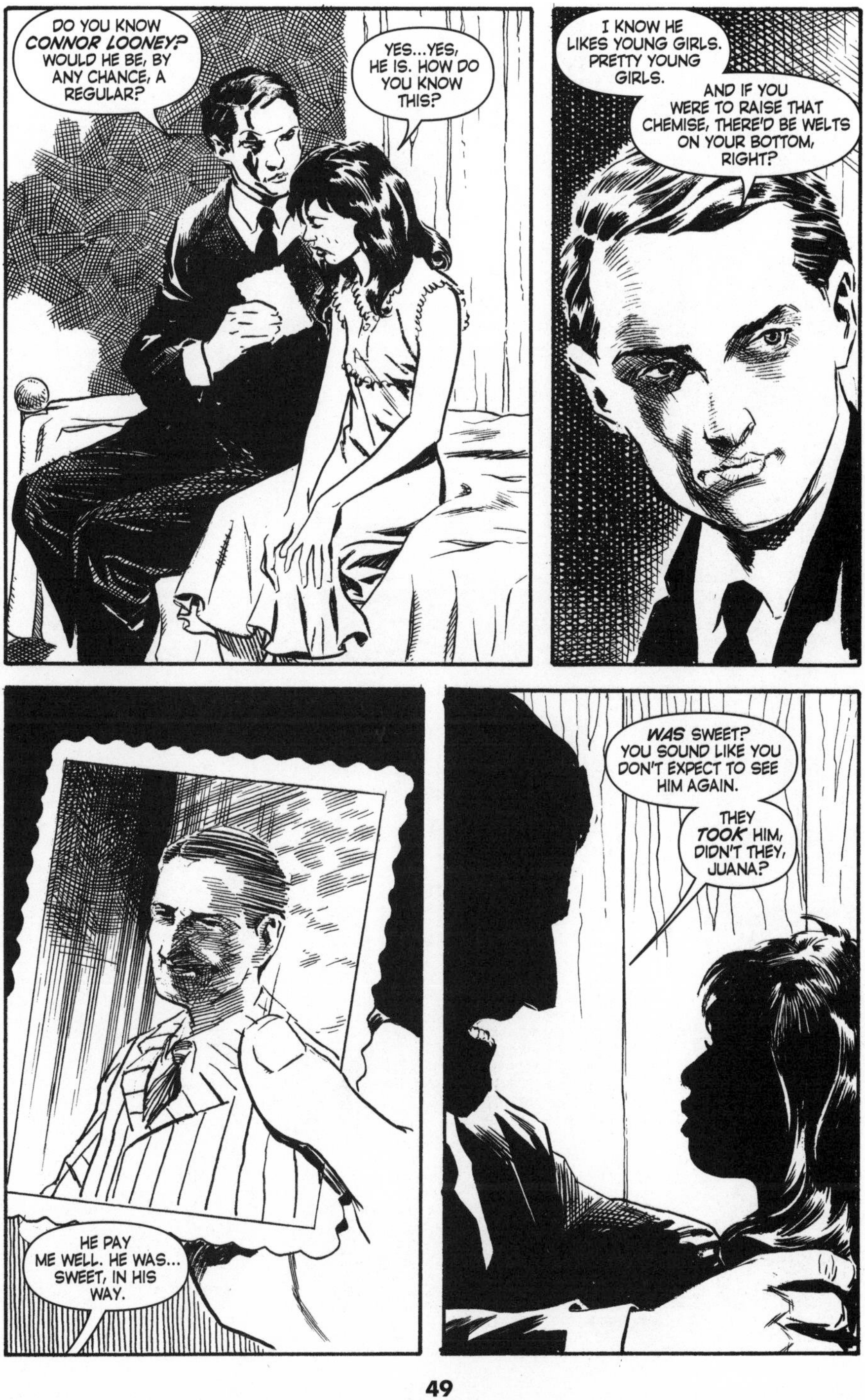
DO YOU KNOW CONNOR LOONEY? WOULD HE BE, BY ANY CHANCE, A REGULAR?
YES...YES, HE IS. HOW DO YOU KNOW THIS?
I KNOW HE LIKES YOUNG GIRLS. PRETTY YOUNG GIRLS.
AND IF YOU WERE TO RAISE THAT CHEMISE, THERE'D BE WELTS ON YOUR BOTTOM, RIGHT?
HE PAY ME WELL. HE WAS... SWEET, IN HIS WAY.
WAS SWEET? YOU SOUND LIKE YOU DON'T EXPECT TO SEE HIM AGAIN.
THEY TOOK HIM, DIDN'T THEY, JUANA?

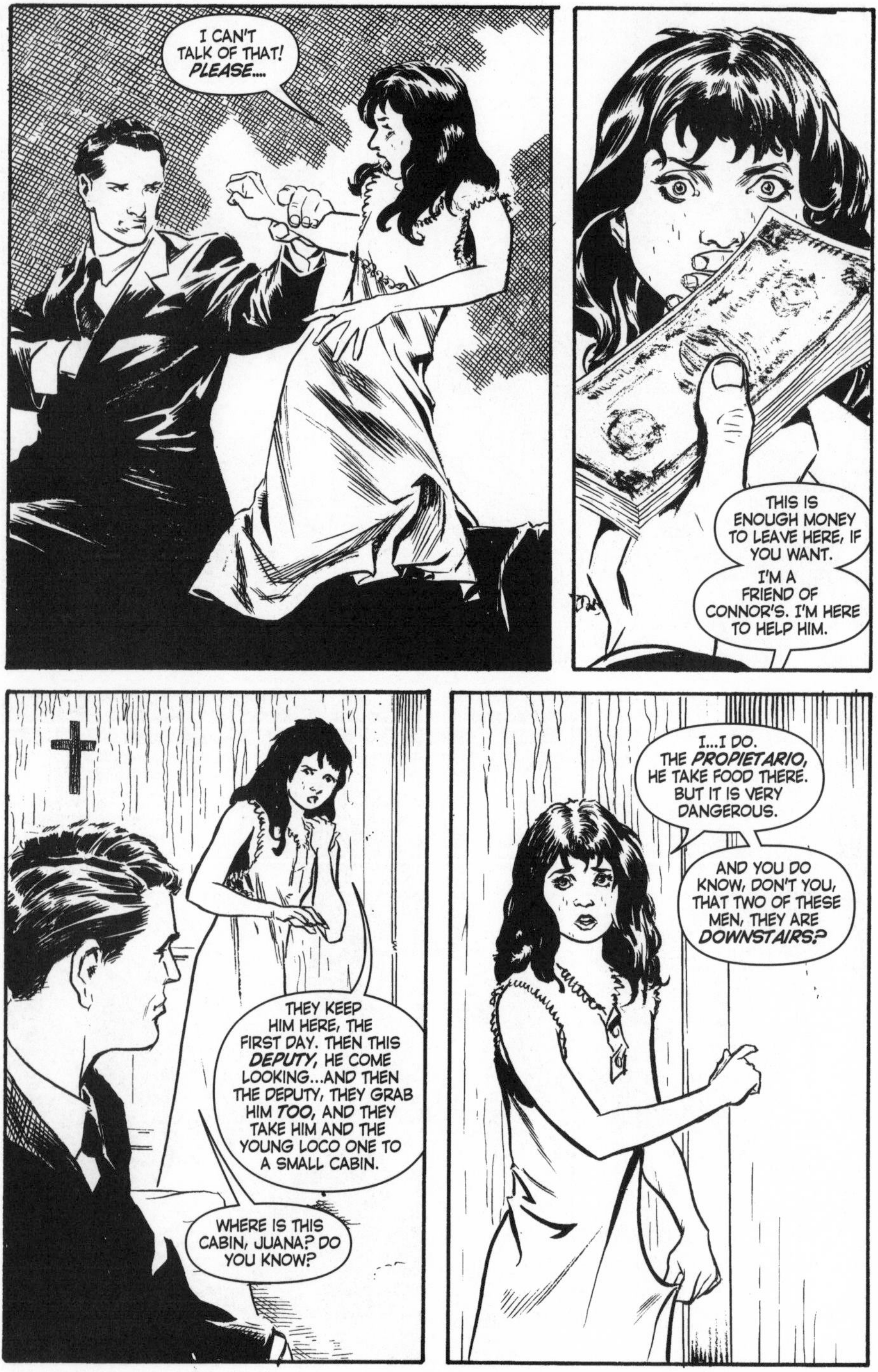
I CAN'T TALK OF THAT! *PLEASE....*
THIS IS ENOUGH MONEY TO LEAVE HERE, IF YOU WANT.
I'M A FRIEND OF CONNOR'S. I'M HERE TO HELP HIM.
THEY KEEP HIM HERE, THE FIRST DAY. THEN THIS *DEPUTY,* HE COME LOOKING...AND THEN THE DEPUTY, THEY GRAB HIM *TOO,* AND THEY TAKE HIM AND THE YOUNG LOCO ONE TO A SMALL CABIN.
WHERE IS THIS CABIN, JUANA? DO YOU KNOW?
I...I DO. THE *PROPIETARIO,* HE TAKE FOOD THERE. BUT IT IS VERY DANGEROUS.
AND YOU DO KNOW, DON'T YOU, THAT TWO OF THESE MEN, THEY ARE *DOWNSTAIRS?*

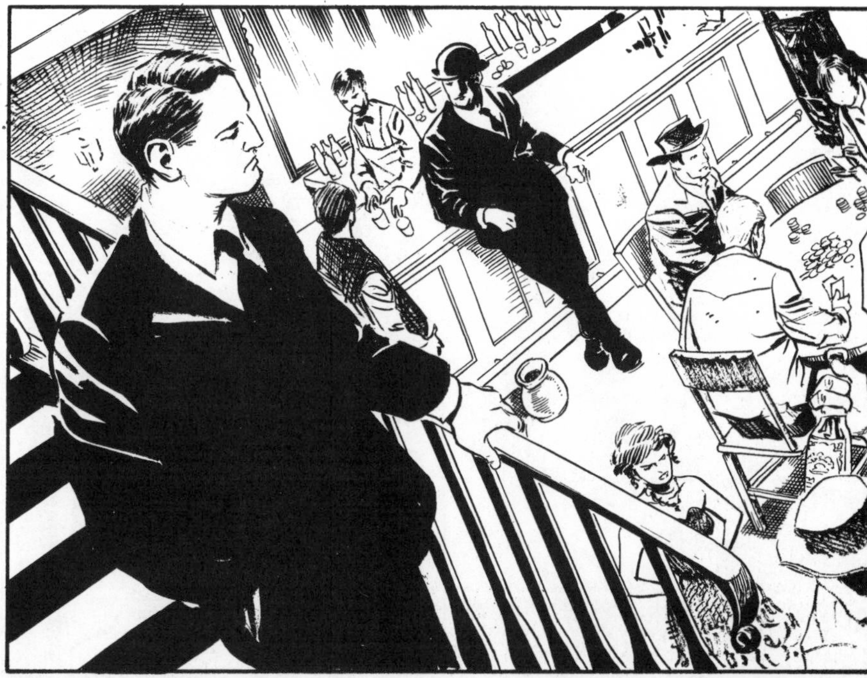

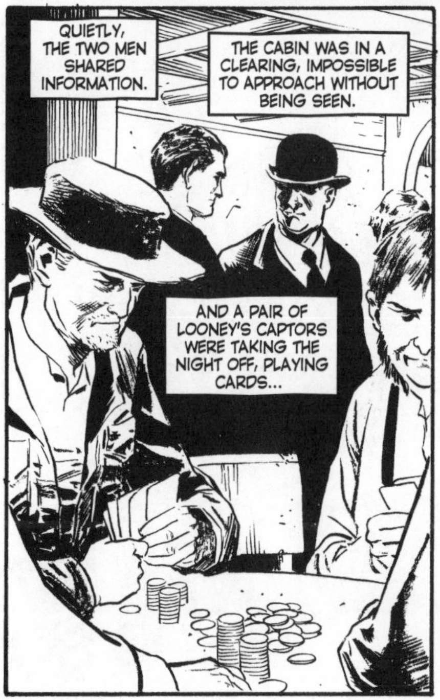
QUIETLY, THE TWO MEN SHARED INFORMATION.
THE CABIN WAS IN A CLEARING, IMPOSSIBLE TO APPROACH WITHOUT BEING SEEN.
AND A PAIR OF LOONEY'S CAPTORS WERE TAKING THE NIGHT OFF, PLAYING CARDS...

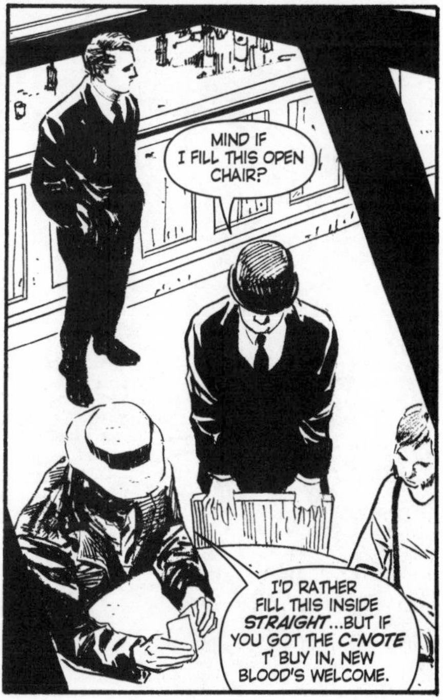
MIND IF I FILL THIS OPEN CHAIR?
I'D RATHER FILL THIS INSIDE STRAIGHT...BUT IF YOU GOT THE C-NOTE T' BUY IN, NEW BLOOD'S WELCOME.

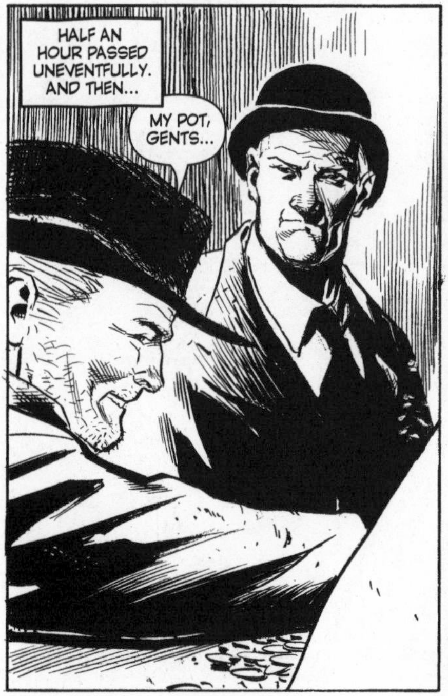
HALF AN HOUR PASSED UNEVENTFULLY. AND THEN...
MY POT, GENTS...

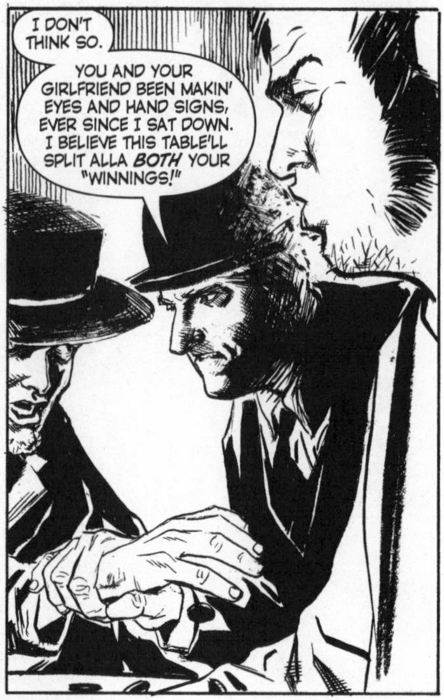
I DON'T THINK SO.
YOU AND YOUR GIRLFRIEND BEEN MAKIN' EYES AND HAND SIGNS, EVER SINCE I SAT DOWN. I BELIEVE THIS TABLE'LL SPLIT ALLA *BOTH* YOUR "WINNINGS!"

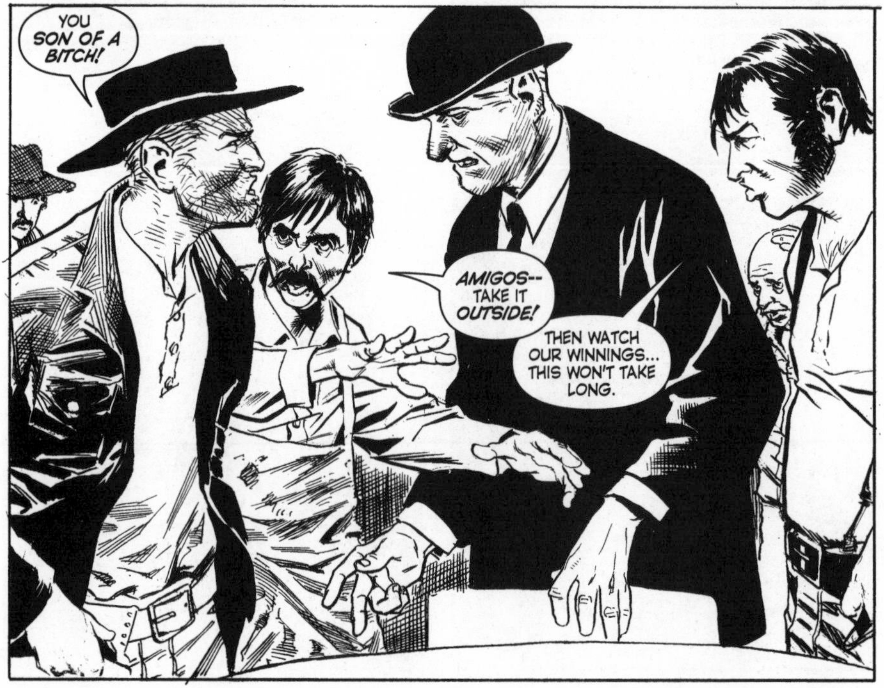
YOU *SON OF A BITCH!*
AMIGOS-- TAKE IT *OUTSIDE!*
THEN WATCH OUR WINNINGS... THIS WON'T TAKE LONG.

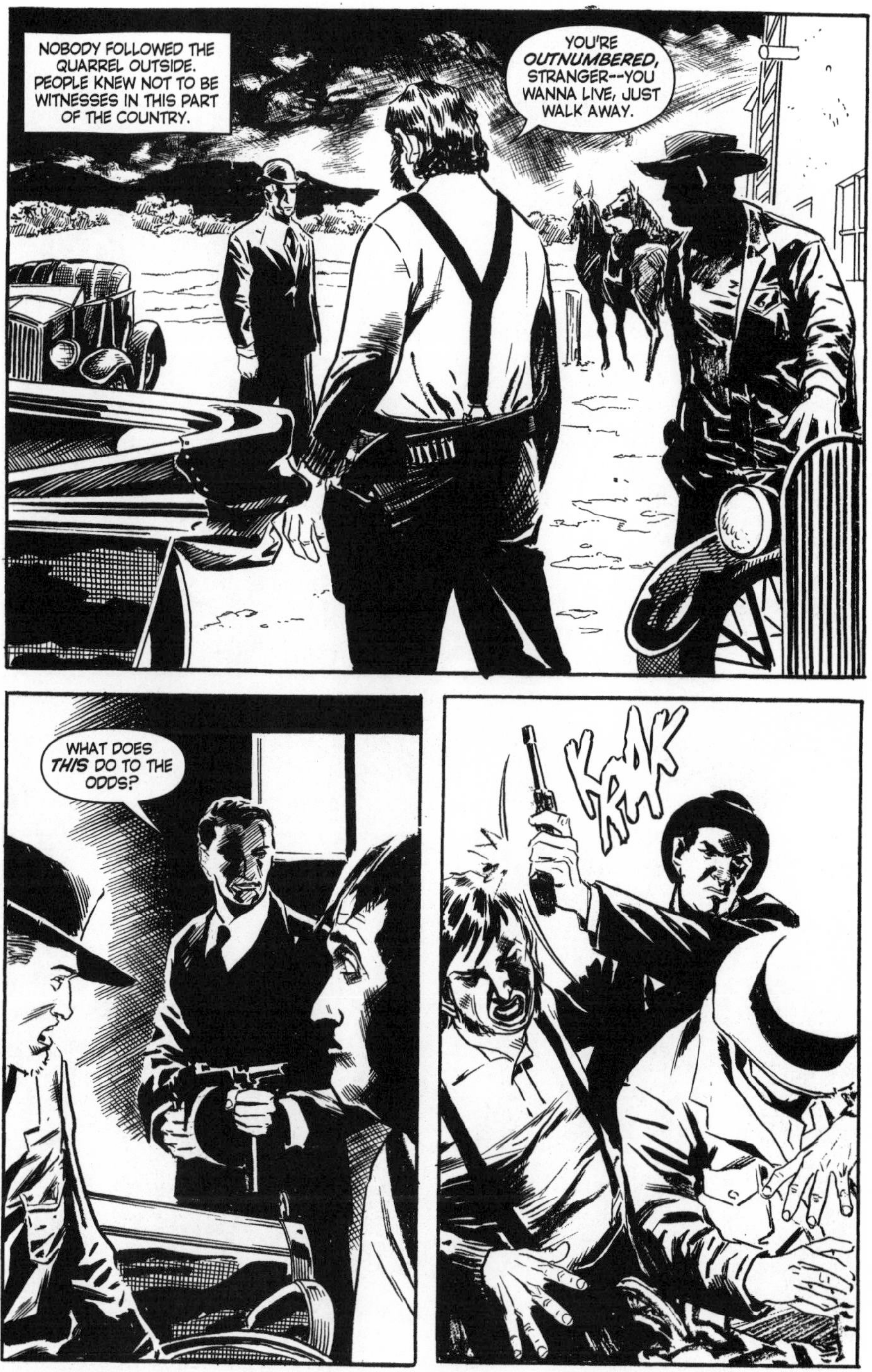
NOBODY FOLLOWED THE QUARREL OUTSIDE. PEOPLE KNEW NOT TO BE WITNESSES IN THIS PART OF THE COUNTRY.
YOU'RE *OUTNUMBERED,* STRANGER--YOU WANNA LIVE, JUST WALK AWAY.
WHAT DOES *THIS* DO TO THE ODDS?
KRAK KRAK

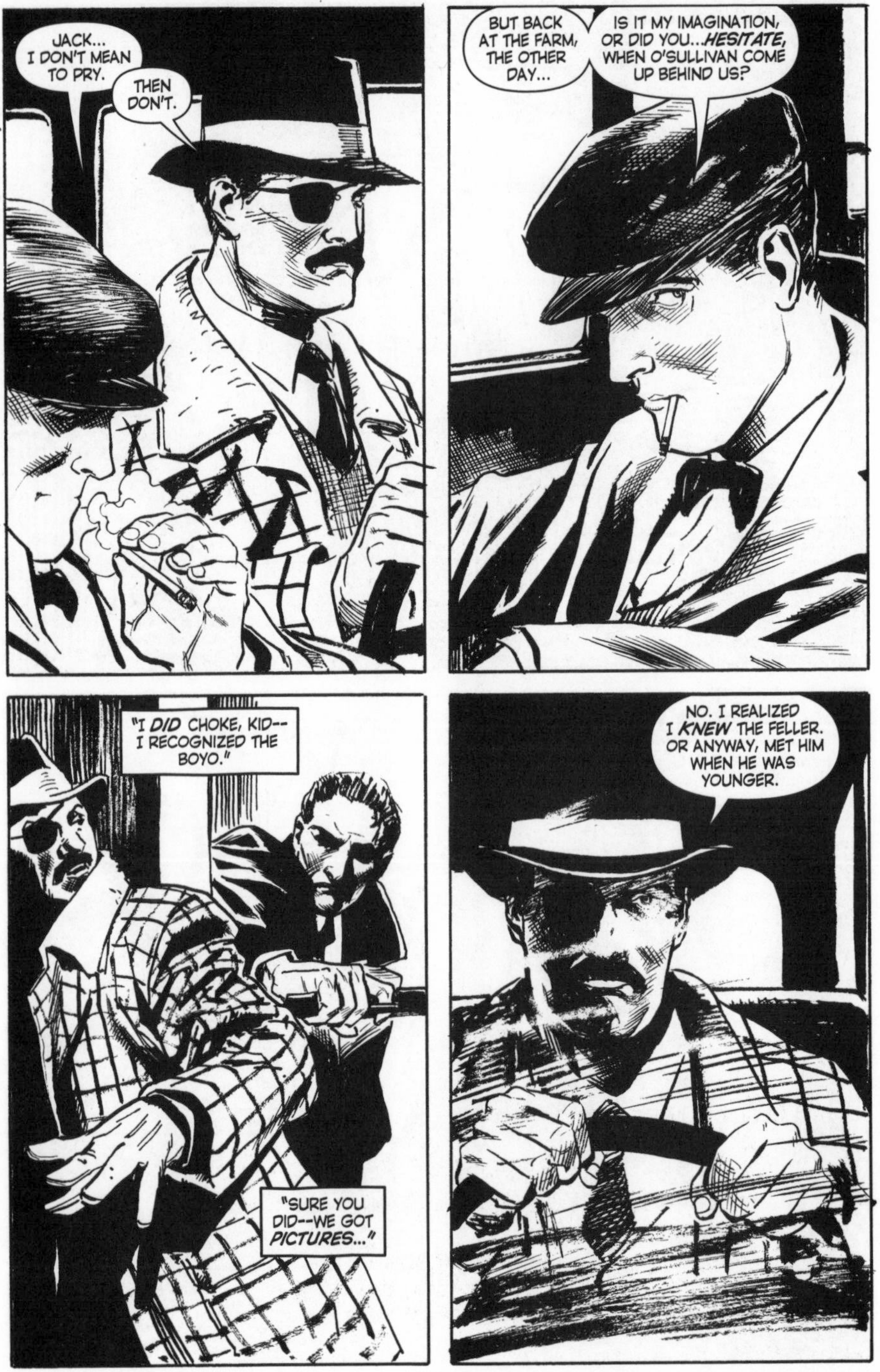
JACK... I DON'T MEAN TO PRY.
THEN DON'T.
BUT BACK AT THE FARM, THE OTHER DAY...
IS IT MY IMAGINATION, OR DID YOU...HESITATE, WHEN O'SULLIVAN COME UP BEHIND US?
"I DID CHOKE, KID-- I RECOGNIZED THE BOYO."
"SURE YOU DID--WE GOT PICTURES..."
NO. I REALIZED I KNEW THE FELLER. OR ANYWAY, MET HIM WHEN HE WAS YOUNGER.

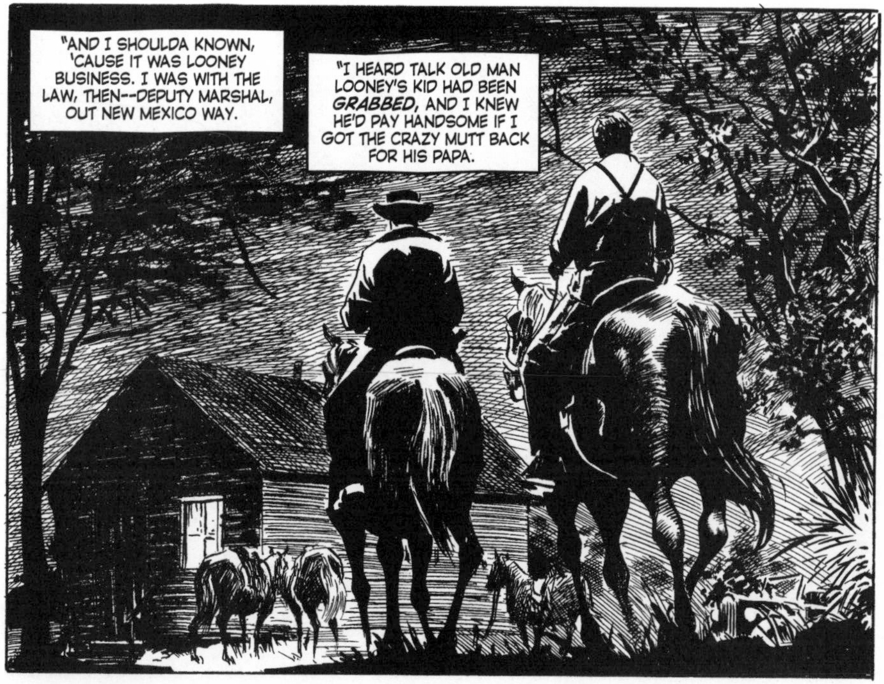
"AND I SHOULDA KNOWN, 'CAUSE IT WAS LOONEY BUSINESS. I WAS WITH THE LAW, THEN--DEPUTY MARSHAL, OUT NEW MEXICO WAY.
"I HEARD TALK OLD MAN LOONEY'S KID HAD BEEN GRABBED, AND I KNEW HE'D PAY HANDSOME IF I GOT THE CRAZY MUTT BACK FOR HIS PAPA.

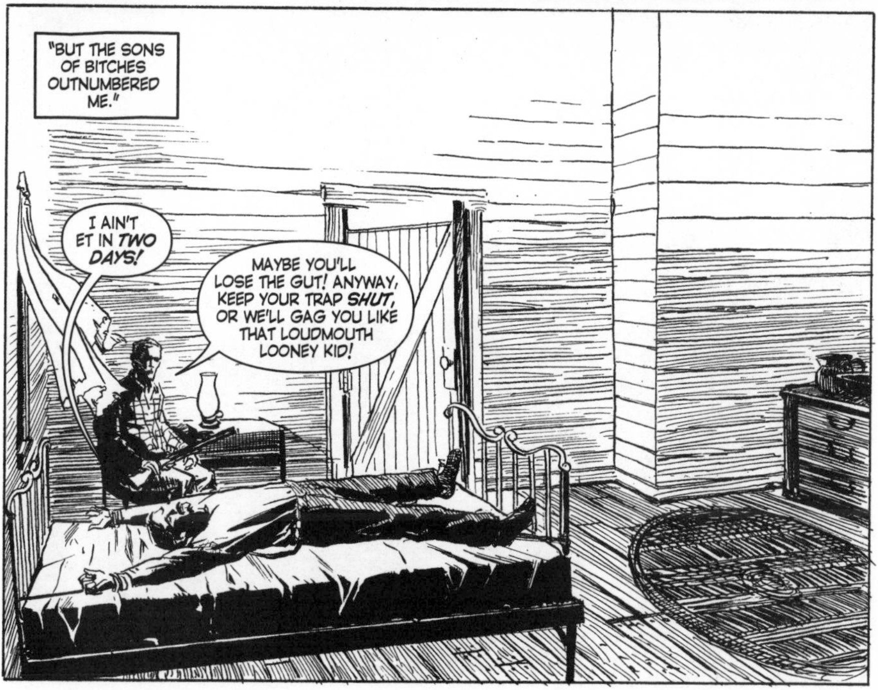
"BUT THE SONS OF BITCHES OUTNUMBERED ME."
I AIN'T ET IN TWO DAYS!
MAYBE YOU'LL LOSE THE GUT! ANYWAY, KEEP YOUR TRAP SHUT, OR WE'LL GAG YOU LIKE THAT LOUDMOUTH LOONEY KID!

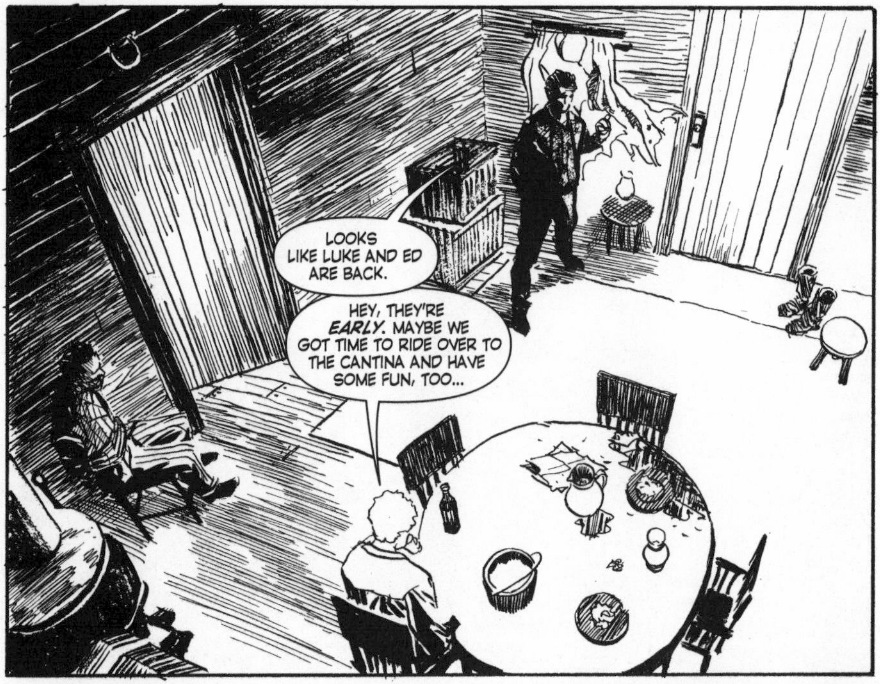
LOOKS LIKE LUKE AND ED ARE BACK.
HEY, THEY'RE *EARLY*. MAYBE WE GOT TIME TO RIDE OVER TO THE CANTINA AND HAVE SOME FUN, TOO...

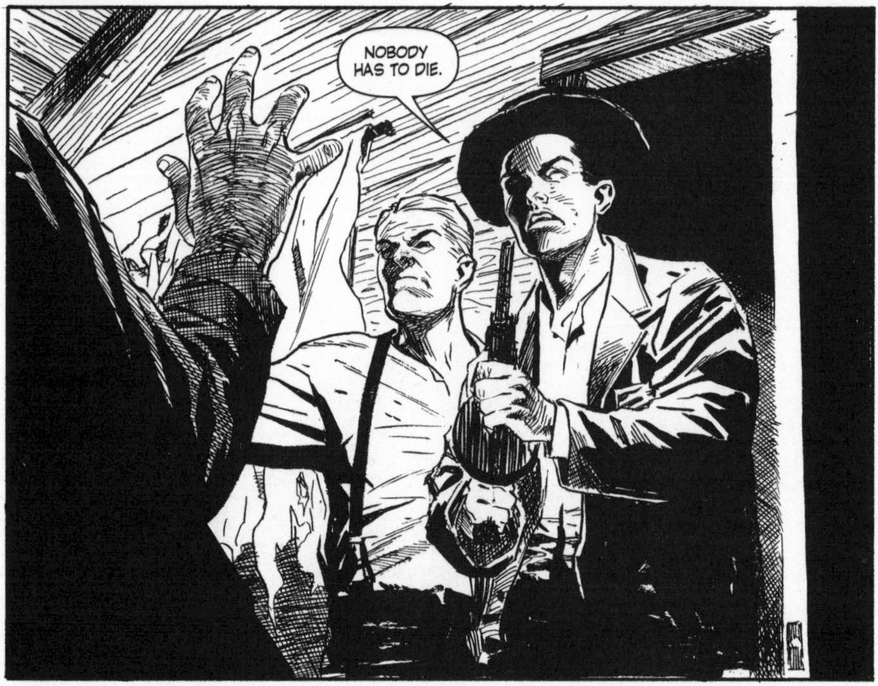
NOBODY HAS TO DIE.

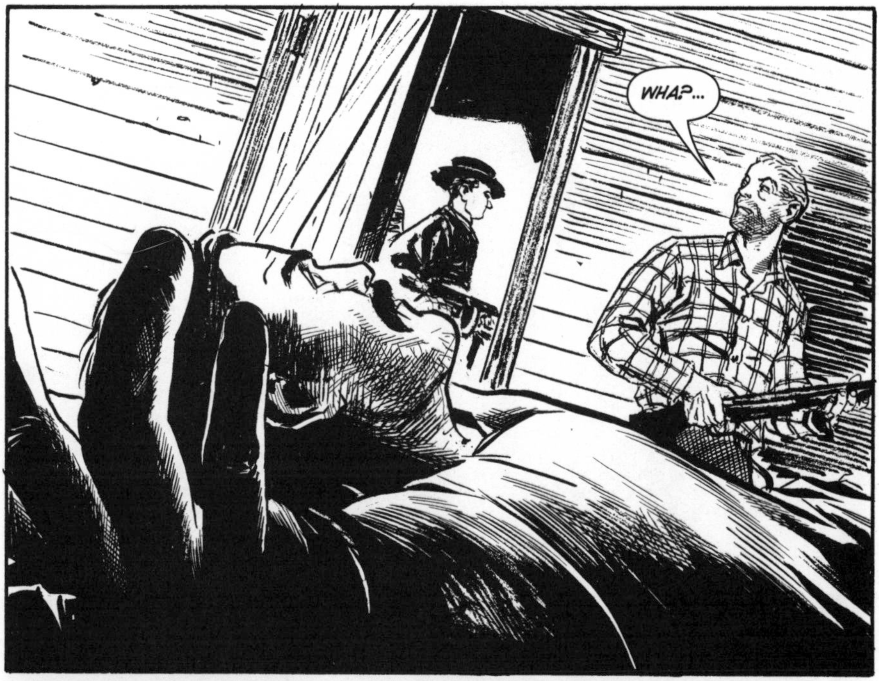
WHAP...

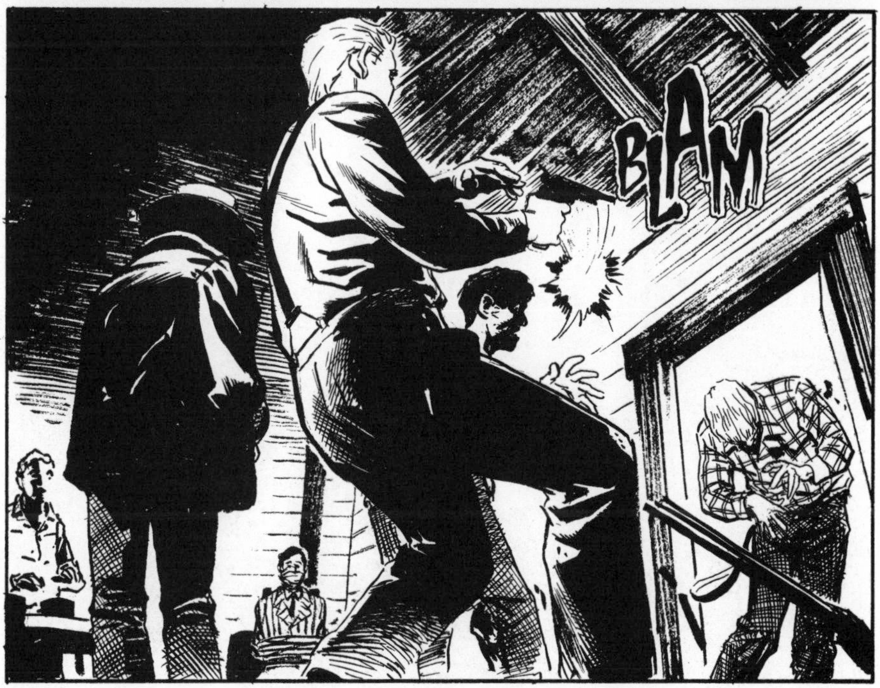
BLAM

BLAM
RAT TAT TAT TAT TAT TAT TAT
BLAM
RAT TAT TAT TAT TAT TAT TAT

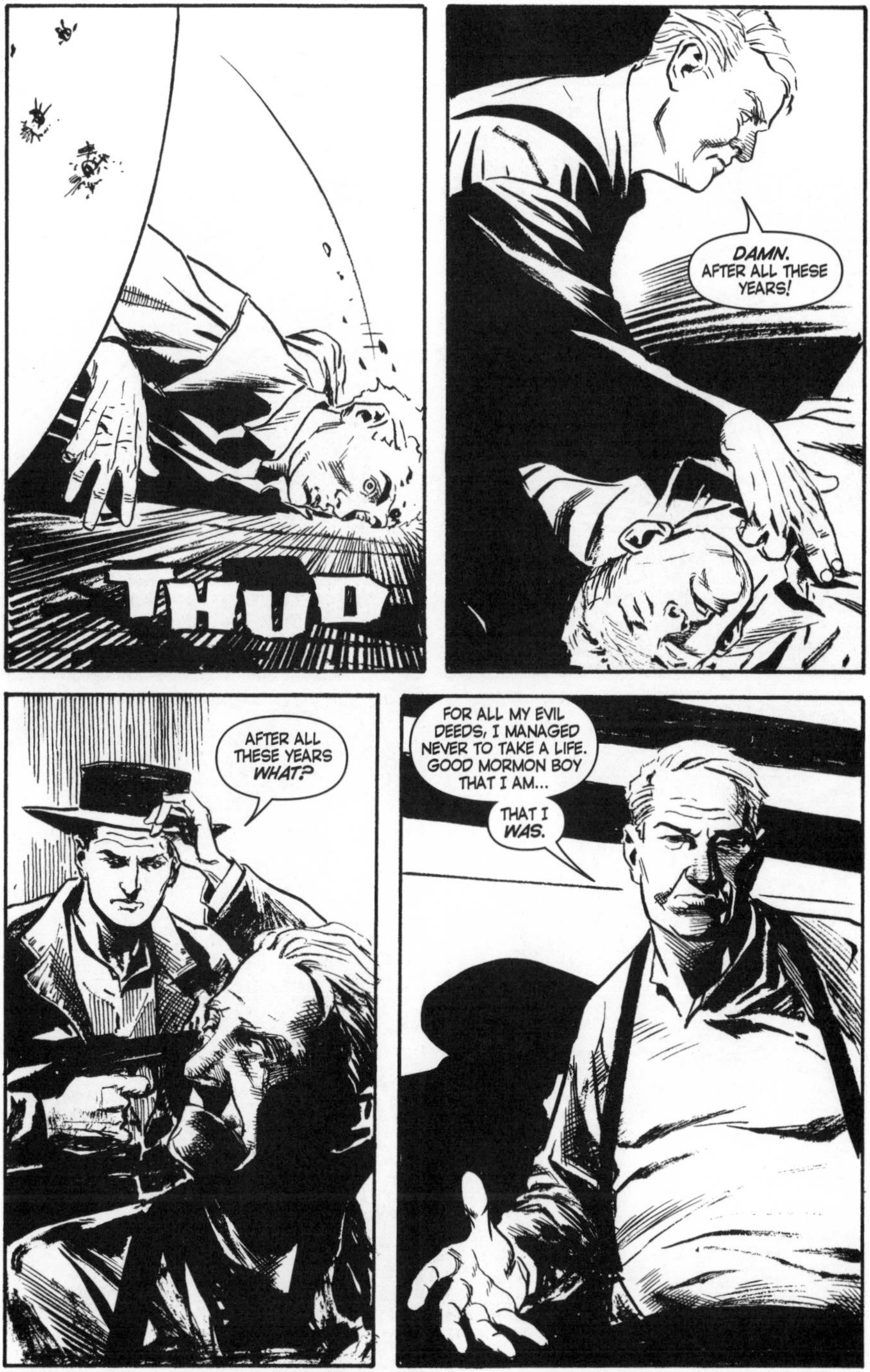
THUD
DAMN. AFTER ALL THESE YEARS!
AFTER ALL THESE YEARS WHAT?
FOR ALL MY EVIL DEEDS, I MANAGED NEVER TO TAKE A LIFE. GOOD MORMON BOY THAT I AM...
THAT I WAS.

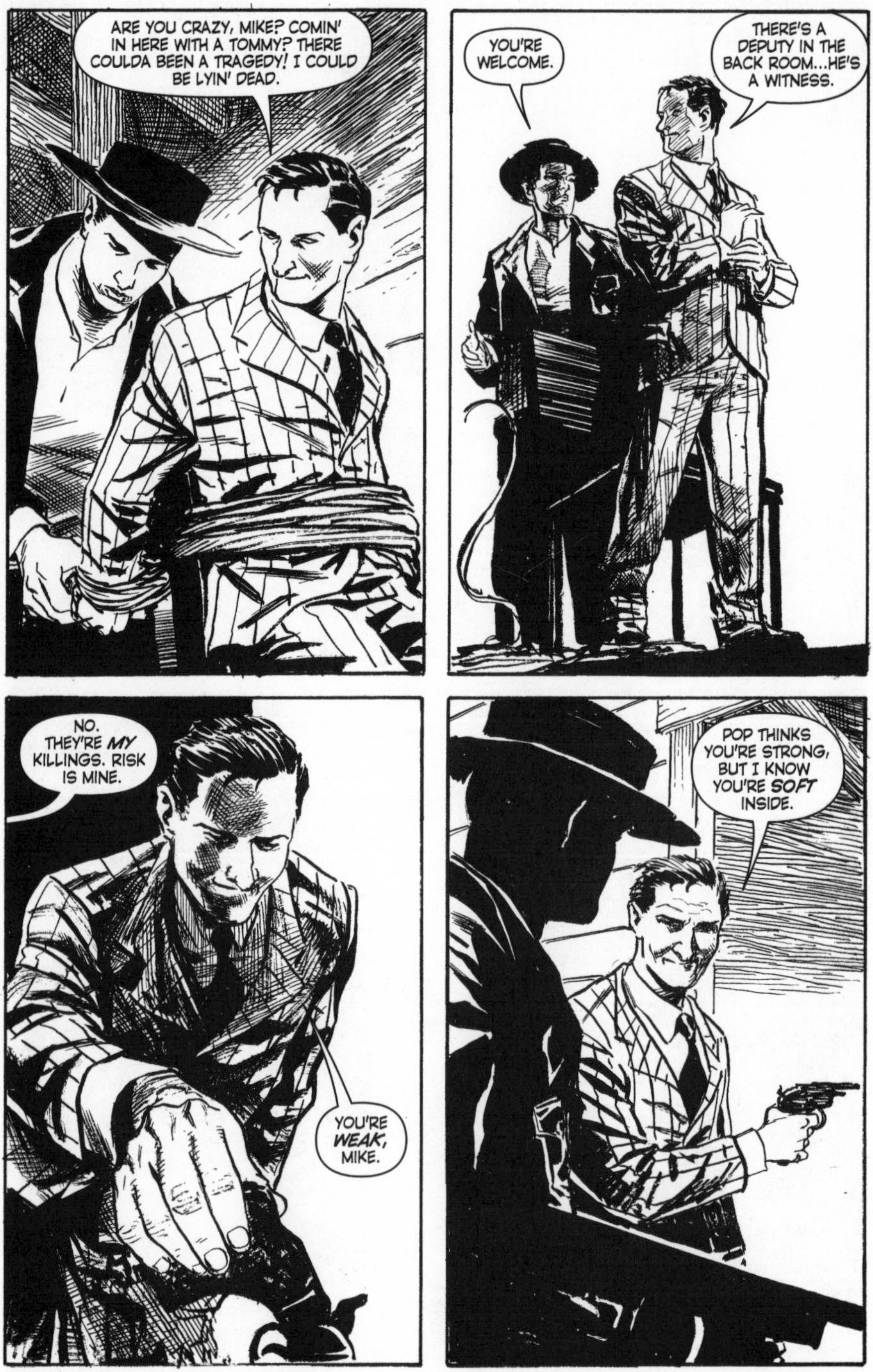
ARE YOU CRAZY, MIKE? COMIN' IN HERE WITH A TOMMY? THERE COULDA BEEN A TRAGEDY! I COULD BE LYIN' DEAD.
YOU'RE WELCOME.
THERE'S A DEPUTY IN THE BACK ROOM...HE'S A WITNESS.
NO. THEY'RE *MY* KILLINGS. RISK IS MINE.
YOU'RE *WEAK,* MIKE.
POP THINKS YOU'RE STRONG, BUT I KNOW YOU'RE *SOFT* INSIDE.

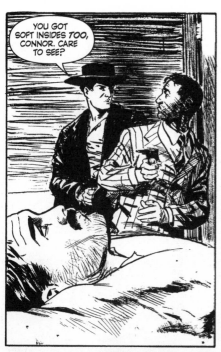

YOU GOT SOFT INSIDES *TOO*, CONNOR. CARE TO SEE?

IT'S ON *YOU*, THEN!

IF HE COMES AFTER US, LAW COMES AFTER US--IT'S ON *YOUR HEAD*, MIKE!

I APPRECIATE THIS. I HAVE NO INTENTION OF--

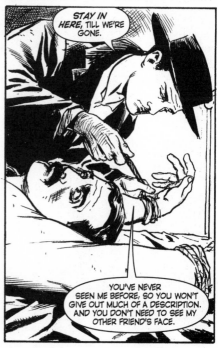

STAY IN *HERE*, TILL WE'RE GONE.

YOU'VE NEVER SEEN ME BEFORE, SO YOU WON'T GIVE OUT MUCH OF A DESCRIPTION. AND YOU DON'T NEED TO SEE MY OTHER FRIEND'S FACE.

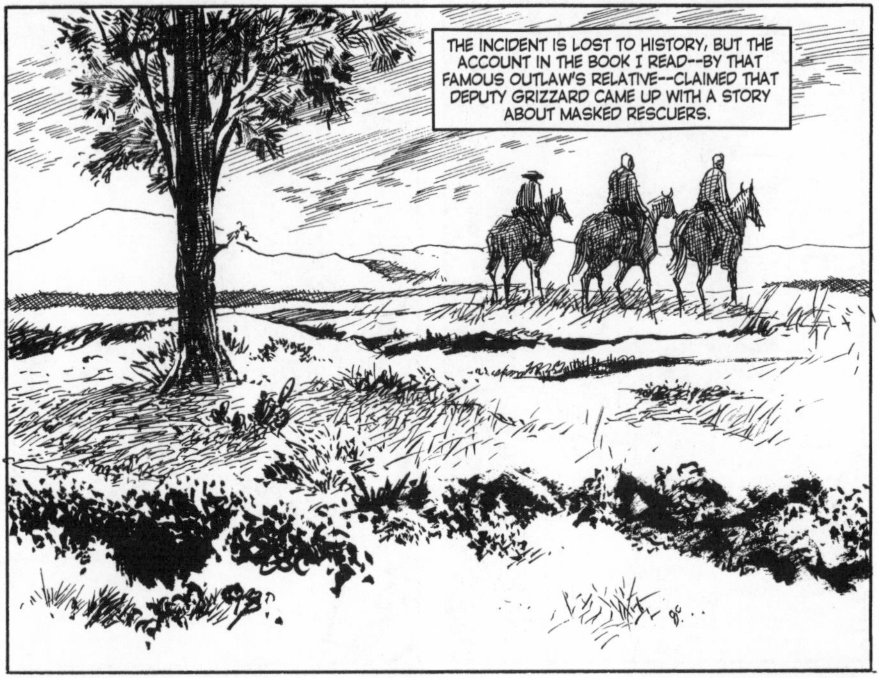
THE INCIDENT IS LOST TO HISTORY, BUT THE ACCOUNT IN THE BOOK I READ--BY THAT FAMOUS OUTLAW'S RELATIVE--CLAIMED THAT DEPUTY GRIZZARD CAME UP WITH A STORY ABOUT MASKED RESCUERS.

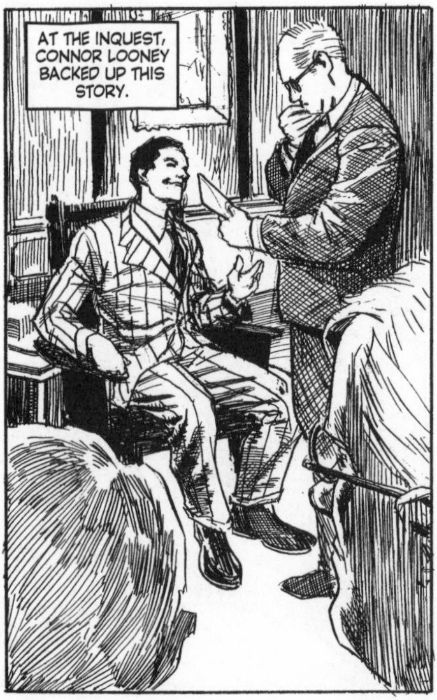
AT THE INQUEST, CONNOR LOONEY BACKED UP THIS STORY.

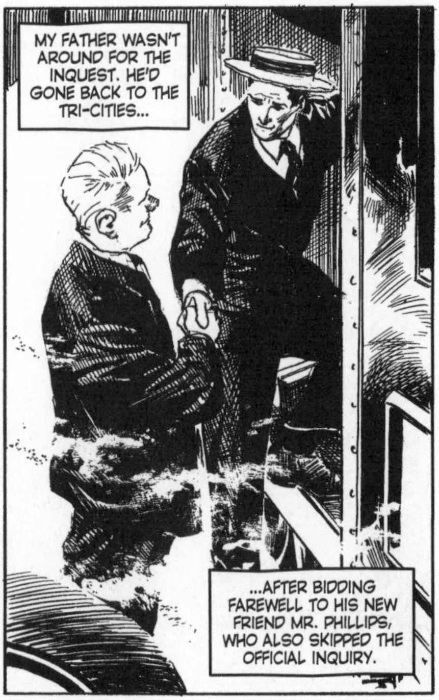
MY FATHER WASN'T AROUND FOR THE INQUEST. HE'D GONE BACK TO THE TRI-CITIES...
...AFTER BIDDING FAREWELL TO HIS NEW FRIEND MR. PHILLIPS, WHO ALSO SKIPPED THE OFFICIAL INQUIRY.

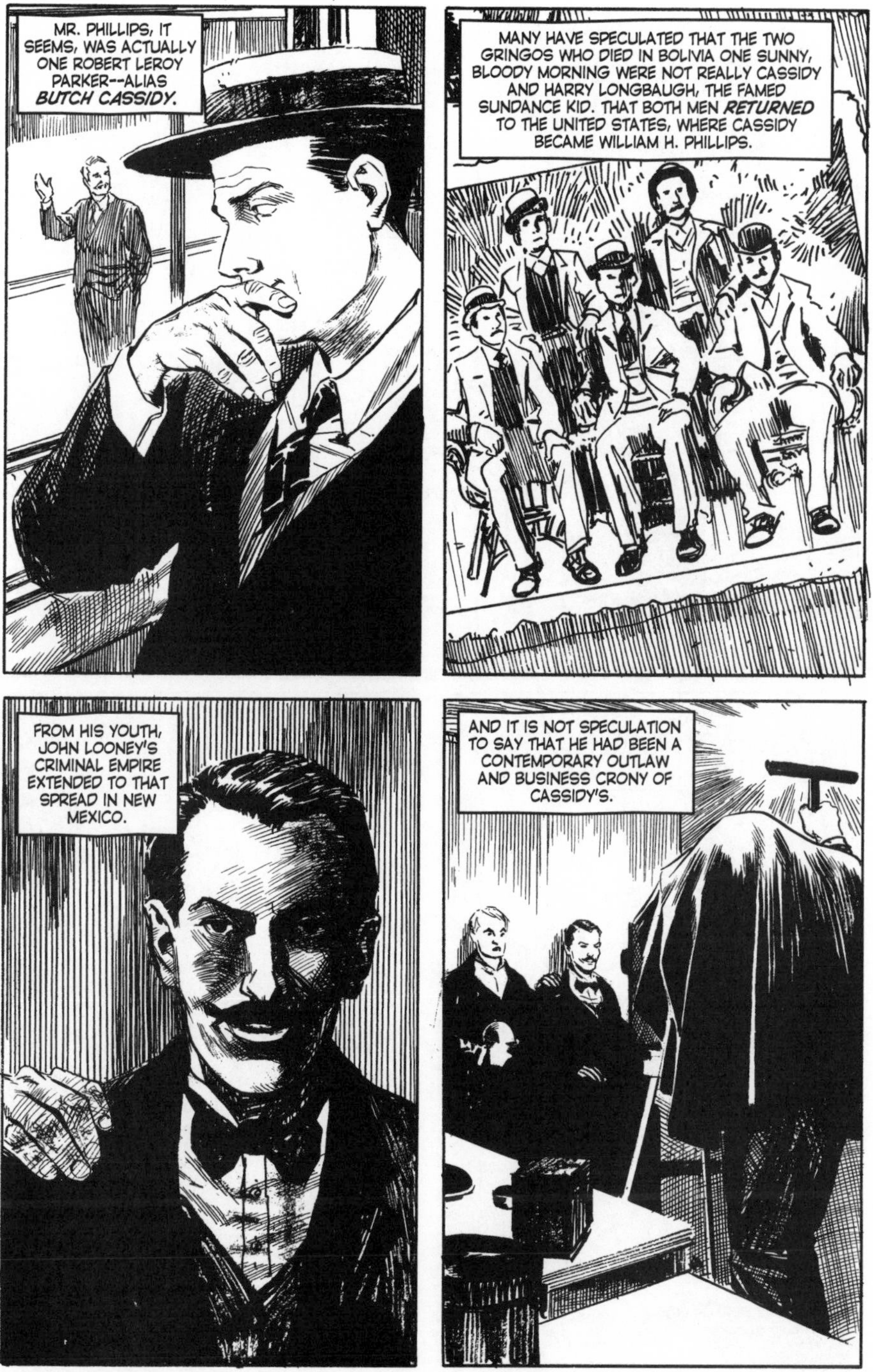
MR. PHILLIPS, IT SEEMS, WAS ACTUALLY ONE ROBERT LEROY PARKER--ALIAS *BUTCH CASSIDY*.
MANY HAVE SPECULATED THAT THE TWO GRINGOS WHO DIED IN BOLIVIA ONE SUNNY, BLOODY MORNING WERE NOT REALLY CASSIDY AND HARRY LONGBAUGH, THE FAMED SUNDANCE KID. THAT BOTH MEN *RETURNED* TO THE UNITED STATES, WHERE CASSIDY BECAME WILLIAM H. PHILLIPS.
FROM HIS YOUTH, JOHN LOONEY'S CRIMINAL EMPIRE EXTENDED TO THAT SPREAD IN NEW MEXICO.
AND IT IS NOT SPECULATION TO SAY THAT HE HAD BEEN A CONTEMPORARY OUTLAW AND BUSINESS CRONY OF CASSIDY'S.

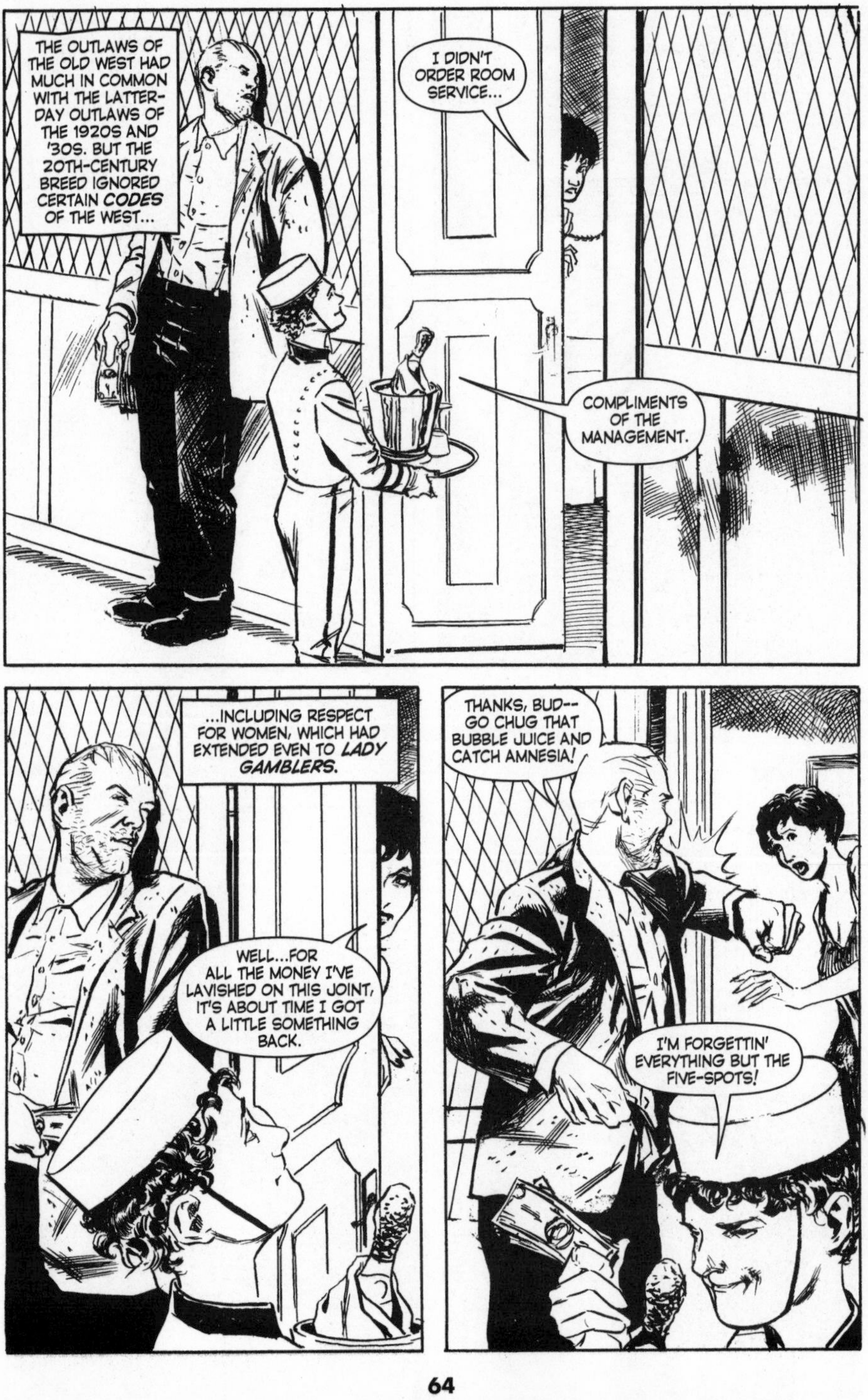
THE OUTLAWS OF THE OLD WEST HAD MUCH IN COMMON WITH THE LATTER-DAY OUTLAWS OF THE 1920S AND '30S. BUT THE 20TH-CENTURY BREED IGNORED CERTAIN *CODES* OF THE WEST...
I DIDN'T ORDER ROOM SERVICE...
COMPLIMENTS OF THE MANAGEMENT.
...INCLUDING RESPECT FOR WOMEN, WHICH HAD EXTENDED EVEN TO *LADY GAMBLERS*.
WELL...FOR ALL THE MONEY I'VE LAVISHED ON THIS JOINT, IT'S ABOUT TIME I GOT A LITTLE SOMETHING BACK.
THANKS, BUD-- GO CHUG THAT BUBBLE JUICE AND CATCH AMNESIA!
I'M FORGETTIN' EVERYTHING BUT THE FIVE-SPOTS!

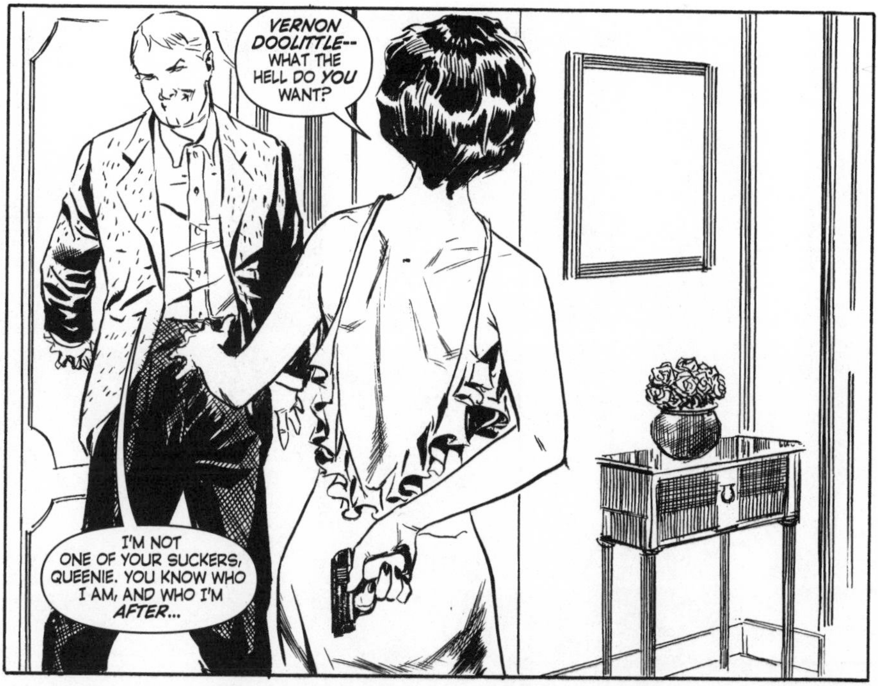
VERNON DOOLITTLE-- WHAT THE HELL DO YOU WANT?
I'M NOT ONE OF YOUR SUCKERS, QUEENIE. YOU KNOW WHO I AM, AND WHO I'M AFTER...

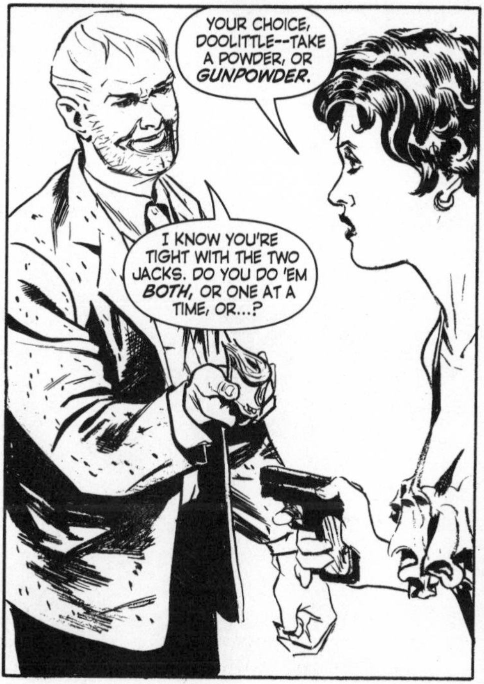
YOUR CHOICE, DOOLITTLE--TAKE A POWDER, OR GUNPOWDER.
I KNOW YOU'RE TIGHT WITH THE TWO JACKS. DO YOU DO 'EM BOTH, OR ONE AT A TIME, OR...?

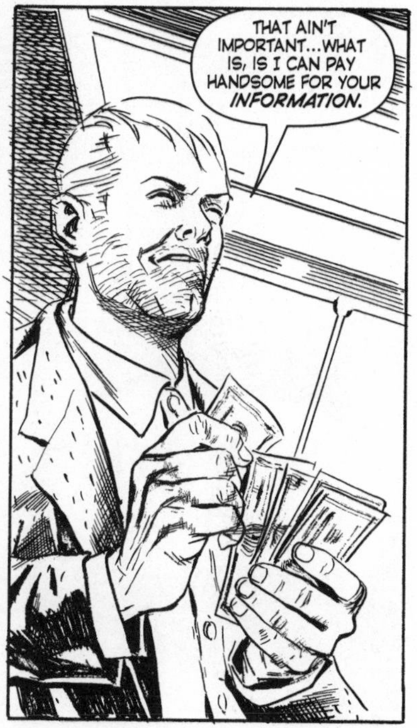
THAT AIN'T IMPORTANT...WHAT IS, IS I CAN PAY HANDSOME FOR YOUR INFORMATION.

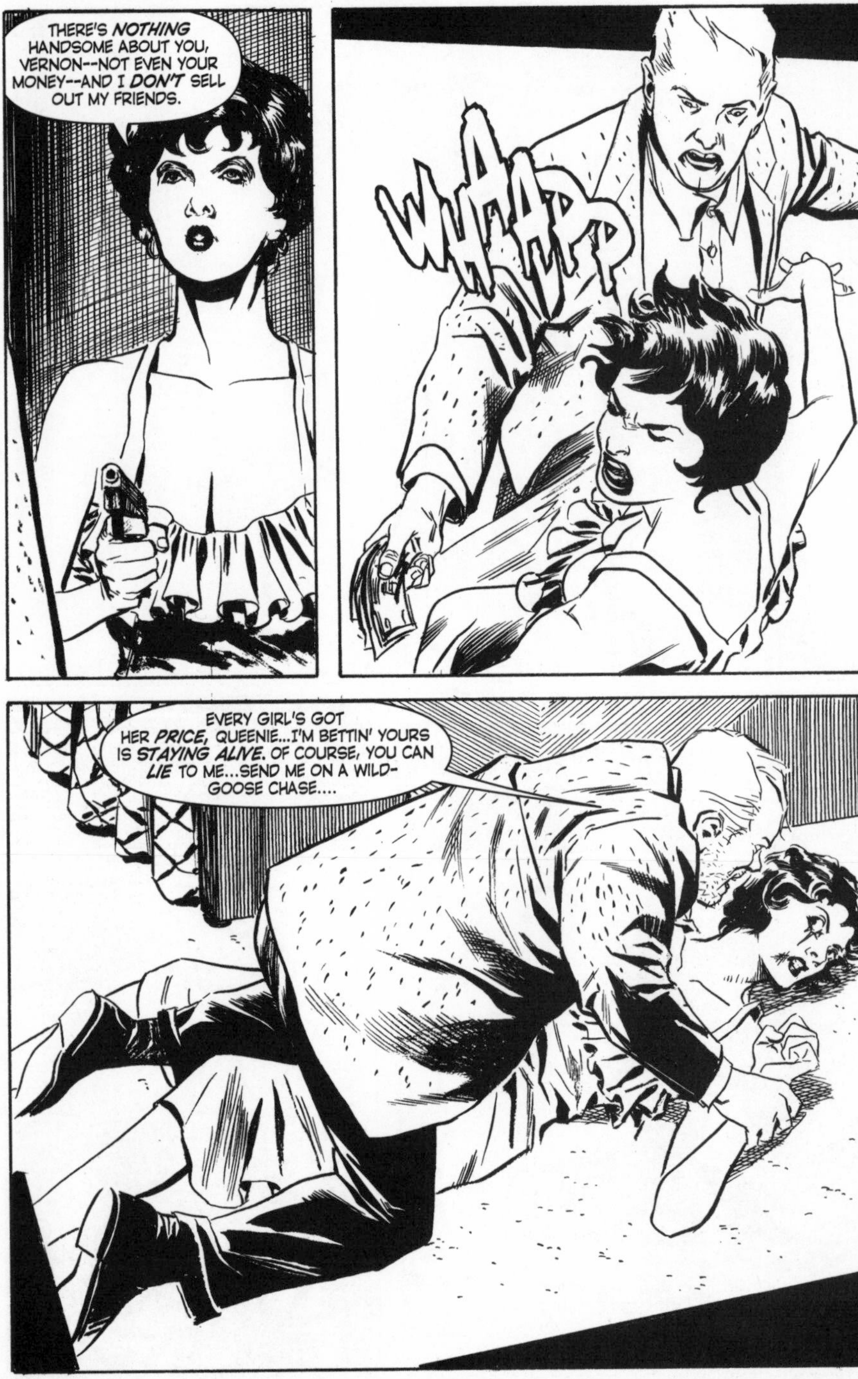
THERE'S NOTHING HANDSOME ABOUT YOU, VERNON--NOT EVEN YOUR MONEY--AND I DON'T SELL OUT MY FRIENDS.
WHAPP
EVERY GIRL'S GOT HER PRICE, QUEENIE...I'M BETTIN' YOURS IS STAYING ALIVE. OF COURSE, YOU CAN LIE TO ME...SEND ME ON A WILD-GOOSE CHASE....

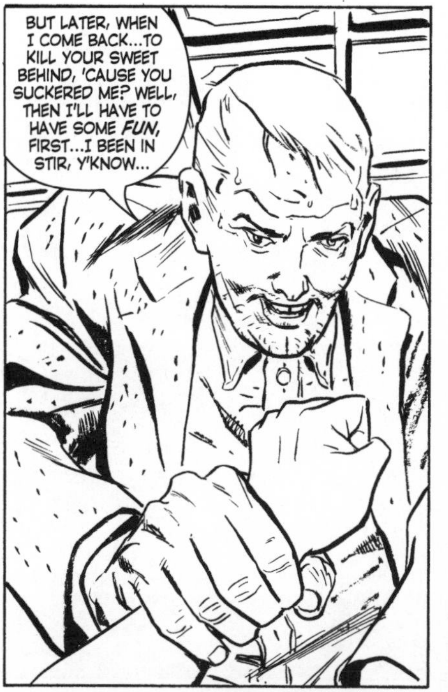
BUT LATER, WHEN I COME BACK...TO KILL YOUR SWEET BEHIND, 'CAUSE YOU SUCKERED ME? WELL, THEN I'LL HAVE TO HAVE SOME *FUN*, FIRST...I BEEN IN STIR, Y'KNOW...

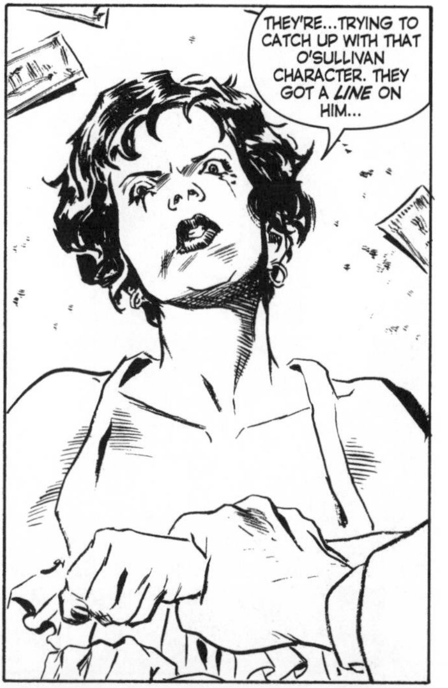
THEY'RE...TRYING TO CATCH UP WITH THAT O'SULLIVAN CHARACTER. THEY GOT A *LINE* ON HIM...

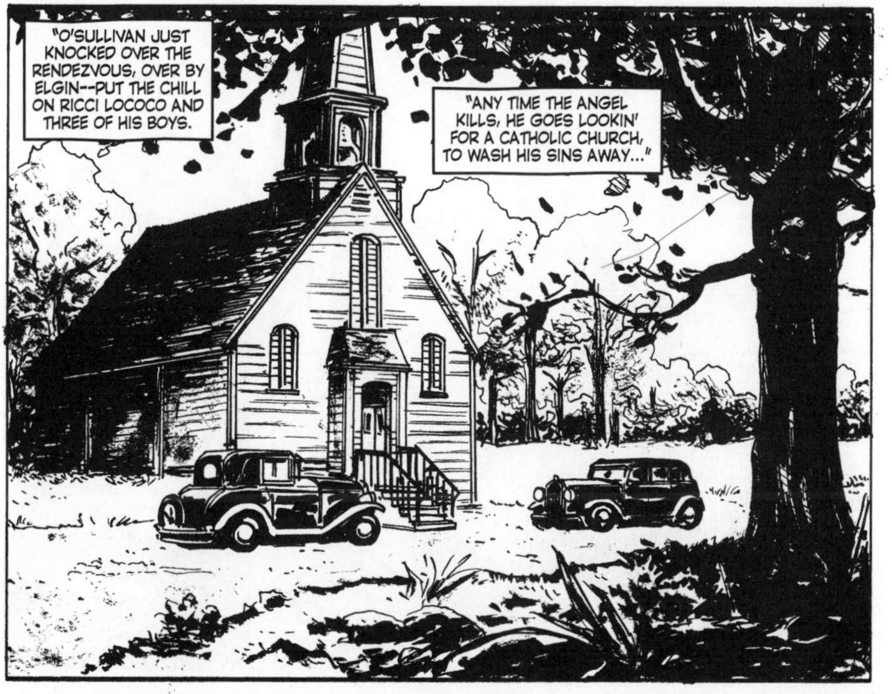
"O'SULLIVAN JUST KNOCKED OVER THE RENDEZVOUS, OVER BY ELGIN--PUT THE CHILL ON RICCI LOCOCO AND THREE OF HIS BOYS.
"ANY TIME THE ANGEL KILLS, HE GOES LOOKIN' FOR A CATHOLIC CHURCH, TO WASH HIS SINS AWAY..."

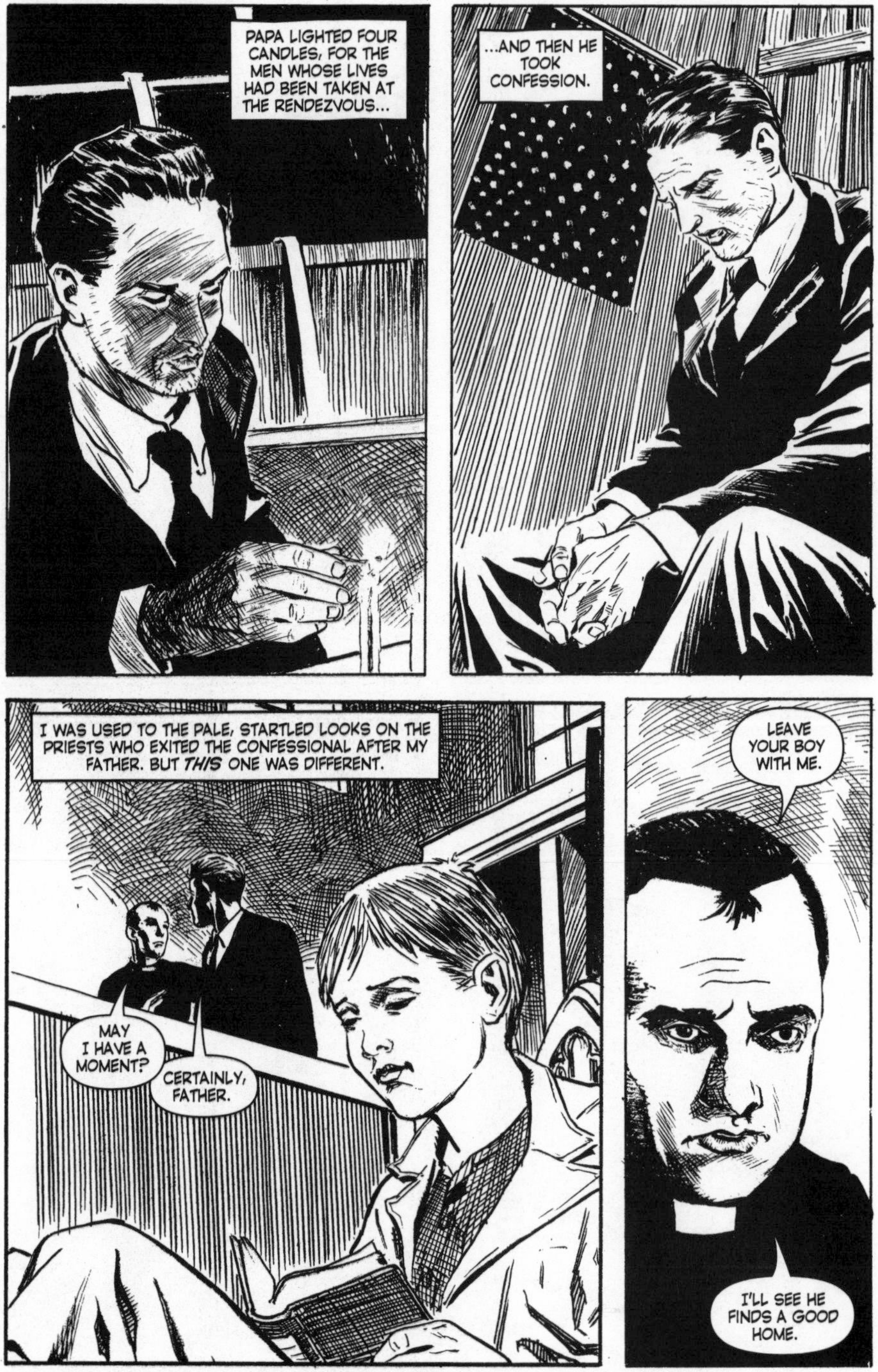
PAPA LIGHTED FOUR CANDLES, FOR THE MEN WHOSE LIVES HAD BEEN TAKEN AT THE RENDEZVOUS...
...AND THEN HE TOOK CONFESSION.
I WAS USED TO THE PALE, STARTLED LOOKS ON THE PRIESTS WHO EXITED THE CONFESSIONAL AFTER MY FATHER. BUT *THIS* ONE WAS DIFFERENT.
MAY I HAVE A MOMENT?
CERTAINLY, FATHER.
LEAVE YOUR BOY WITH ME.
I'LL SEE HE FINDS A GOOD HOME.

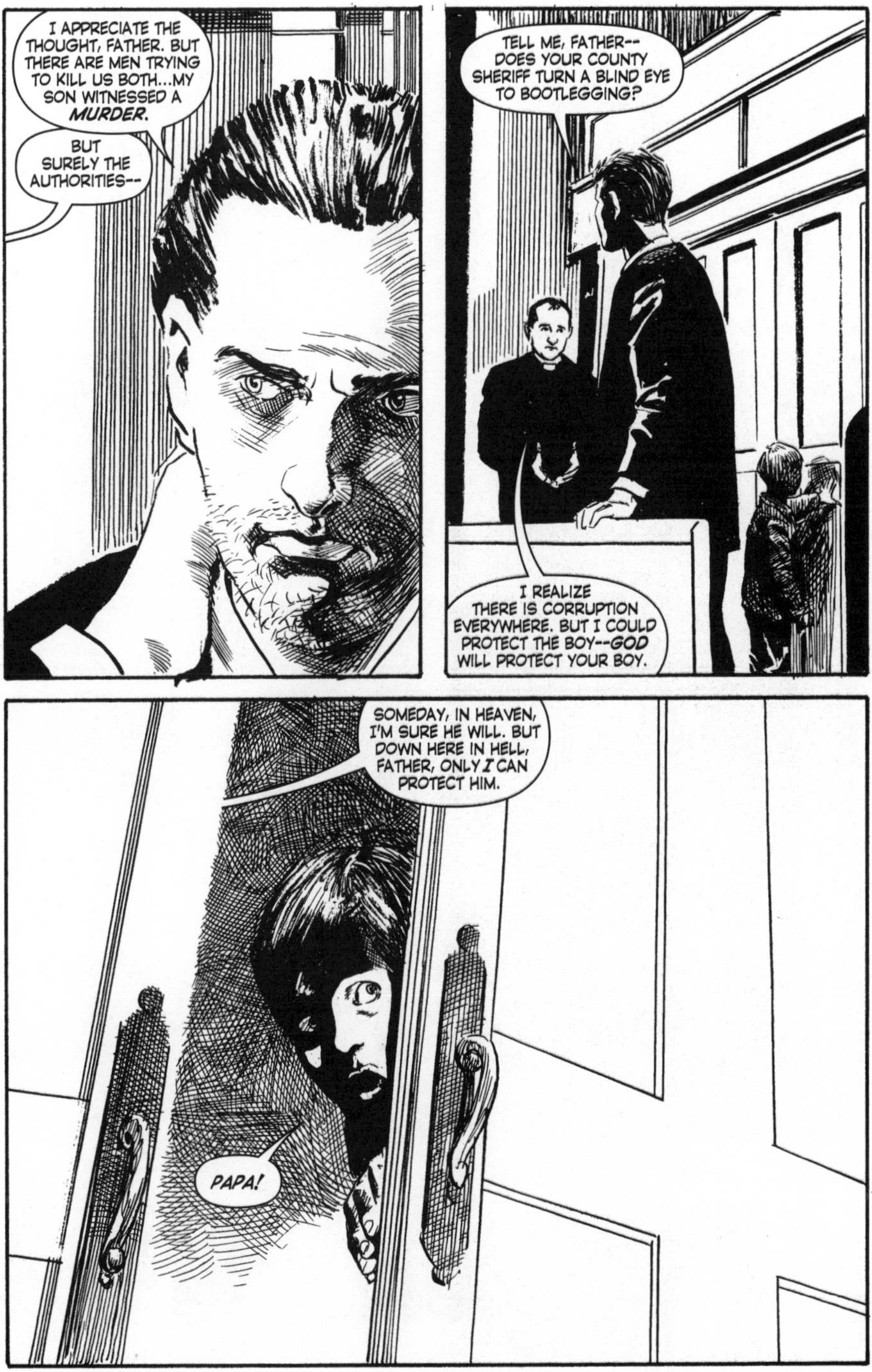
I APPRECIATE THE THOUGHT, FATHER. BUT THERE ARE MEN TRYING TO KILL US BOTH...MY SON WITNESSED A *MURDER*.
BUT SURELY THE AUTHORITIES--
TELL ME, FATHER-- DOES YOUR COUNTY SHERIFF TURN A BLIND EYE TO BOOTLEGGING?
I REALIZE THERE IS CORRUPTION EVERYWHERE. BUT I COULD PROTECT THE BOY--*GOD* WILL PROTECT YOUR BOY.
SOMEDAY, IN HEAVEN, I'M SURE HE WILL. BUT DOWN HERE IN HELL, FATHER, ONLY *I* CAN PROTECT HIM.
PAPA!

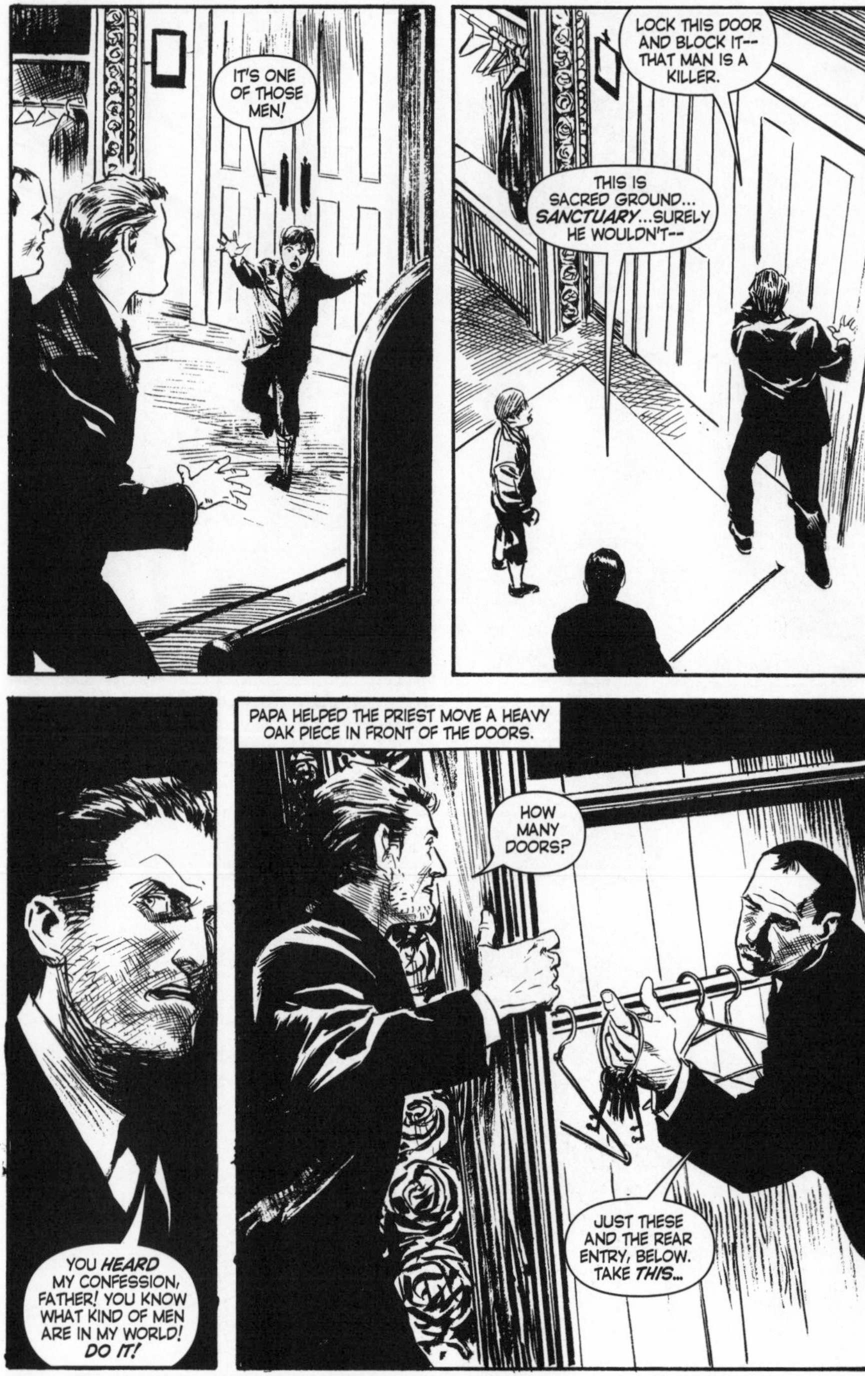
IT'S ONE OF THOSE MEN!
LOCK THIS DOOR AND BLOCK IT-- THAT MAN IS A KILLER.
THIS IS SACRED GROUND... SANCTUARY...SURELY HE WOULDN'T--
YOU HEARD MY CONFESSION, FATHER! YOU KNOW WHAT KIND OF MEN ARE IN MY WORLD! DO IT!
PAPA HELPED THE PRIEST MOVE A HEAVY OAK PIECE IN FRONT OF THE DOORS.
HOW MANY DOORS?
JUST THESE AND THE REAR ENTRY, BELOW. TAKE THIS...

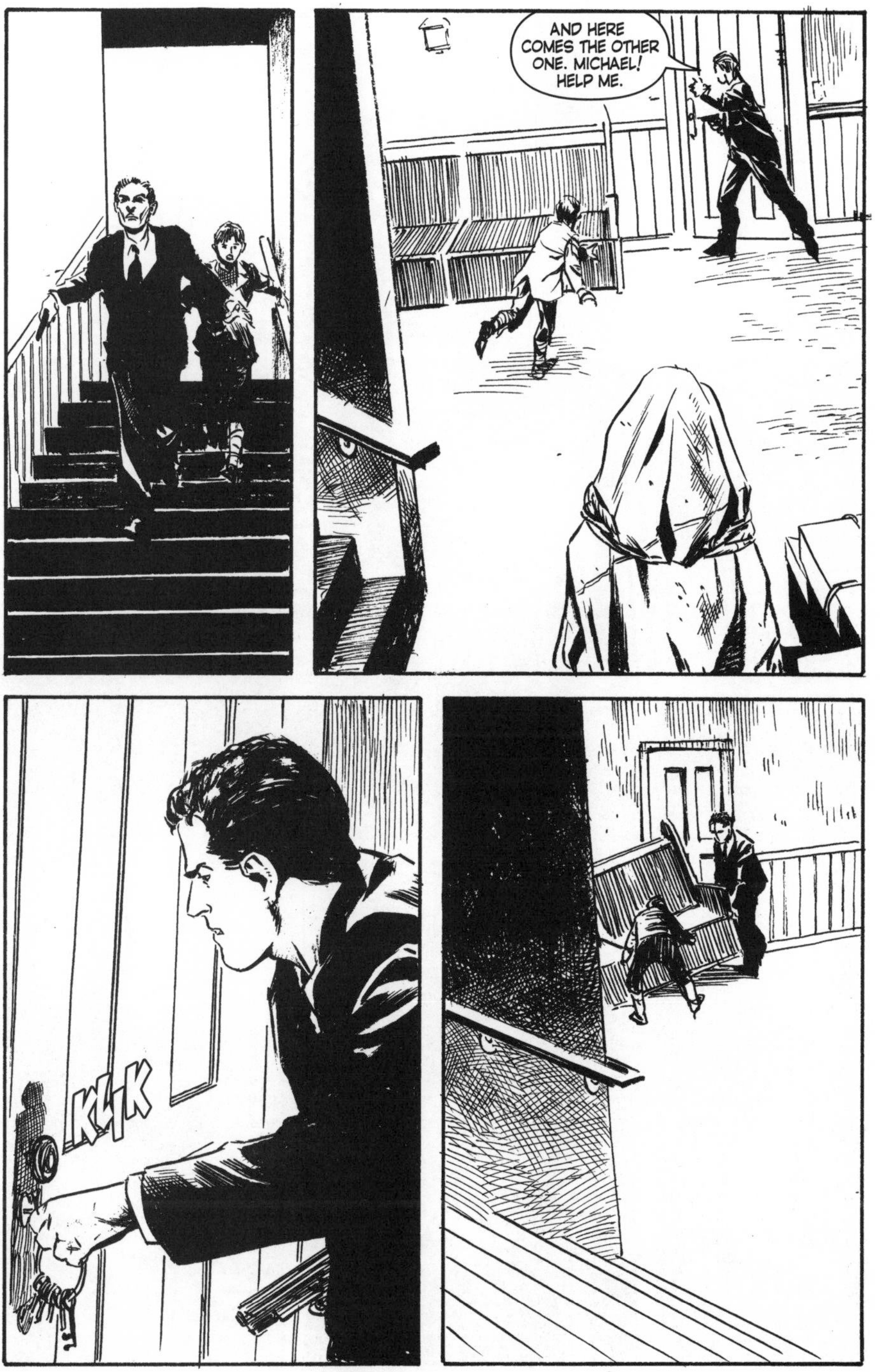
AND HERE COMES THE OTHER ONE. MICHAEL! HELP ME.
KLIK

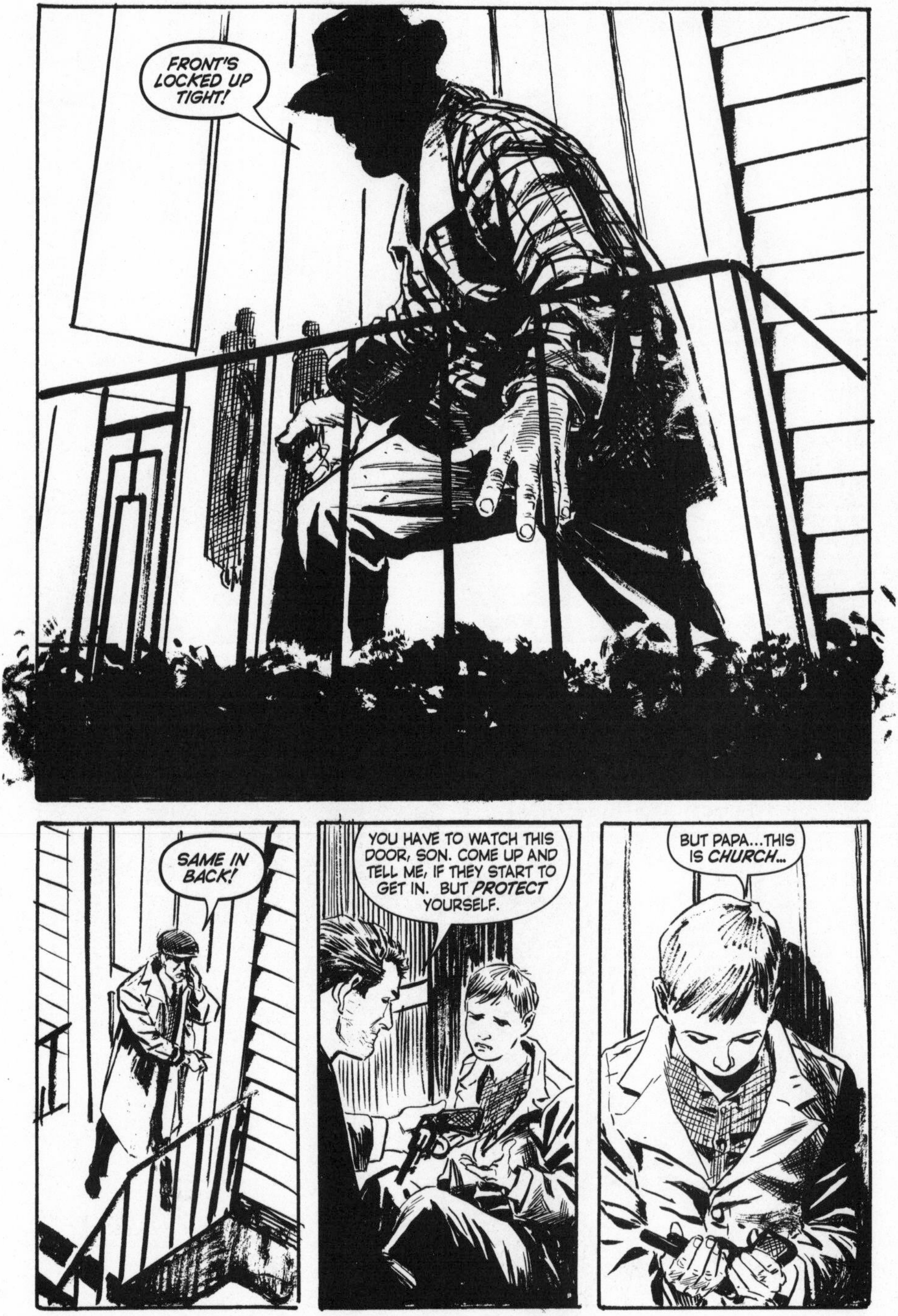
FRONT'S LOCKED UP TIGHT!
SAME IN BACK!
YOU HAVE TO WATCH THIS DOOR, SON. COME UP AND TELL ME, IF THEY START TO GET IN. BUT *PROTECT* YOURSELF.
BUT PAPA...THIS IS *CHURCH*...

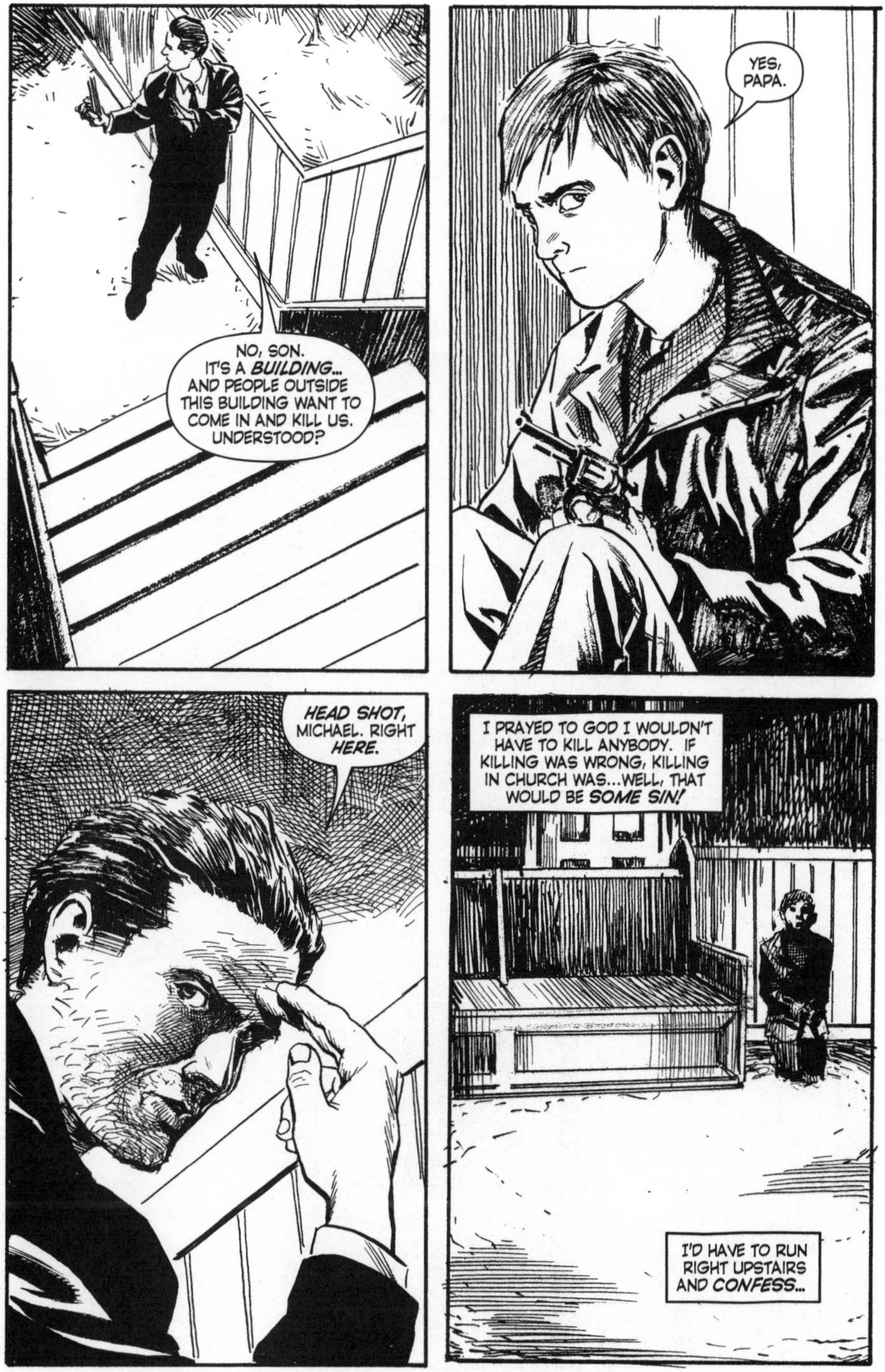
NO, SON. IT'S A *BUILDING*... AND PEOPLE OUTSIDE THIS BUILDING WANT TO COME IN AND KILL US. UNDERSTOOD?
YES, PAPA.
HEAD SHOT, MICHAEL. RIGHT *HERE*.
I PRAYED TO GOD I WOULDN'T HAVE TO KILL ANYBODY. IF KILLING WAS WRONG, KILLING IN CHURCH WAS...WELL, THAT WOULD BE *SOME SIN!*
I'D HAVE TO RUN RIGHT UPSTAIRS AND *CONFESS*...

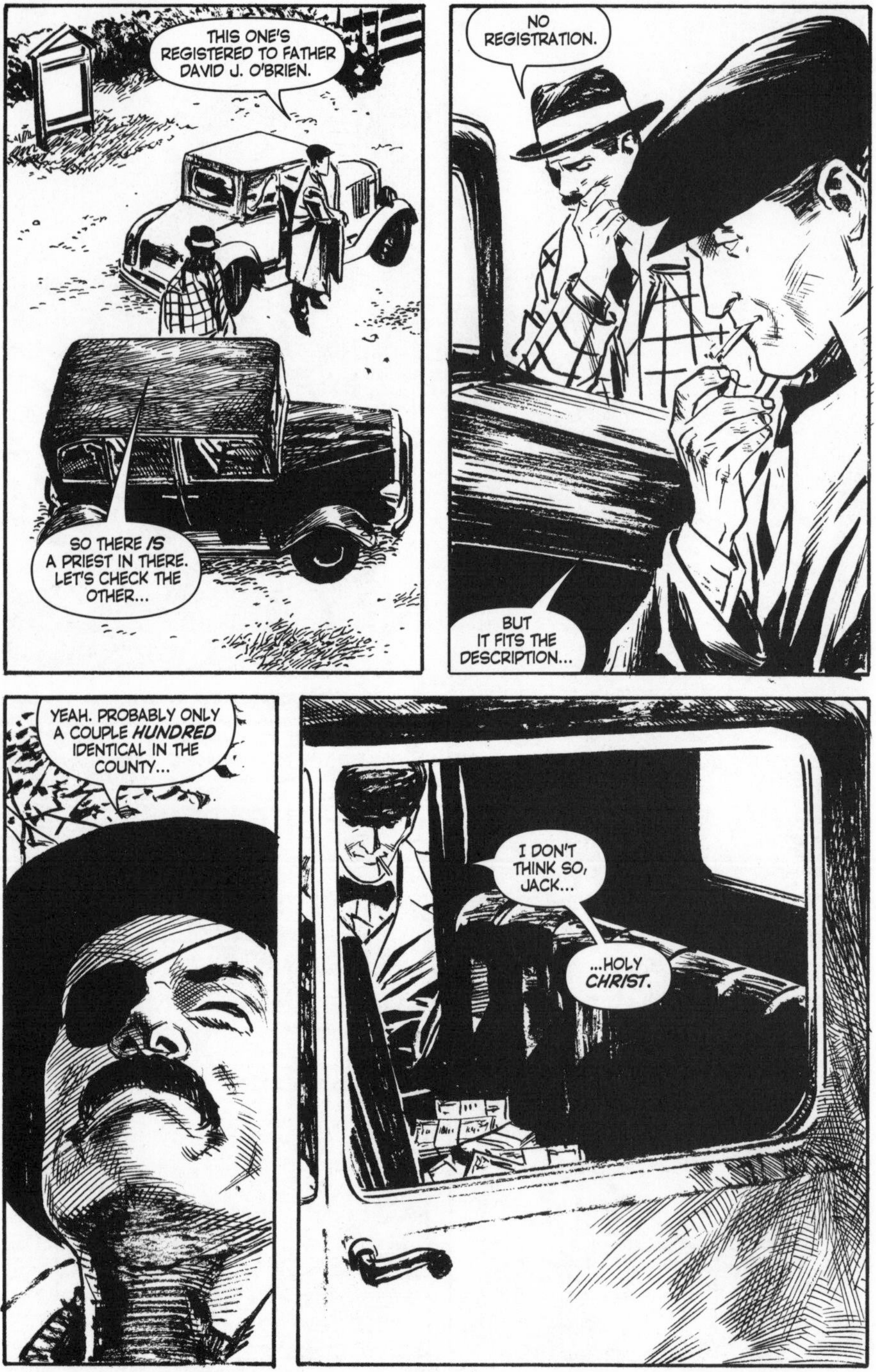
THIS ONE'S REGISTERED TO FATHER DAVID J. O'BRIEN.
SO THERE *IS* A PRIEST IN THERE. LET'S CHECK THE OTHER...
NO REGISTRATION.
BUT IT FITS THE DESCRIPTION...
YEAH. PROBABLY ONLY A COUPLE *HUNDRED* IDENTICAL IN THE COUNTY...
I DON'T THINK SO, JACK...
...HOLY *CHRIST*.

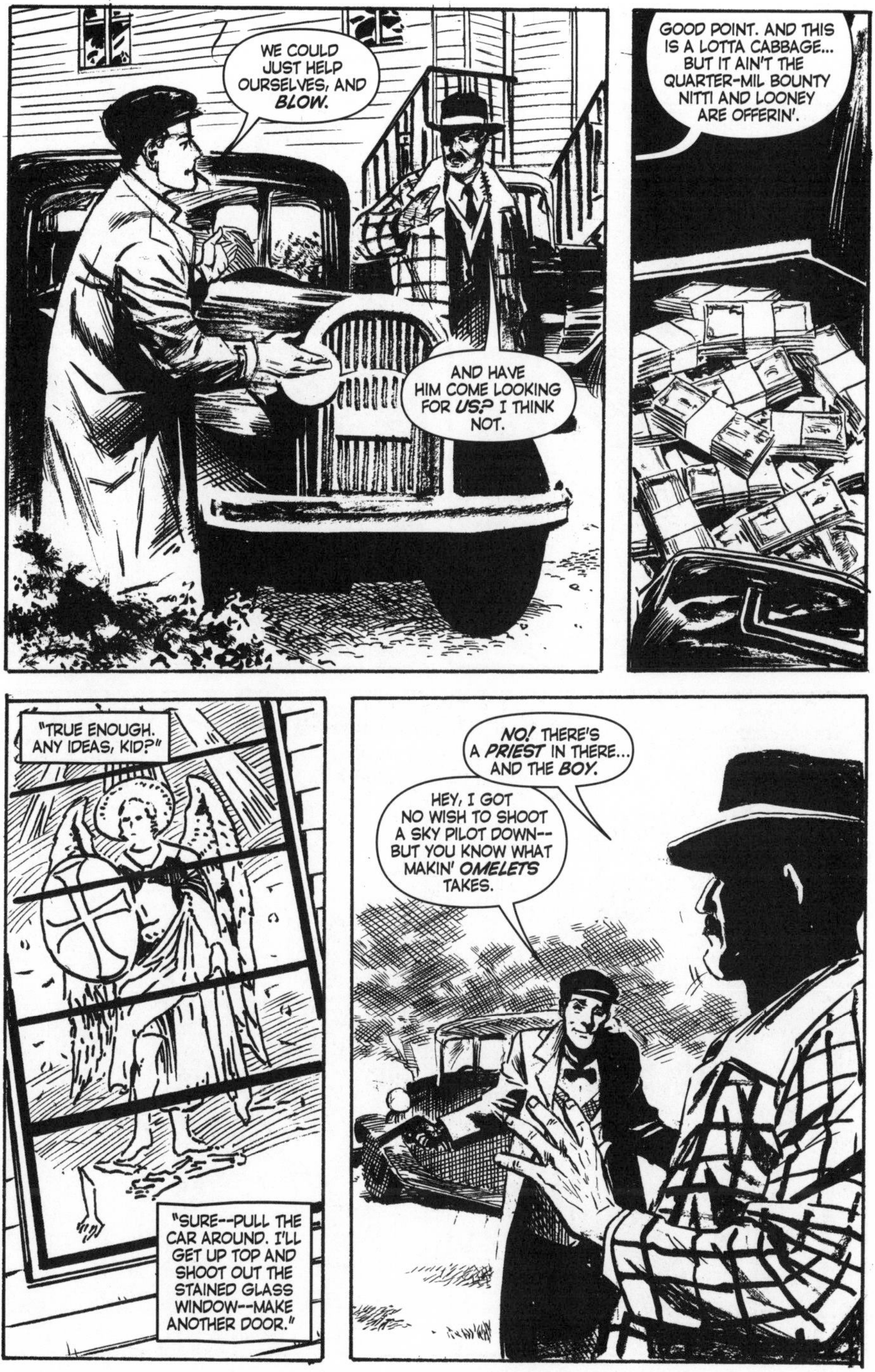
WE COULD JUST HELP OURSELVES, AND BLOW.
AND HAVE HIM COME LOOKING FOR US? I THINK NOT.
GOOD POINT. AND THIS IS A LOTTA CABBAGE... BUT IT AIN'T THE QUARTER-MIL BOUNTY NITTI AND LOONEY ARE OFFERIN'.
"TRUE ENOUGH. ANY IDEAS, KID?"
"SURE--PULL THE CAR AROUND. I'LL GET UP TOP AND SHOOT OUT THE STAINED GLASS WINDOW--MAKE ANOTHER DOOR."
NO! THERE'S A PRIEST IN THERE... AND THE BOY.
HEY, I GOT NO WISH TO SHOOT A SKY PILOT DOWN-- BUT YOU KNOW WHAT MAKIN' OMELETS TAKES.

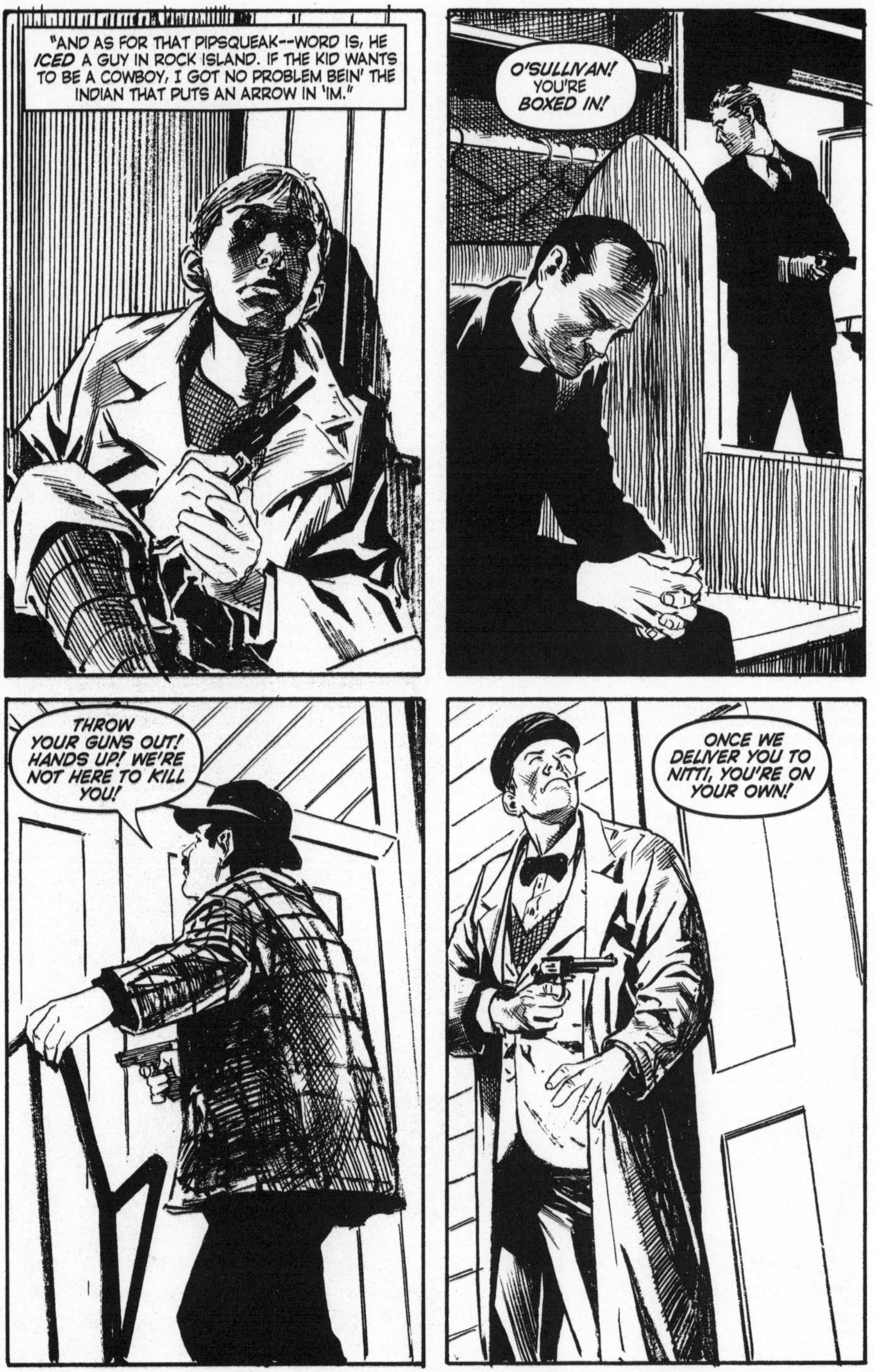
"AND AS FOR THAT PIPSQUEAK--WORD IS, HE ICED A GUY IN ROCK ISLAND. IF THE KID WANTS TO BE A COWBOY, I GOT NO PROBLEM BEIN' THE INDIAN THAT PUTS AN ARROW IN 'IM."
O'SULLIVAN! YOU'RE BOXED IN!
THROW YOUR GUNS OUT! HANDS UP! WE'RE NOT HERE TO KILL YOU!
ONCE WE DELIVER YOU TO NITTI, YOU'RE ON YOUR OWN!

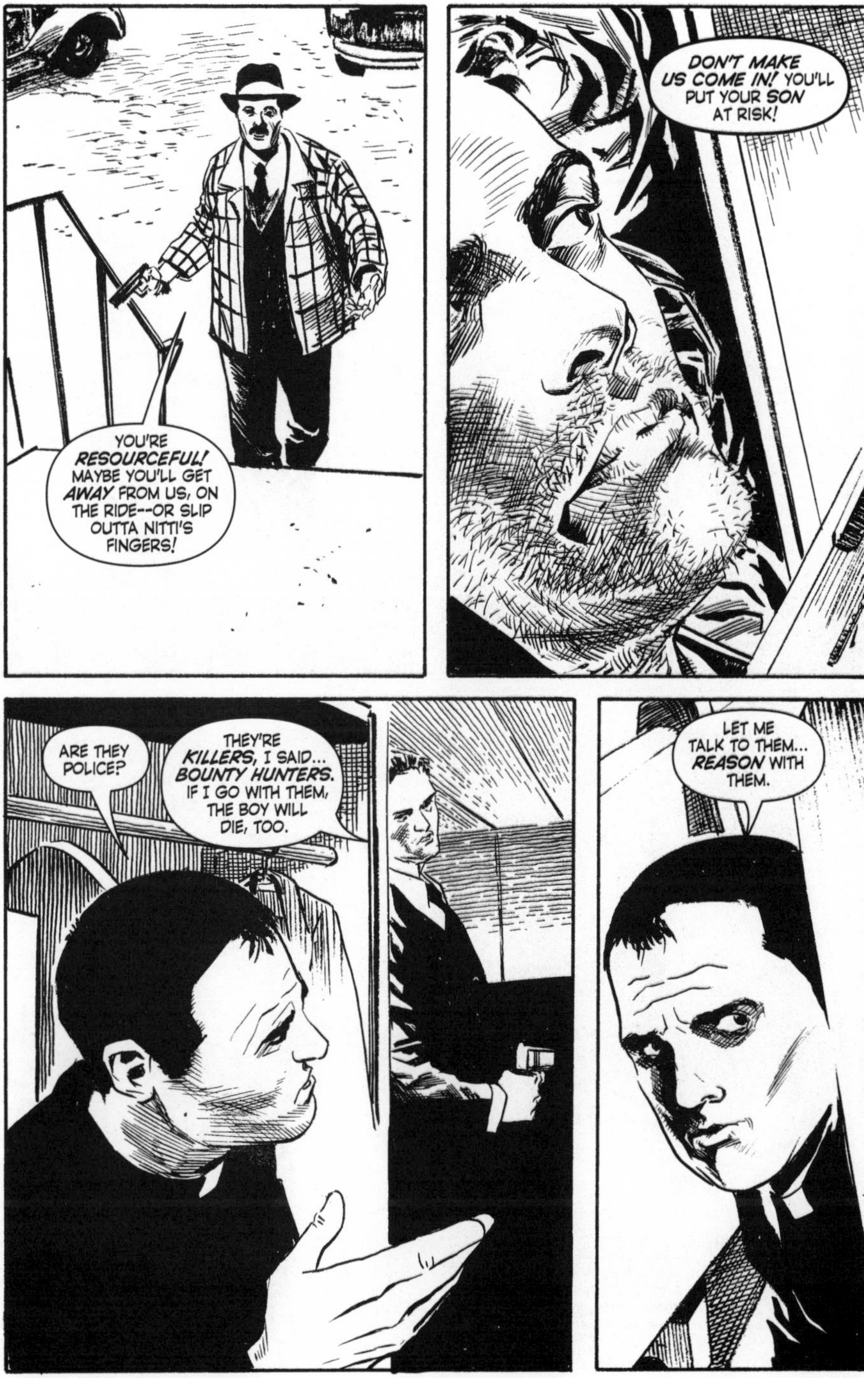
YOU'RE RESOURCEFUL! MAYBE YOU'LL GET AWAY FROM US, ON THE RIDE--OR SLIP OUTTA NITTI'S FINGERS!
DON'T MAKE US COME IN! YOU'LL PUT YOUR SON AT RISK!
ARE THEY POLICE?
THEY'RE KILLERS, I SAID... BOUNTY HUNTERS. IF I GO WITH THEM, THE BOY WILL DIE, TOO.
LET ME TALK TO THEM... REASON WITH THEM.

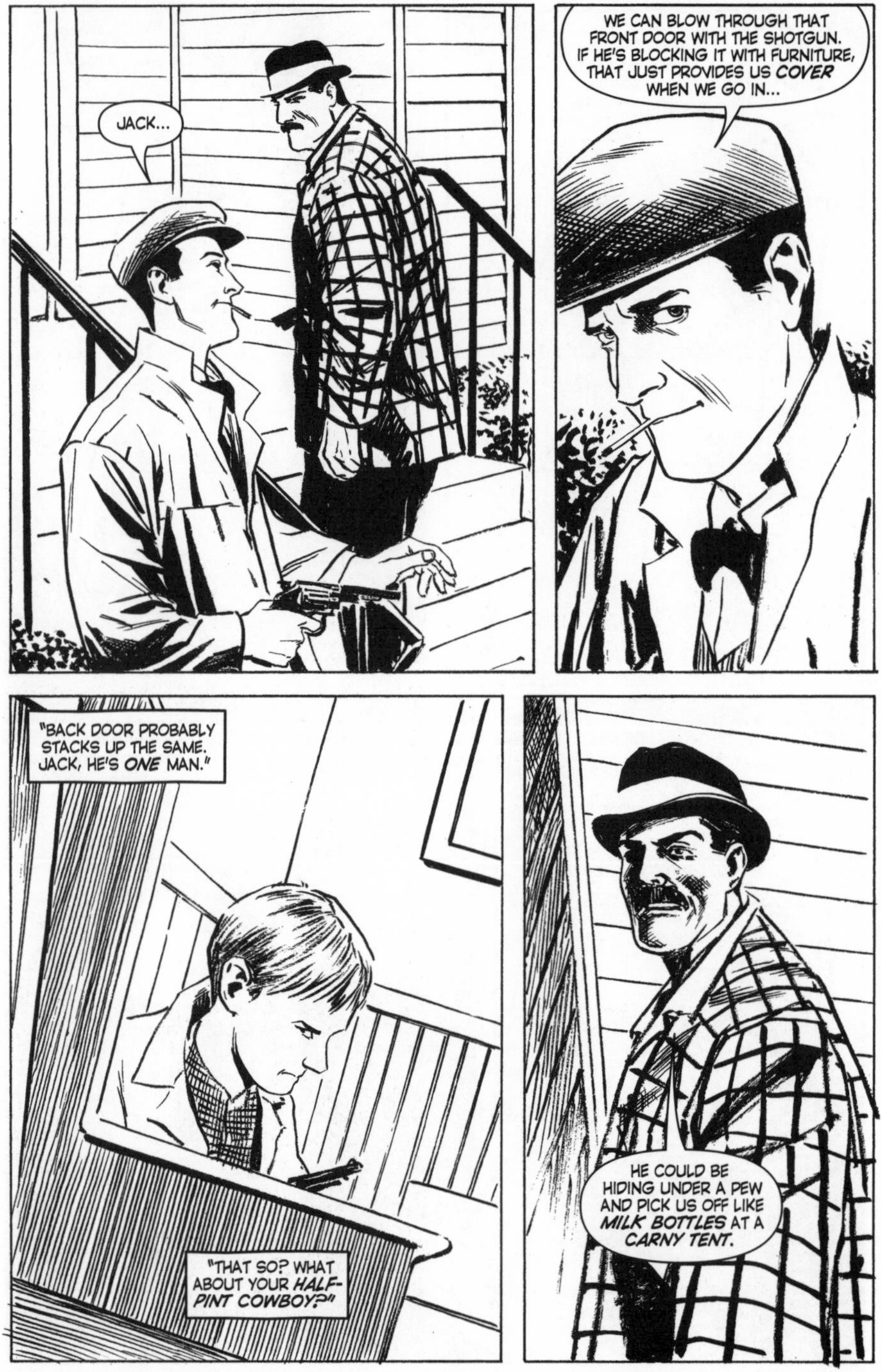
JACK...
WE CAN BLOW THROUGH THAT FRONT DOOR WITH THE SHOTGUN. IF HE'S BLOCKING IT WITH FURNITURE, THAT JUST PROVIDES US *COVER* WHEN WE GO IN...
"BACK DOOR PROBABLY STACKS UP THE SAME. JACK, HE'S *ONE* MAN."
"THAT SO? WHAT ABOUT YOUR *HALF-PINT COWBOY?*"
HE COULD BE HIDING UNDER A PEW AND PICK US OFF LIKE *MILK BOTTLES* AT A *CARNY TENT.*

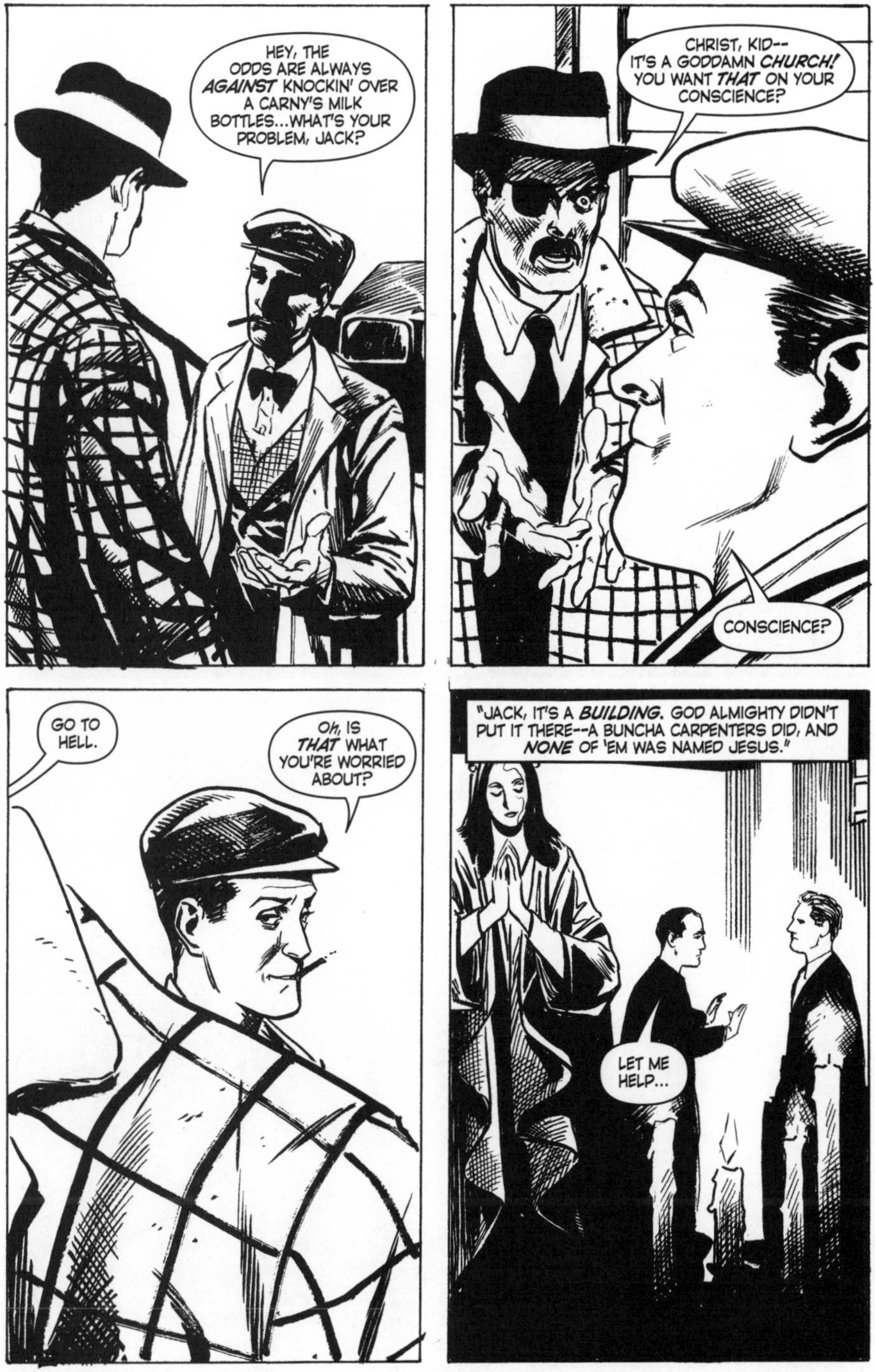
HEY, THE ODDS ARE ALWAYS AGAINST KNOCKIN' OVER A CARNY'S MILK BOTTLES...WHAT'S YOUR PROBLEM, JACK?
CHRIST, KID-- IT'S A GODDAMN CHURCH! YOU WANT THAT ON YOUR CONSCIENCE?
CONSCIENCE?
GO TO HELL.
OH, IS THAT WHAT YOU'RE WORRIED ABOUT?
"JACK, IT'S A BUILDING. GOD ALMIGHTY DIDN'T PUT IT THERE--A BUNCHA CARPENTERS DID, AND NONE OF 'EM WAS NAMED JESUS."
LET ME HELP...

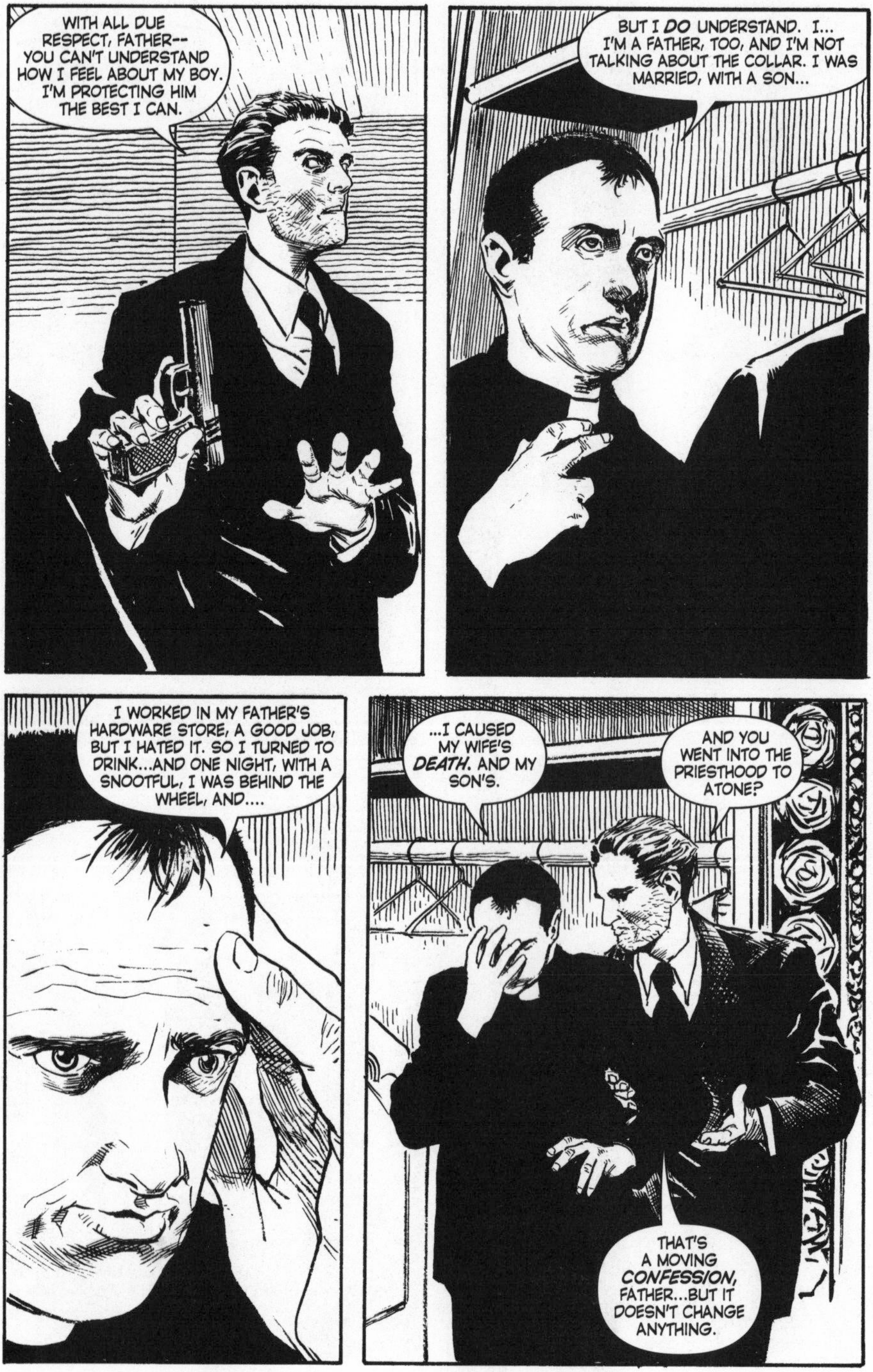
WITH ALL DUE RESPECT, FATHER-- YOU CAN'T UNDERSTAND HOW I FEEL ABOUT MY BOY. I'M PROTECTING HIM THE BEST I CAN.
BUT I DO UNDERSTAND. I... I'M A FATHER, TOO, AND I'M NOT TALKING ABOUT THE COLLAR. I WAS MARRIED, WITH A SON...
I WORKED IN MY FATHER'S HARDWARE STORE, A GOOD JOB, BUT I HATED IT. SO I TURNED TO DRINK...AND ONE NIGHT, WITH A SNOOTFUL, I WAS BEHIND THE WHEEL, AND....
...I CAUSED MY WIFE'S DEATH. AND MY SON'S.
AND YOU WENT INTO THE PRIESTHOOD TO ATONE?
THAT'S A MOVING CONFESSION, FATHER...BUT IT DOESN'T CHANGE ANYTHING.

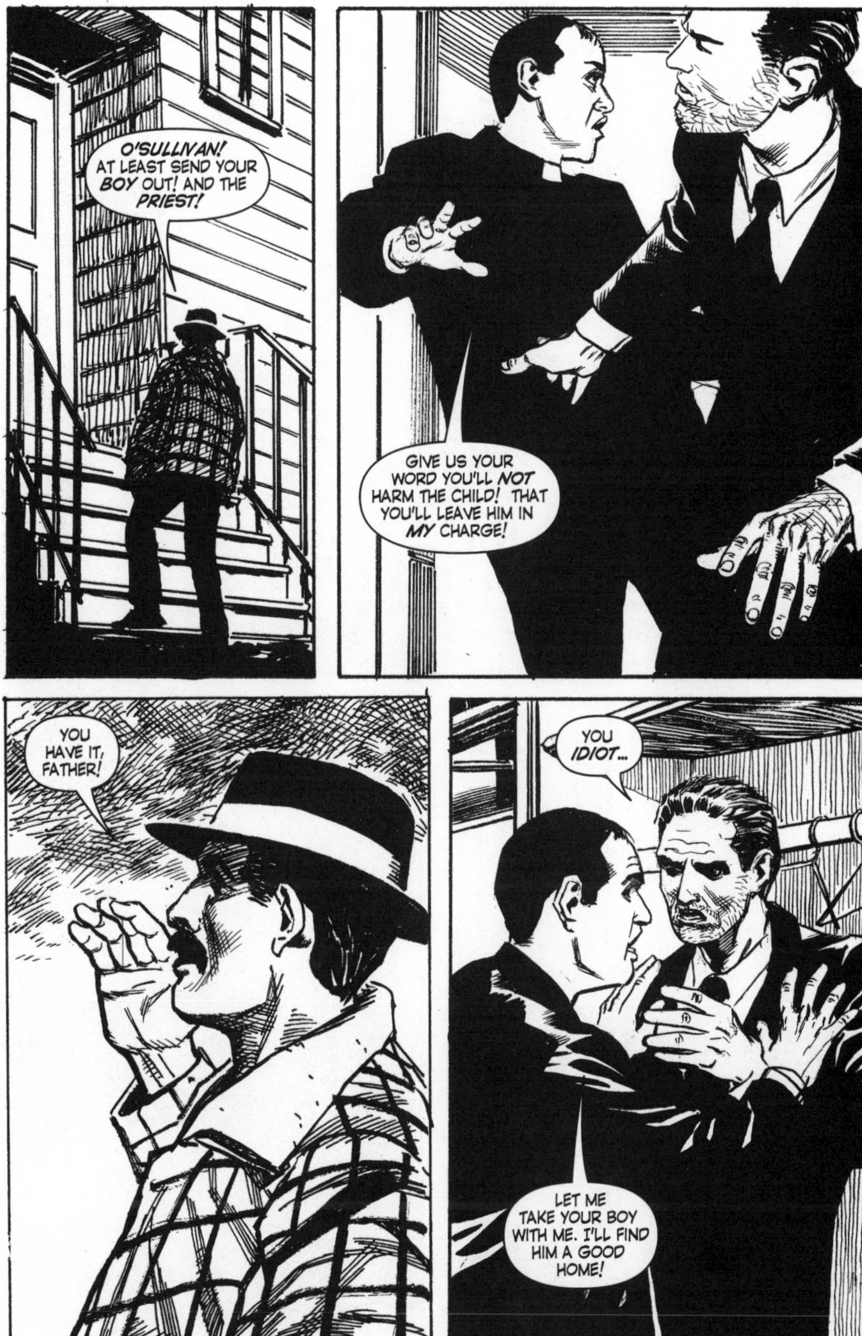
O'SULLIVAN! AT LEAST SEND YOUR BOY OUT! AND THE PRIEST!
GIVE US YOUR WORD YOU'LL NOT HARM THE CHILD! THAT YOU'LL LEAVE HIM IN MY CHARGE!
YOU HAVE IT, FATHER!
YOU IDIOT...
LET ME TAKE YOUR BOY WITH ME. I'LL FIND HIM A GOOD HOME!

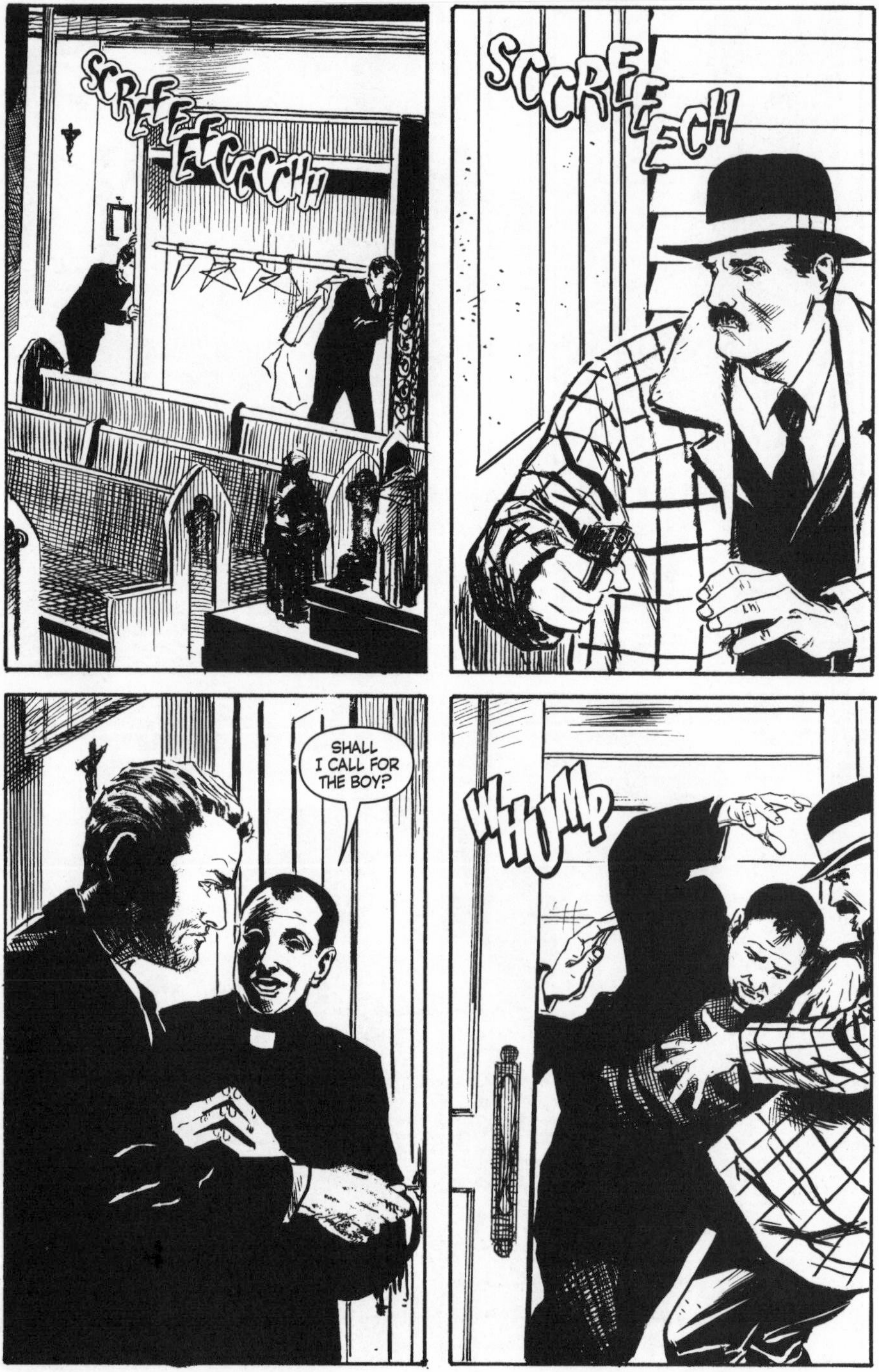
SCREEEEECCCCHH
SCCREEECH
SHALL I CALL FOR THE BOY?
WHUMP

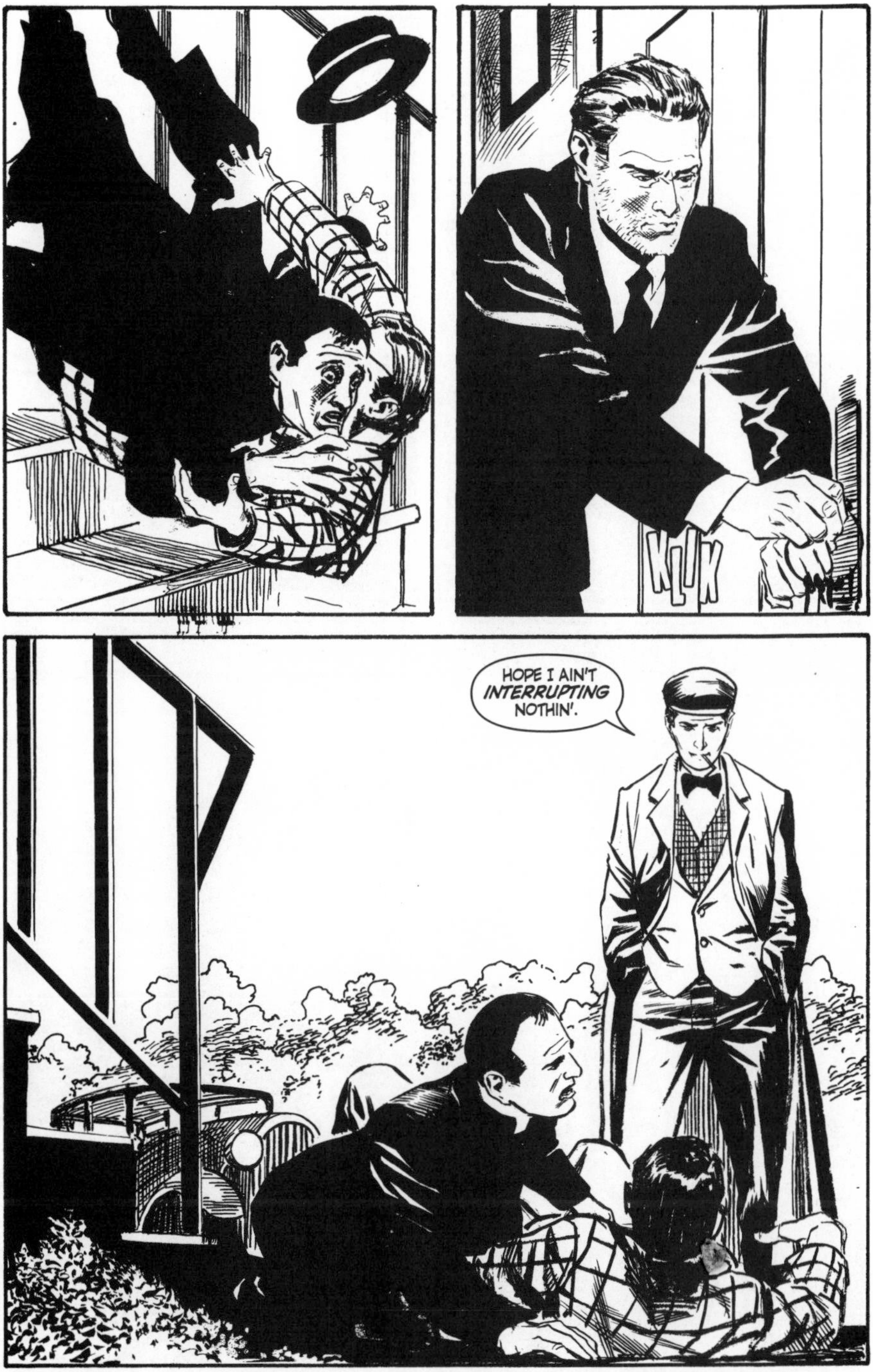
KLIK
HOPE I AIN'T *INTERRUPTING* NOTHIN'.

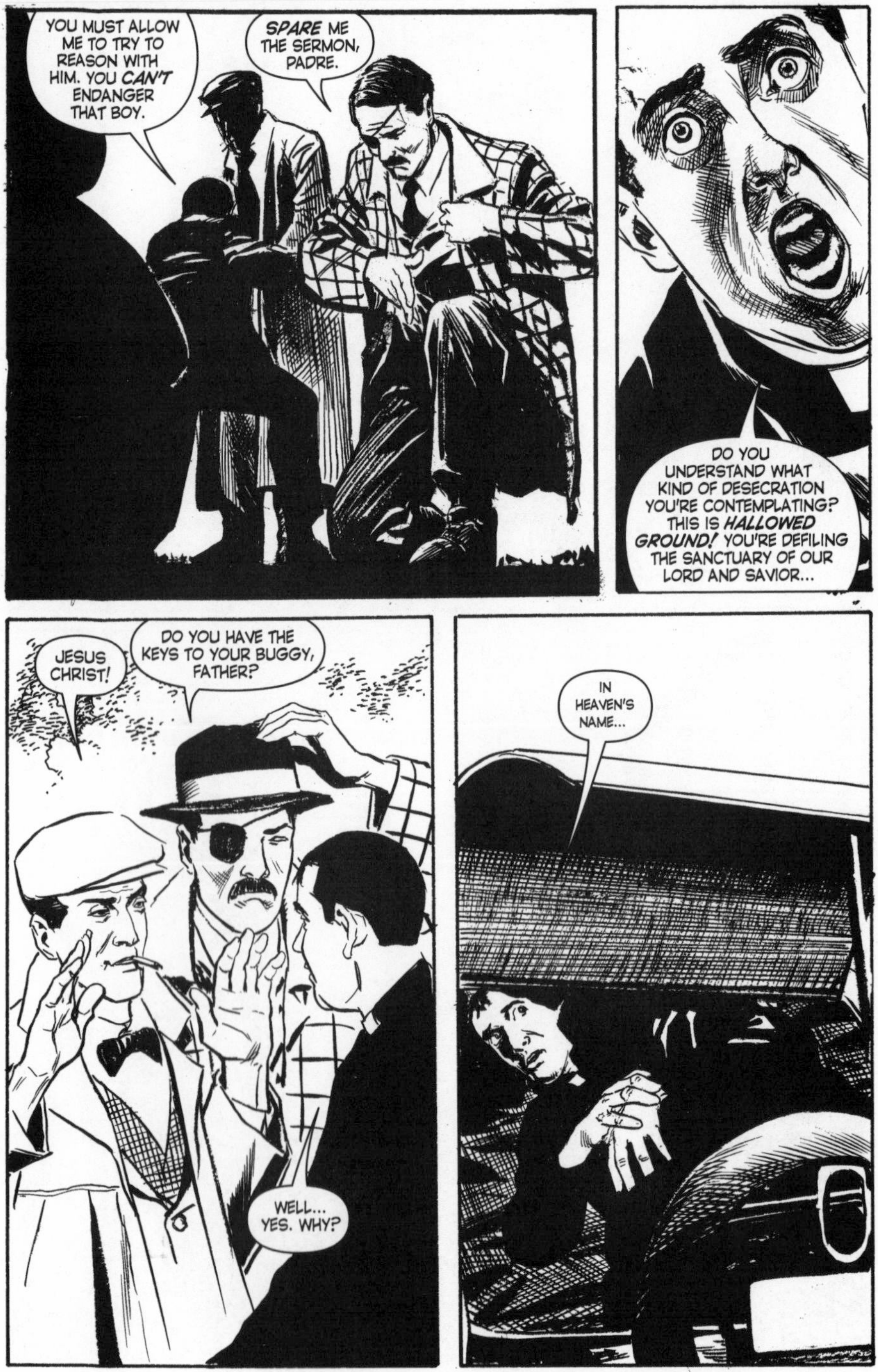
YOU MUST ALLOW ME TO TRY TO REASON WITH HIM. YOU *CAN'T* ENDANGER THAT BOY.
SPARE ME THE SERMON, PADRE.
DO YOU UNDERSTAND WHAT KIND OF DESECRATION YOU'RE CONTEMPLATING? THIS IS ***HALLOWED GROUND!*** YOU'RE DEFILING THE SANCTUARY OF OUR LORD AND SAVIOR...
JESUS CHRIST!
DO YOU HAVE THE KEYS TO YOUR BUGGY, FATHER?
WELL... YES. WHY?
IN HEAVEN'S NAME...

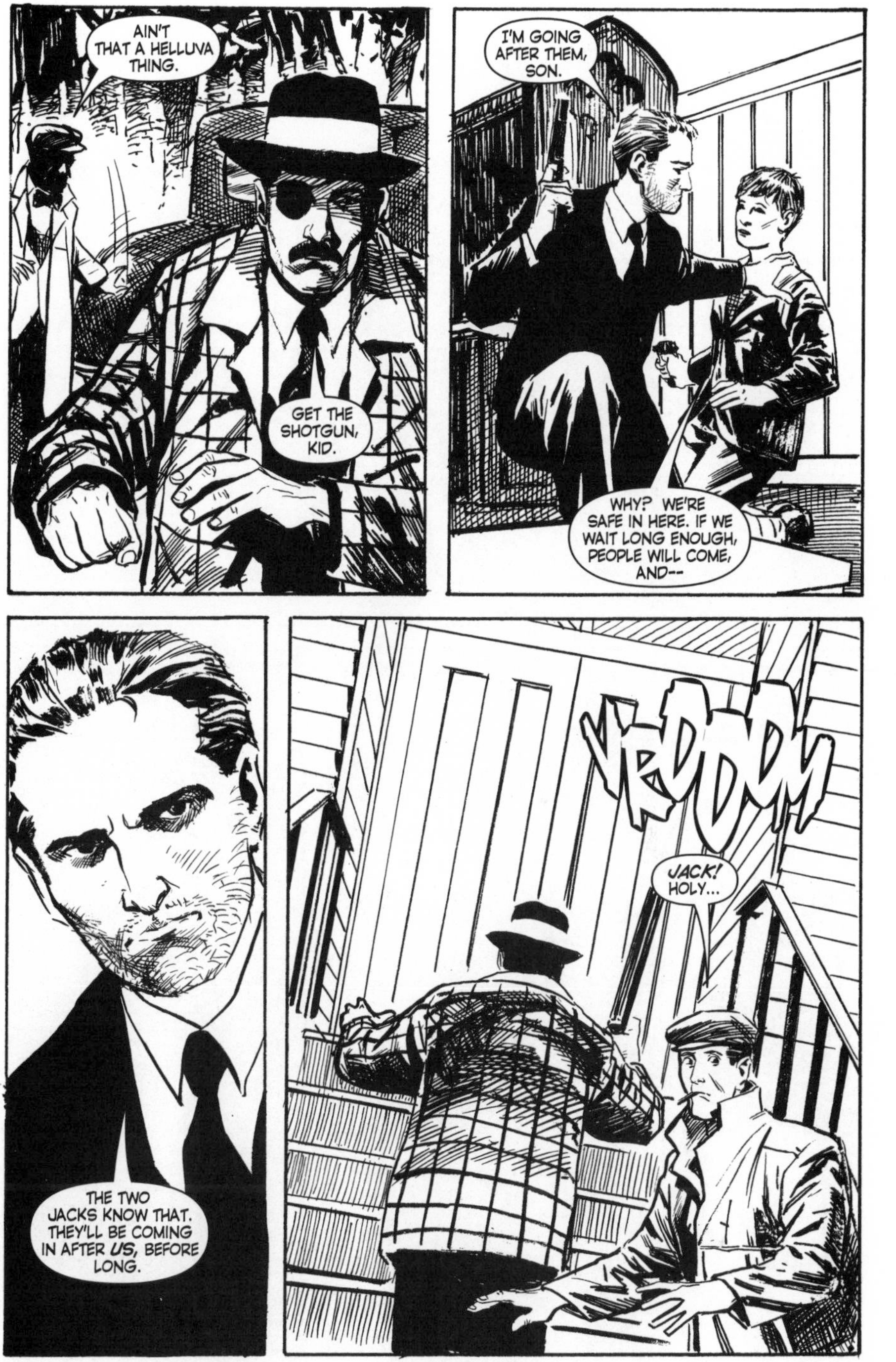

AIN'T THAT A HELLUVA THING.
GET THE SHOTGUN, KID.
I'M GOING AFTER THEM, SON.
WHY? WE'RE SAFE IN HERE. IF WE WAIT LONG ENOUGH, PEOPLE WILL COME, AND--
THE TWO JACKS KNOW THAT. THEY'LL BE COMING IN AFTER *US*, BEFORE LONG.
JACK! HOLY...

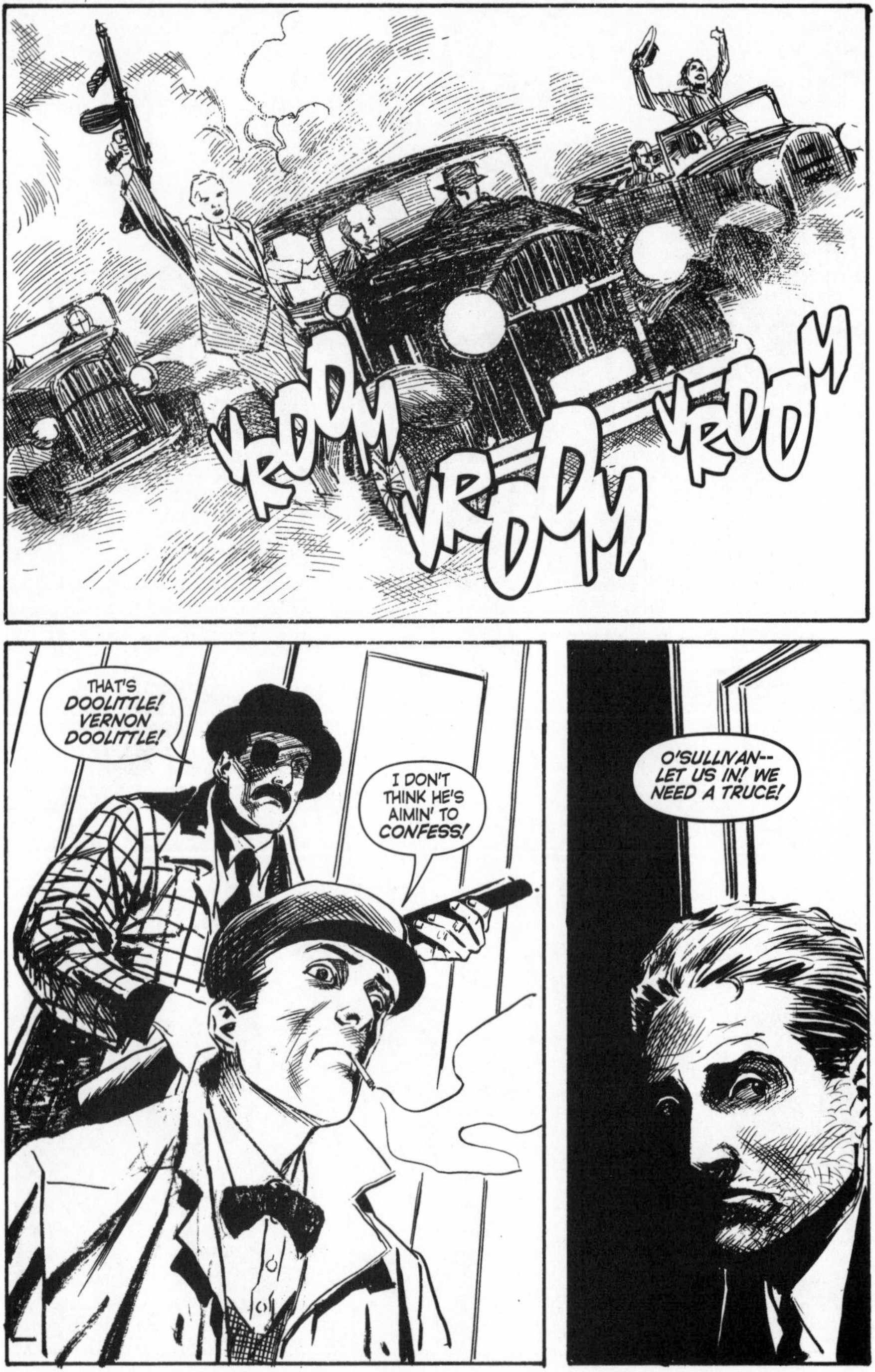
VROOM
VROOM
VROOM
THAT'S *DOOLITTLE!* VERNON DOOLITTLE!
I DON'T THINK HE'S AIMIN' TO *CONFESS!*
O'SULLIVAN-- LET US IN! WE NEED A TRUCE!

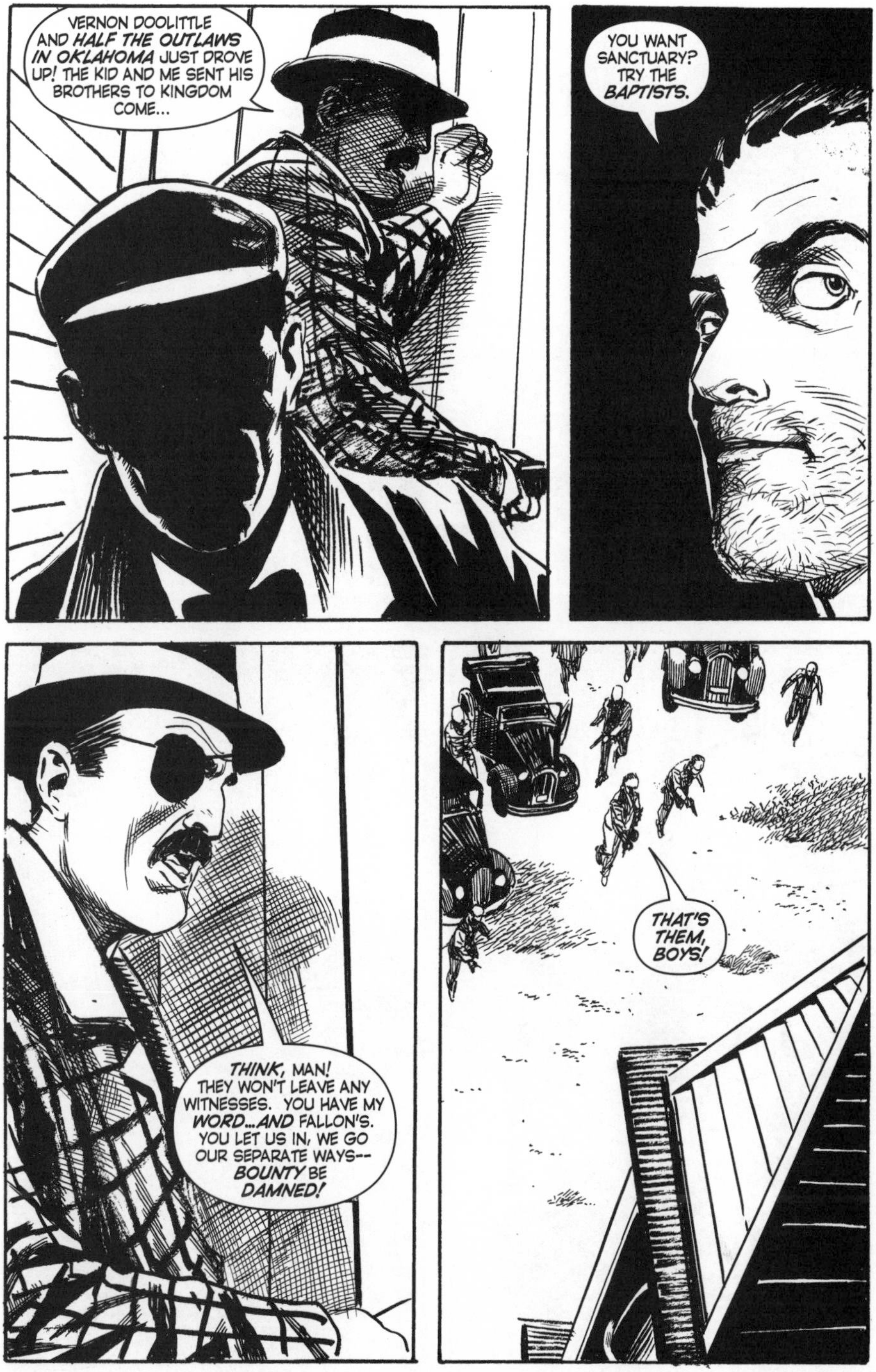
VERNON DOOLITTLE AND HALF THE OUTLAWS IN OKLAHOMA JUST DROVE UP! THE KID AND ME SENT HIS BROTHERS TO KINGDOM COME...
YOU WANT SANCTUARY? TRY THE BAPTISTS.
THINK, MAN! THEY WON'T LEAVE ANY WITNESSES. YOU HAVE MY WORD...AND FALLON'S. YOU LET US IN, WE GO OUR SEPARATE WAYS-- BOUNTY BE DAMNED!
THAT'S THEM, BOYS!

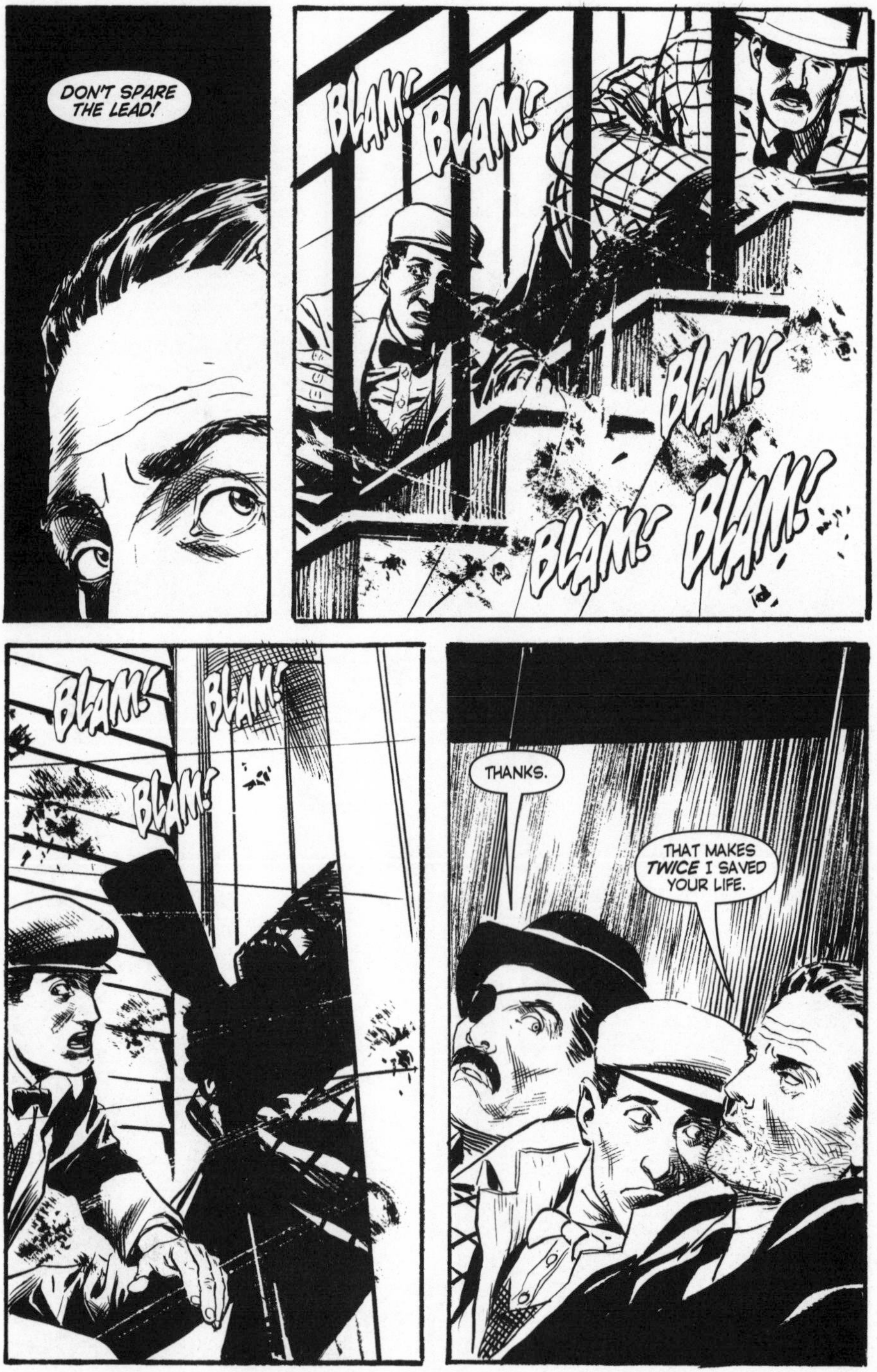
DON'T SPARE THE LEAD!
BLAM!
BLAM!
BLAM!
BLAM!
BLAM!
BLAM!
BLAM!
BLAM!
THANKS.
THAT MAKES *TWICE* I SAVED YOUR LIFE.

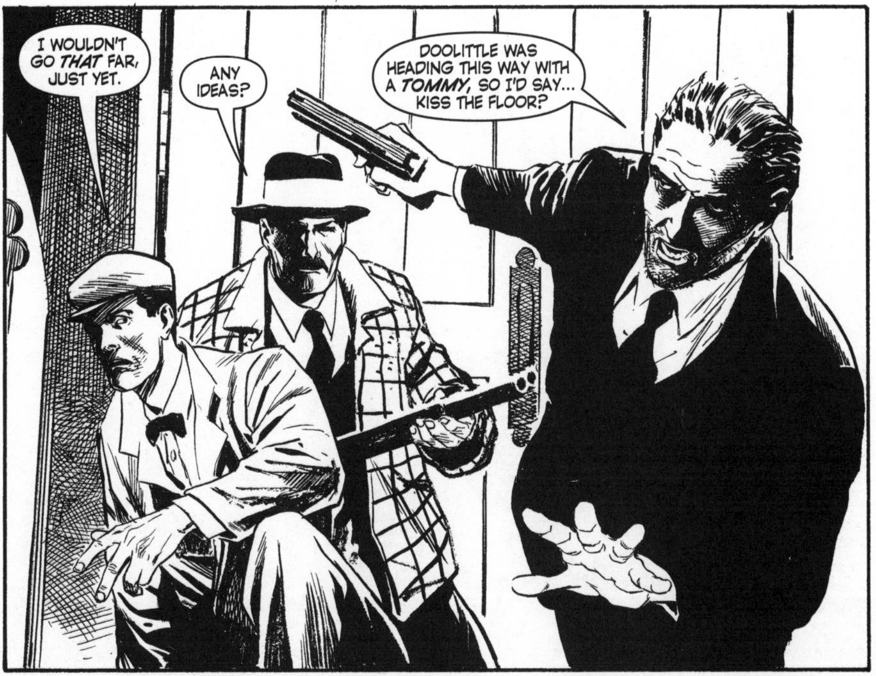
I WOULDN'T GO *THAT* FAR, JUST YET.
ANY IDEAS?
DOOLITTLE WAS HEADING THIS WAY WITH A *TOMMY*, SO I'D SAY... KISS THE FLOOR?

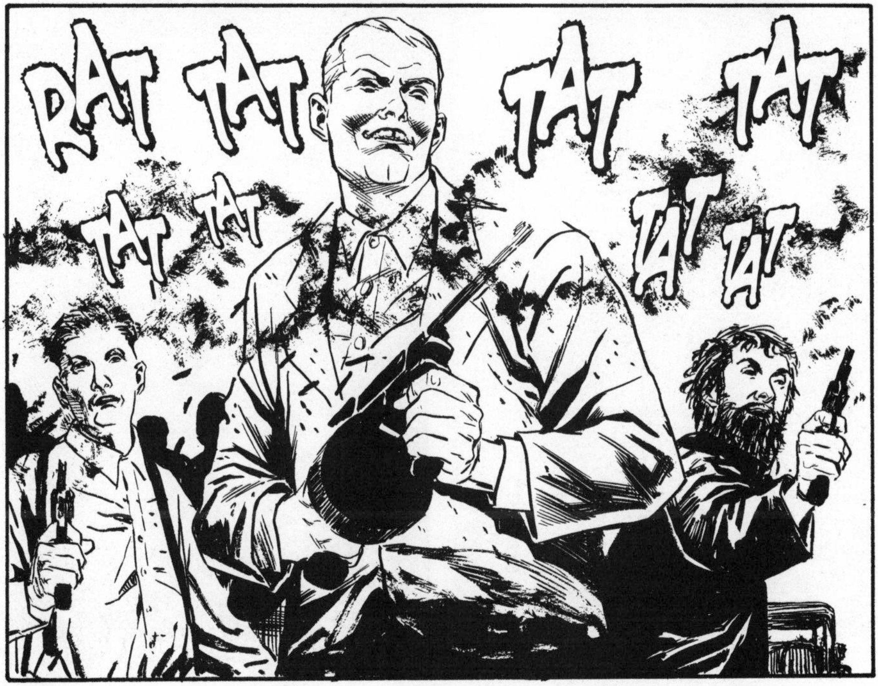
RAT TAT TAT TAT
TAT TAT TAT TAT

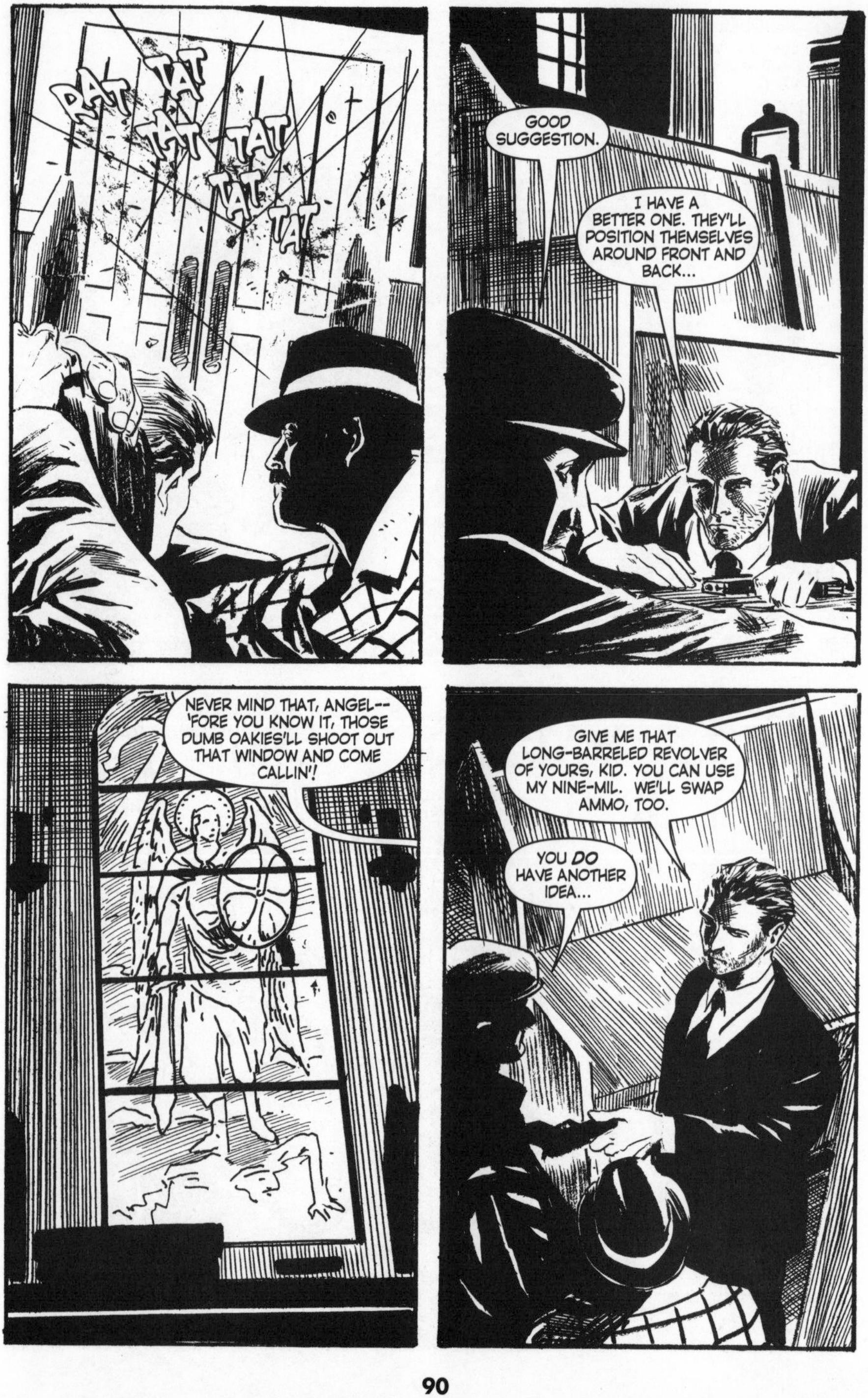
RAT TAT TAT TAT TAT TAT
GOOD SUGGESTION.
I HAVE A BETTER ONE. THEY'LL POSITION THEMSELVES AROUND FRONT AND BACK...
NEVER MIND THAT, ANGEL-- 'FORE YOU KNOW IT, THOSE DUMB OAKIES'LL SHOOT OUT THAT WINDOW AND COME CALLIN'!
GIVE ME THAT LONG-BARRELED REVOLVER OF YOURS, KID. YOU CAN USE MY NINE-MIL. WE'LL SWAP AMMO, TOO.
YOU **DO** HAVE ANOTHER IDEA...

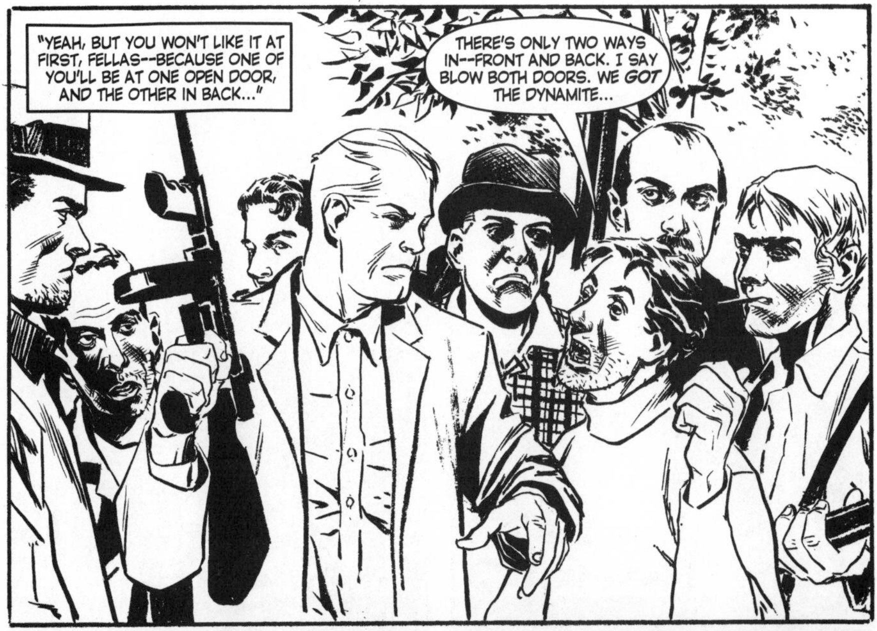
"YEAH, BUT YOU WON'T LIKE IT AT FIRST, FELLAS--BECAUSE ONE OF YOU'LL BE AT ONE OPEN DOOR, AND THE OTHER IN BACK..."
THERE'S ONLY TWO WAYS IN--FRONT AND BACK. I SAY BLOW BOTH DOORS. WE GOT THE DYNAMITE...

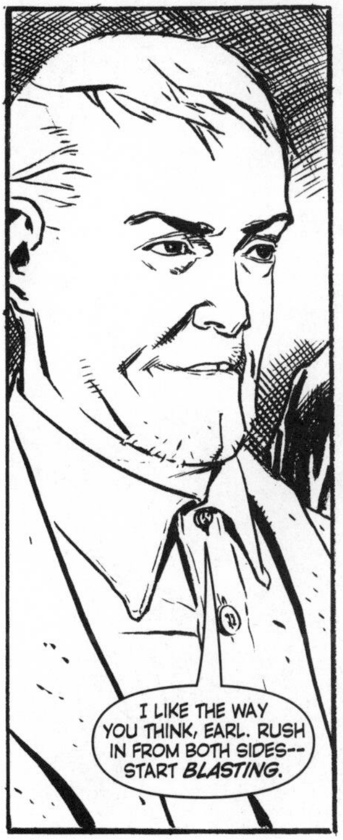
I LIKE THE WAY YOU THINK, EARL. RUSH IN FROM BOTH SIDES--START BLASTING.

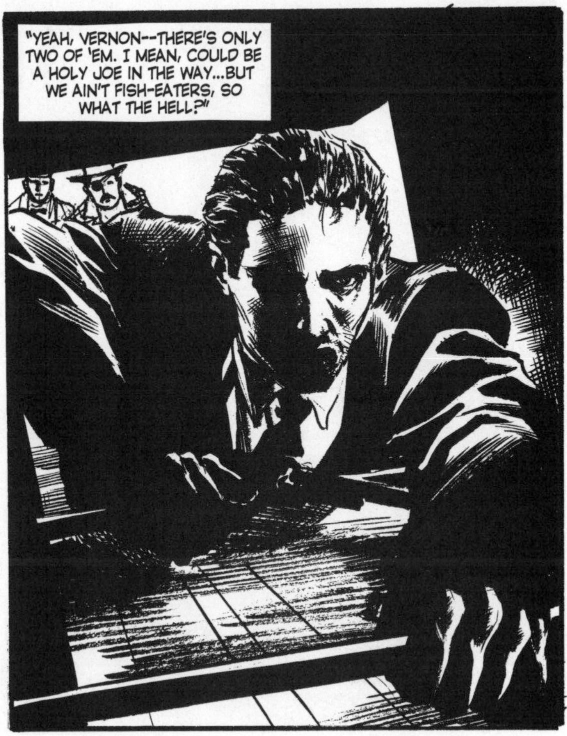
"YEAH, VERNON--THERE'S ONLY TWO OF 'EM. I MEAN, COULD BE A HOLY JOE IN THE WAY...BUT WE AIN'T FISH-EATERS, SO WHAT THE HELL?"

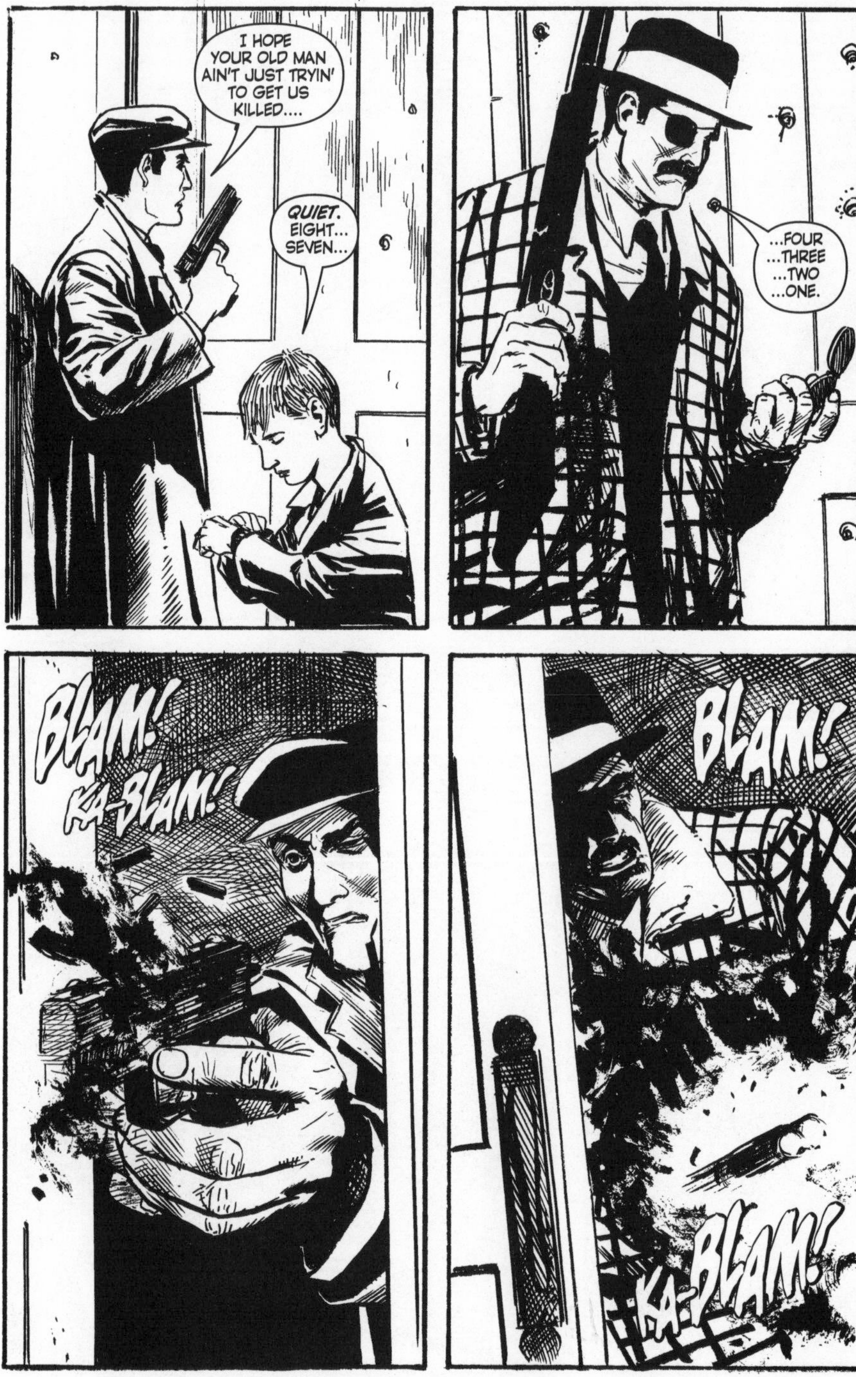
I HOPE YOUR OLD MAN AIN'T JUST TRYIN' TO GET US KILLED....
QUIET. EIGHT... SEVEN...
...FOUR ...THREE ...TWO ...ONE.
BLAM!
KA-BLAM!
BLAM!
KA-BLAM!

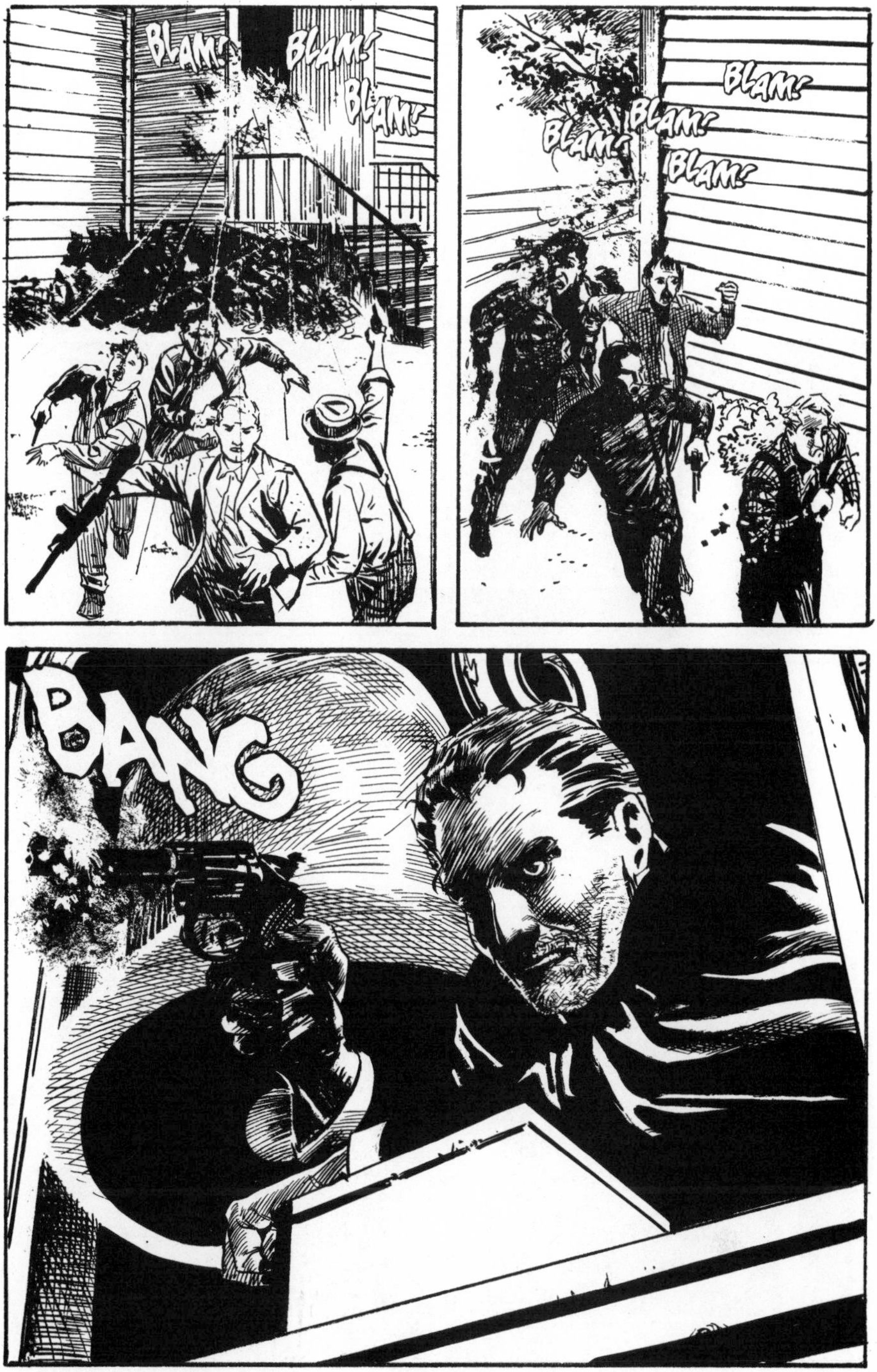
BLAM!
BLAM!
BLAM!
BLAM!
BLAM!
BLAM!
BLAM!
BANG

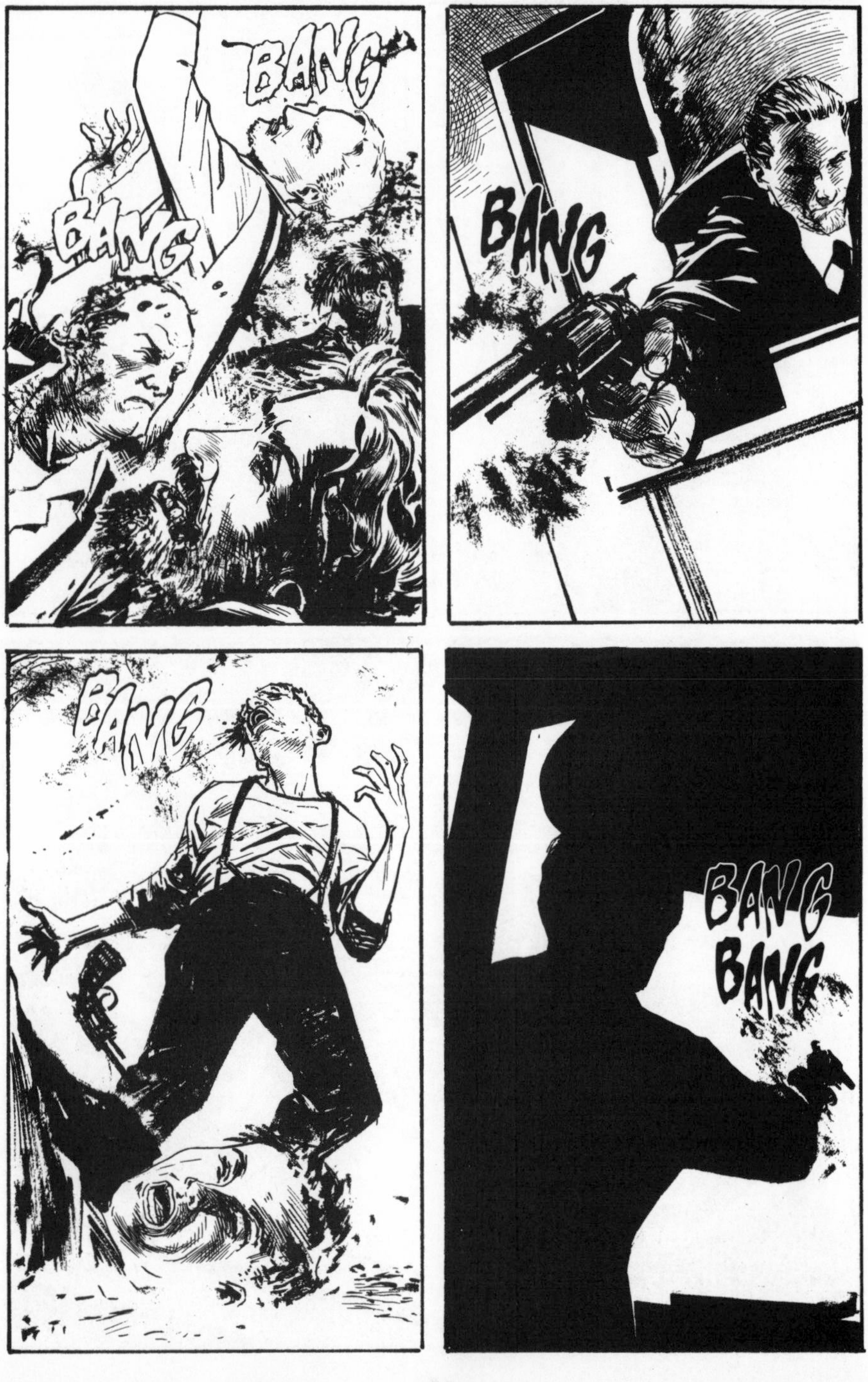
BANG
BANG
BANG
BANG
BANG
BANG

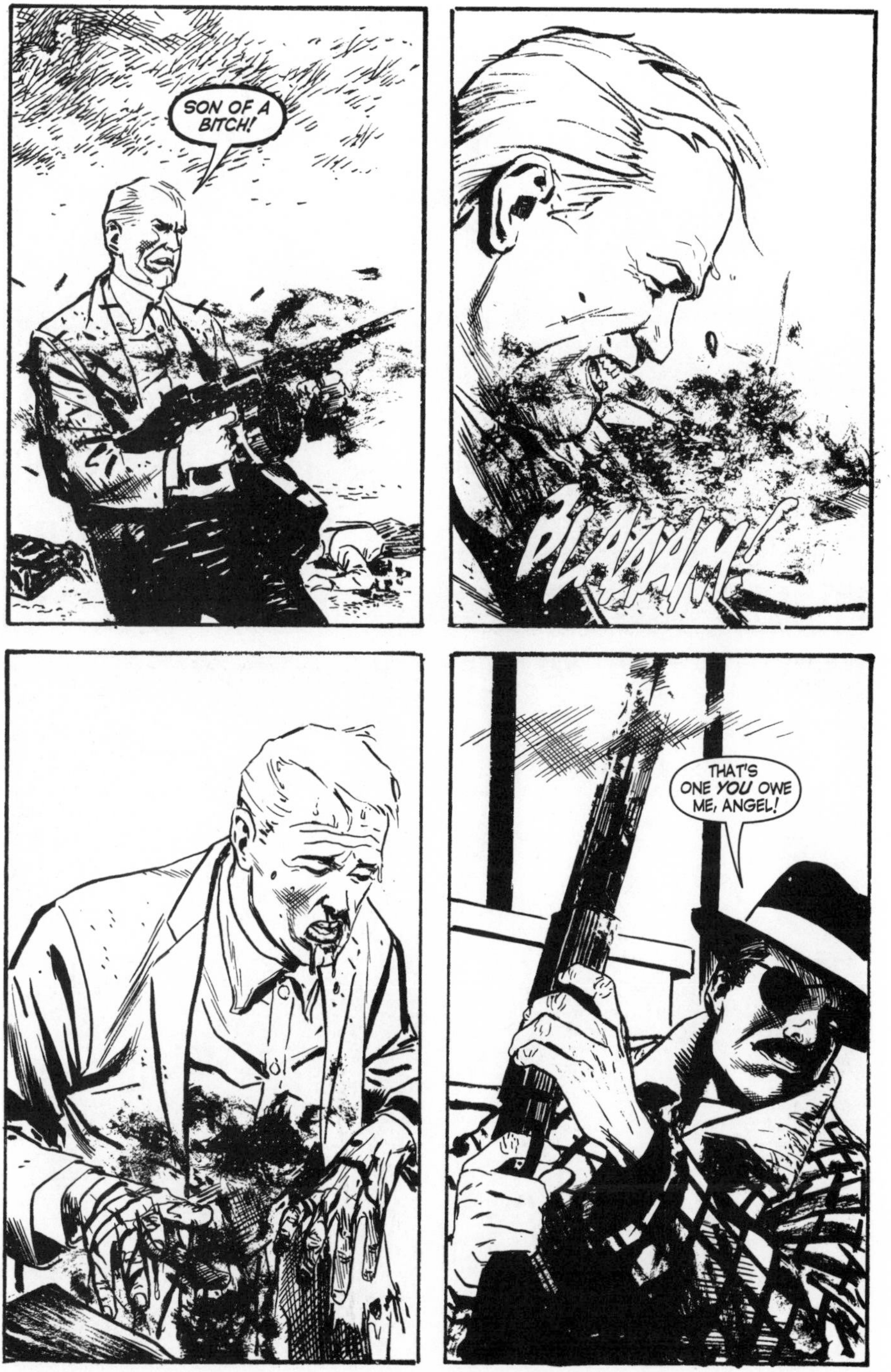
SON OF A BITCH!
BLAAAM!
THAT'S ONE YOU OWE ME, ANGEL!

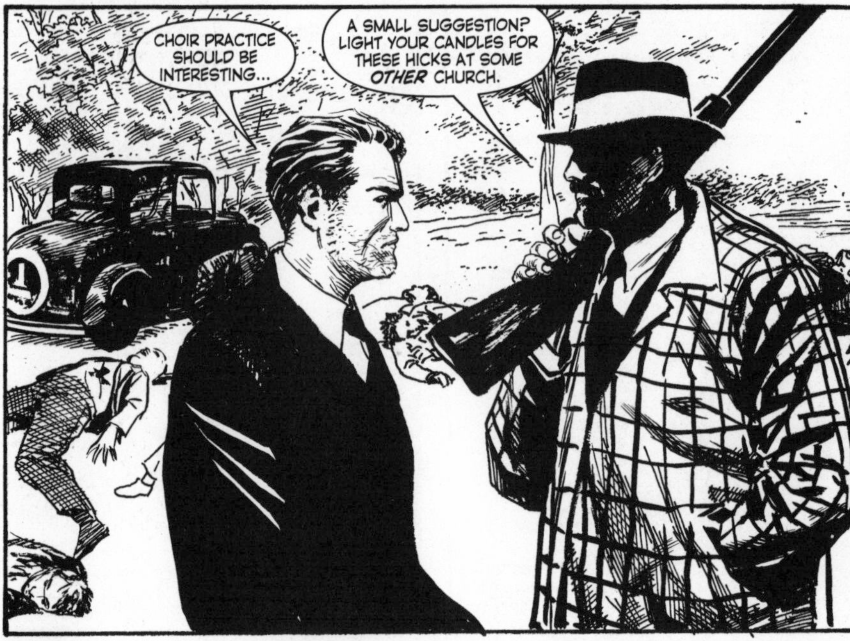
CHOIR PRACTICE SHOULD BE INTERESTING...
A SMALL SUGGESTION? LIGHT YOUR CANDLES FOR THESE HICKS AT SOME *OTHER* CHURCH.

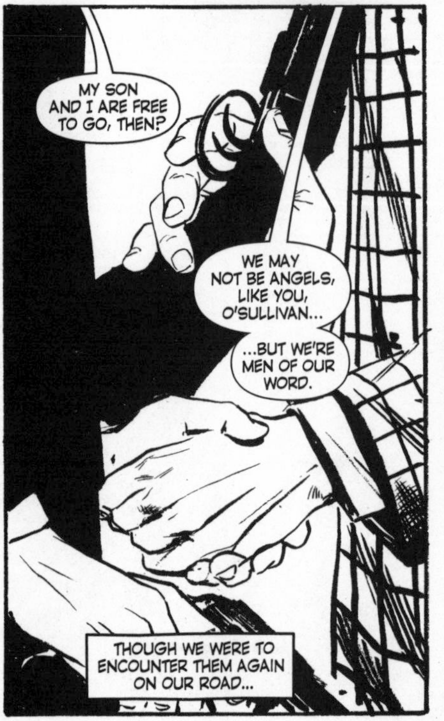
MY SON AND I ARE FREE TO GO, THEN?
WE MAY NOT BE ANGELS, LIKE YOU, O'SULLIVAN...
...BUT WE'RE MEN OF OUR WORD.
THOUGH WE WERE TO ENCOUNTER THEM AGAIN ON OUR ROAD...

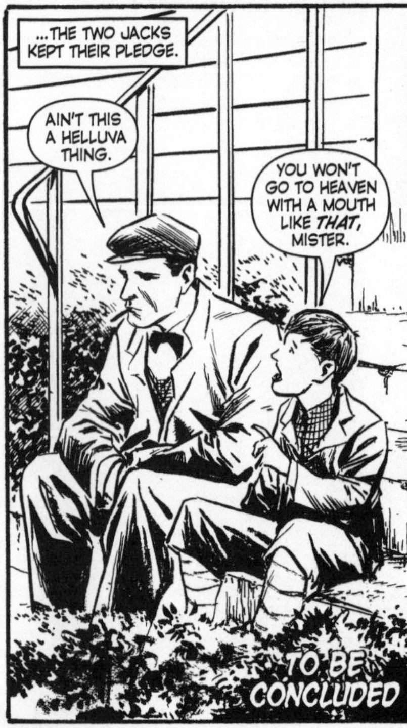
...THE TWO JACKS KEPT THEIR PLEDGE.
AIN'T THIS A HELLUVA THING.
YOU WON'T GO TO HEAVEN WITH A MOUTH LIKE *THAT*, MISTER.
TO BE CONCLUDED